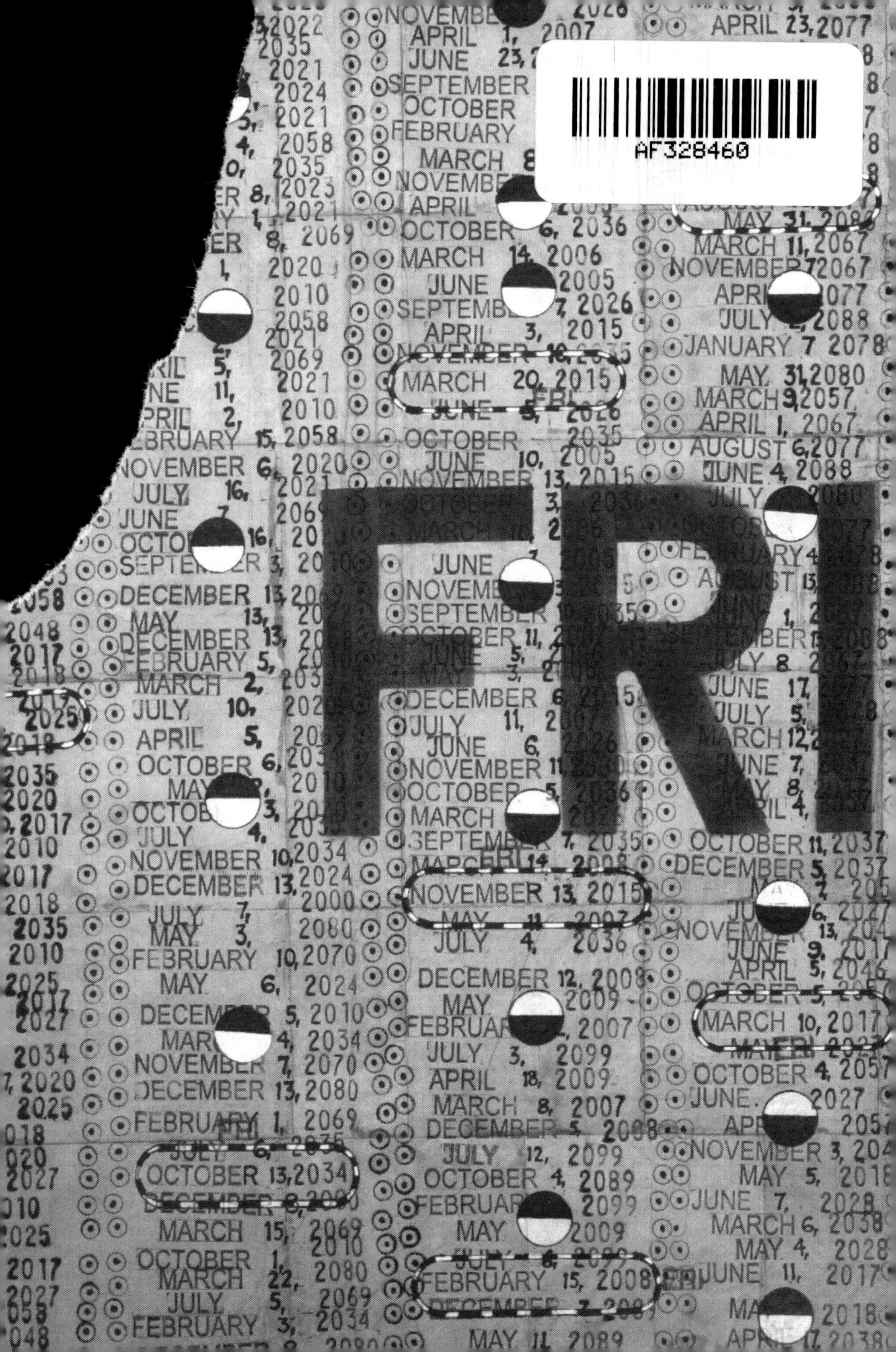

AF328460
FRI

DAY

FLIP-FLOP

JUNE ..., 2095
MAY ..., 2094
AUGUST 5, 2084
JUNE 3, 2073
APRIL 7, 2095
OCTOBER ..., 2094
AUGUST ..., 2005
MAY ..., 2073
JUNE 16, 2084
OCTOBER 5, 2063
DECEMBER 6, 2043
APRIL 4, 2094
JULY 2, 2044
MAY 7, 2084
NOVEMBER ..., 2073
MAY ..., 2043
DECEMBER 7, 2045
JULY 1, 2073
MAY 14, 2063
APRIL 5, 2044
JULY 8, 2063
DECEMBER 11, 2045
MAY 8, 2005
APRIL 4, 20...
FEBRUARY ..., 2063
DECEMBER ..., 2044
OCTOBER 7, 20...
JANUARY 12, 20...
APRIL 8, 2073
OCTOBER 3, 2044
DECEMBER 1, 2043
FEBRUARY 6, 2044
OCTOBER 11, 2049
DECEMBER 7, 2038
AUGUST 3, 2045
JANUARY ..., 2049
DECEMBER ..., 2048
SEPTEMBER 1, 2045
MAY 3, 2049
AUGUST 7, 2048
JULY 8, 2038
NOVEMBER ..., 2046
FEBRUARY 1, 2045
JULY 10, 2049
JANUARY 11, 2046
MARCH 8, 2049
JUNE 12, 2038
DECEMBER 7, 2063
MAY 4, 2046
APRIL 8, 2049
OCTOBER ..., 2049
AUGUST ..., 2048
FEBRUARY ..., 2046

FEBRUARY 3, 2081
OCTOBER 1, 2071
APRIL 3, 2061
JANUARY 5, 2081
OCTOBER 4, 2061
APRIL 8, 2092
JULY 3, 2071
SEPTEMBER 5, 2081
JULY 3, 2071
MAY 2, 2081
JUNE 3, 2002

NOVEMBER 7, 2081

FEBRUARY 2, 2002
JULY ..., 2071
JUNE 1, 2081
OCTOBER 3, 2002
JULY 5, 2081
AUGUST 1, 2092
MAY ..., 2061
JULY 3, 2071
JUNE 1, 2081
APRIL 4, 2082
MARCH 3, 2002
JUNE 6, 2081
MAY 10, 2092
OCTOBER 2, 2002
FEBRUARY 2, 2002
JULY 5, 2081
AUGUST 3, 2002
NOVEMBER 1, 2082
FEBRUARY ..., 2051
AUGUST 12, 2056
APRIL 8, 2055
AUGUST ..., 2055
JANUARY ..., 2055
JUNE ..., 2053
MAY ..., 2047
APRIL 4, 20...
OCTOBER 11, 20...
FEBRUARY 7, 2055
JULY 4, ...

JANUARY 1, 2049 FRI ⟷ JANUARY 1, 9402 FRI

JANUARY 2, 2071 FRI ⟷ JANUARY 2, 1702 FRI

OCTOBER 8, 2044
SEPTEMBER 7, ...
JULY 10, 2044

JANUARY 31, 2095 FRI ⟷ JANUARY 31, 9502 FRI

JUNE ..., 2043
OCTOBER ..., 2044

MAY ...
APRIL ...
JANUARY ...
JUNE ...
MAY ...
JULY ...
APRIL 3, ...
FEBRUARY 6, ...
OCTOBER 15, ...
JUNE 13, ...
APRIL 5, 20...
NOVEMBER 7, 20...
AUGUST ..., 20...
FEBRUARY 4, 2031
MARCH 10, 2022
MAY 5, 2031
JULY 10, 2021
OCTOBER 5, 2031
NOVEMBER 6, 2033
DECEMBER 4, 2021
FEBRUARY 7, 2043
MARCH 15, 2032
JULY 4, 2031
FEBRUARY 5, 2021
SEPTEMBER 16, 2033

DECEMBER 17, 2021

FEBRUARY 15, 2043
MARCH 5, 2032
JULY 5, 2033
DECEMBER 23, 2022
JUNE 4, 2032
JANUARY ..., 2043
MARCH ..., 2022
MARCH ..., 2032

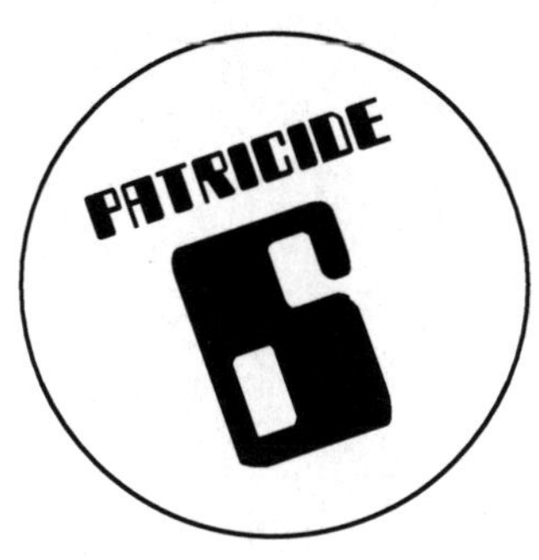

THe OutSider

edited by Neil Coombs

first edition

Published by
Dark Windows Press
72 Llandudno Road
Rhos-on-Sea
LL28 4EJ
UK

www.darkwindows.co.uk
info@darkwindows.co.uk

All rights reserved

No portion of this book may be reproduced in any form without prior written permission of the publisher.

Copyright © 2013 Neil Coombs

First Edition 2013

1

Printed in the UK

ISSN: 2043-6610
ISBN-13: 978-1-909769-00-7

Design, and layout by Neil Coombs

Cover image by Chris Hipkiss

Images on endpapers are details from George Widener 'Friday' 2009 Mixed media on paper 41½ x 74½ inches (image courtesy Ricco/ Maresca Gallery, New York)

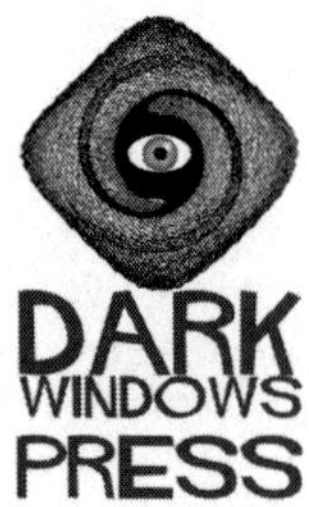

Contents

There is a current trend to describe a particular stratum of society as *the precariat*. The proletariat, balancing on the edge of something, forever waiting to slip or jump from the ledge. The notion of *precariat* with its indication of borders, liminality or 'edgeness' seems to suggest that there is some abyss beyond society into which we can fall. It is from this imagined place, somewhere beyond society (a lived experience for many) that we see the outsider emerging. A mythical, revolutionary, liberatory figure.

This book is an investigation into the idea of the outsider – particularly an attempt to explore the point at which the inside and the outside might be unified. Renay Kerkman argues in her short piece on the *outlier* that we may now live in a world where the outsiders outnumber the insiders. Perhaps we are all outside of society looking in on its spectacle, the illusion of inclusion suppressing the true functioning of our thought?

It is the way in which the outsider refuses either to solicit approval or to develop a career as an artist, the ways in which they appear impelled to explore the marvellous nature of everyday experience, which attracts us to their work. Of course there are some artists that are isolated from society and others who are incarcerated by society but there are few 21st century crea-

tors who are working entirely from their own inner experience. It is more likely that these artists are confronting and interpreting a disquieting external reality – something outside themselves.

We have invited writers and encouraged open submissions for this edition of Patricide and, from the resulting body of work, a few themes have emerged… Many artists who have found themselves nominated as outsiders, whilst recognising the opportunity that exhibiting work in this context may give them, have found it difficult to disassociate themselves from the label. A desire for equality emerges in artists and those who work with them: an aspiration to search for equivalences between, and parity with, artists that have not been defined as outside.

Perhaps when considering outsider art, given that there are far more artists outside of the gallery system than inside, we should effectively ignore institutions such as the art market, art galleries, archives and publications. We should allow these cultural asylums to draw their own borders around what is inside or outside their field of interest.

We have avoided the temptation to develop a taxonomy of outsiders or to separate artists, writers, critics and curators into separate sections but have divided the book into two parts: The first part *Concerning the Outsider* includes writing and visual work about outsider art and the experiences of outsider artists. The second section *Responding to the Outsider* includes responses to the broader notion of the term outsider – exploring the idea through poetry, prose and visual art.

It is not the goal of this book to attempt a definition of outsider art but Patricide's investigation has yielded some results. There appears to be an agreement among contributors that the value of outsider art lies in the psychic purity of the work: that the artefacts created by outsider artists contain what Roger Cardinal describes as "an undeviating honesty and urgency". The work is perhaps the closest we have to what André Breton describes as "Psychic automatism in its pure state", it speaks to us about our own humanity and our existence as social beings in a way that art produced for institutions or fiscal gain never can. That these works may subsequently acquire a financial value and be absorbed into a marketplace is a key area of debate but is beyond the scope of this investigation. Hopefully the combination of work in this book will suggest further areas of research into the outsider world and the precarious relationship between the internal and external.

Thank you to all those who contributed to this edition of Patricide: those that are inside the book and those that are outside. Particular thanks to Henry Boxer for allowing the reproduction of images from his collection and to Roger Cardinal for his support and encouragement.

Part 1: Concerning the Outsider

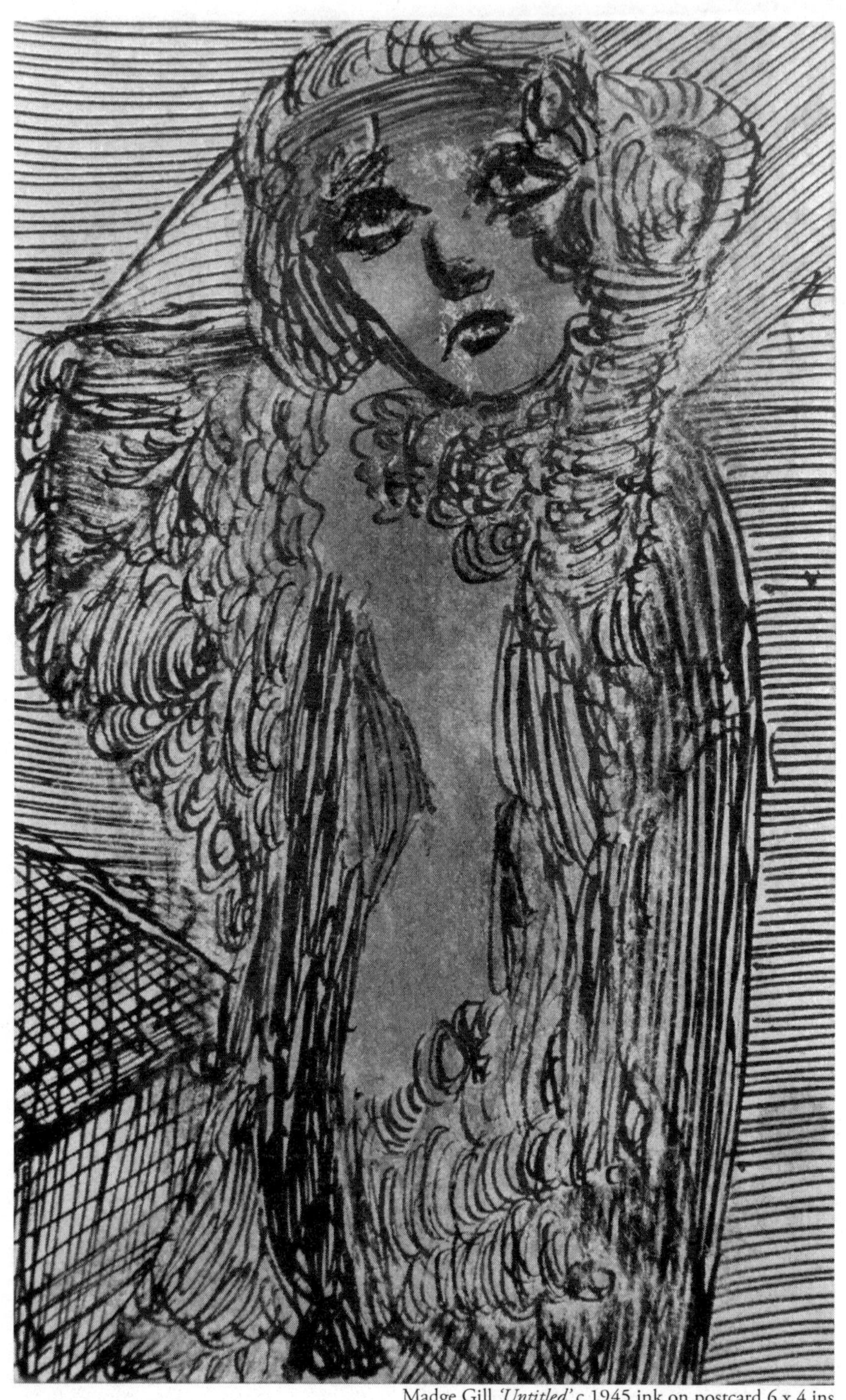

Madge Gill *'Untitled'* c.1945 ink on postcard 6 x 4 ins
image courtesy Henry Boxer Gallery

> *It's when a man finds himself alone, sinking into boredom, when he cannot count on any sort of distraction or pleasure coming from outside himself... that the conditions are ripe for the emergence within him of an impulse to construct – entirely independently and exploiting his own resources for his own personal use – a whole theatre of festivities and enchantments.*
>
> Jean Dubuffet, *Honneur aux valeurs sauvages*

Mystery is not a novelty but a commonplace. Sit quietly in a room and look around: you will find no end of little enigmas in the form of phenomena that are hard to comprehend or that resist easy explanation. Questions arise by the dozen. Why is glass so transparent? What regulates the way the daylight pierces the window and divides an interior space into light and shade? By what processes was this wooden table brought to its present shape? Are those marks on its surface accidental or deliberate? What underlies that wooden surface? Is this an inert and meaningless object, or are we to believe that it is teeming with invisible life?

Such questions take on greater sharpness once other people enter the room. Who are these individuals? How should I name them? What genetic laws and what physical contingencies have given that man his distinctive physique? Why is this woman wearing such a distraught expression? Are these strangers attentive to the same things as I? Do they have unspoken purposes? Are they empty vessels – inert and meaningless? Or should I suppose that each possesses an inner dimension, a private realm sustained by a unique and independent consciousness; and if so, can I have any sort of access to it?

There is a sense in which we are all 'outsiders', eager to participate, to make contact with objects or other social beings in a way which can satisfy our hunger for meaning and security. Once something or someone escapes our understanding, we feel a tremor of panic, for what slips from us seems to diminish our grip on reality at large. Usually, we can fall back on some basic explanation which provides reassurance. Yet mystery leaves a strong aftertaste, provocative and inescapable.

The poet Joë Bousquet observes that "in this world where nothing is explained, we can be sure that mystery is what is least rare"; he goes on to recommend that we approach this mystery "with a very light touch". If indeed ignorance and perplexity are fundamentals of our condition, perhaps it is wise to be cautious and develop a strategy for dealing with the unknown, even the unknowable. I suggest that a creative affinity with enigma can be cultivated which is nothing less than a way of gambling upon the possibility of eventually grasping the coherence of what at first seems indecipherable. And even if full illumination should elude us, we can still strive for fulfilment, adopting a stance which honours intuition as much as intellect. A tolerance of strangeness and a tender alertness to the world and its contents can encourage them to rise into meaningful focus and allow us to feel more at home.

*

Artworks are a perfect instance of objects steeped in mystery which, nevertheless, exhibit the potential to be meaningful. They are exceptional in that their import always transcends the mere sum of their physical properties (weight, size, texture, colour, etc.). They are indeed embodiments of expressivity and intentionality, in so far as their characteristic aspects and configurations originate in human drives, emotions, thoughts and gestures. It is a truism to say of artworks that, given that they derive from the activities of other human beings, they must concern us *as* humans. We are hard put to deny that they tend to be striking, even demanding: for when we come across an individual artwork, it appears to ask that we give it our full attention, that we treat it with respect as we seek some measure of insight or pleasure among its specific forms. To explain the behaviour of light or the physical composition of glass or wood is to engage in an objective enquiry into natural phenomena whose properties are regulated by impersonal laws with no relation to human purposes. By contrast, cultural artefacts take on significance in so far as they are apprehended by human minds conditioned by cultural assumptions, uppermost of which is the expectation of an intent to communicate, a desire to convey meaning.

In an essay entitled 'La Vie profonde', the poet Maurice Maeterlinck writes that "each man must find for himself a particular way of carving out a superior life within the humble and inevitable reality of the everyday". He goes on to contend that everyone has a link to the infinite which they should seek to enhance, and that, at some point in their lives, everyone is granted a revelation of their true spiritual being. I believe that those ignored and often underprivileged people whom we have come to designate as 'Outsider artists' are essentially people who have had such a revelation – an abrupt recognition that there is more to existence than its immediate, humdrum shell – and who have been bold enough to try to cast light upon the dark and profound aspects of their experience. Their artmaking will resemble a journey of exploration which penetrates the surface of normal consciousness and exhibits what the metaphysical painter Giorgio de Chirico refers to as "the revealing symptom of the *inhabited depth*".

Outsider artists are typically people who approach existence as if 'from scratch' – without prejudice, and with a minimum of educational or institutional safeguards. Defying any social, intellectual or physical deficit, they seem each to arrive at a critical moment in their lives when they feel the necessity to stand alone and tackle the mystery of their condition without flinching. Outsider artists feel compelled to address the strangeness of existence; they like to ruminate upon its shapes and textures, and to fret over issues of metaphysical understanding which the average person has no time for. Often they show signs of mental and behavioural non-conformity, among which is an unusual passion for artmaking. In their daily lives, they are disinclined to bother about other people's notions of what is right and proper; and the same applies to their art. Orthodoxy is simply not their concern. Their artefacts may come across to other people as obscure, grotesque or upsetting. In their own eyes, their work is not so much beautiful as *appropriate*, perfectly tailored to their individual expressive project. Of course, there are many people who persist in deprecating the efforts of those who ignore the support-systems of communal knowledge, commonsense and a ritually sanctioned *modus operandi*. Yet the autodidact has the inestimable advantage of being able to test his or her results against a single standard – the intuitive sense of what is directly meaningful to him or her. And nothing is quite as meaningful as the meaning one has carved out *for oneself*.

It has become clear that Outsider Art (*Art brut*) offers a disturbing challenge to the art traditions of our Western society, and above all to the notion of cultural acceptability. By its nature, it is an art of immediacy; it is self-reliant and self-regulating. It has no truck with publicly accredited art: it solicits no instruction and no subsidies. Thus liberated from external strictures, it exhibits an intensity of will which seems excessive and extravagant when compared with that displayed by conventional or academic artists. It nourishes itself on secrecy and shadows: its domain is not the public arena lit by other people's complacent expectations and good advice, but the dark alcoves and anarchic corridors where solitary intent holds sway. Unrepentantly self-engrossed, Outsider Art is the record of a naked grappling with an immediate and sometimes frightening reality, the articulation of what Vassily Kandinsky called "inner necessity", rather than of received ideas.

Above all, our conception of Outsider Art implies the recognition of the singular value of the creative subject. The documenting of one person's idiosyncratic view of life can hardly be a matter of recycling cultural clichés or conventions.

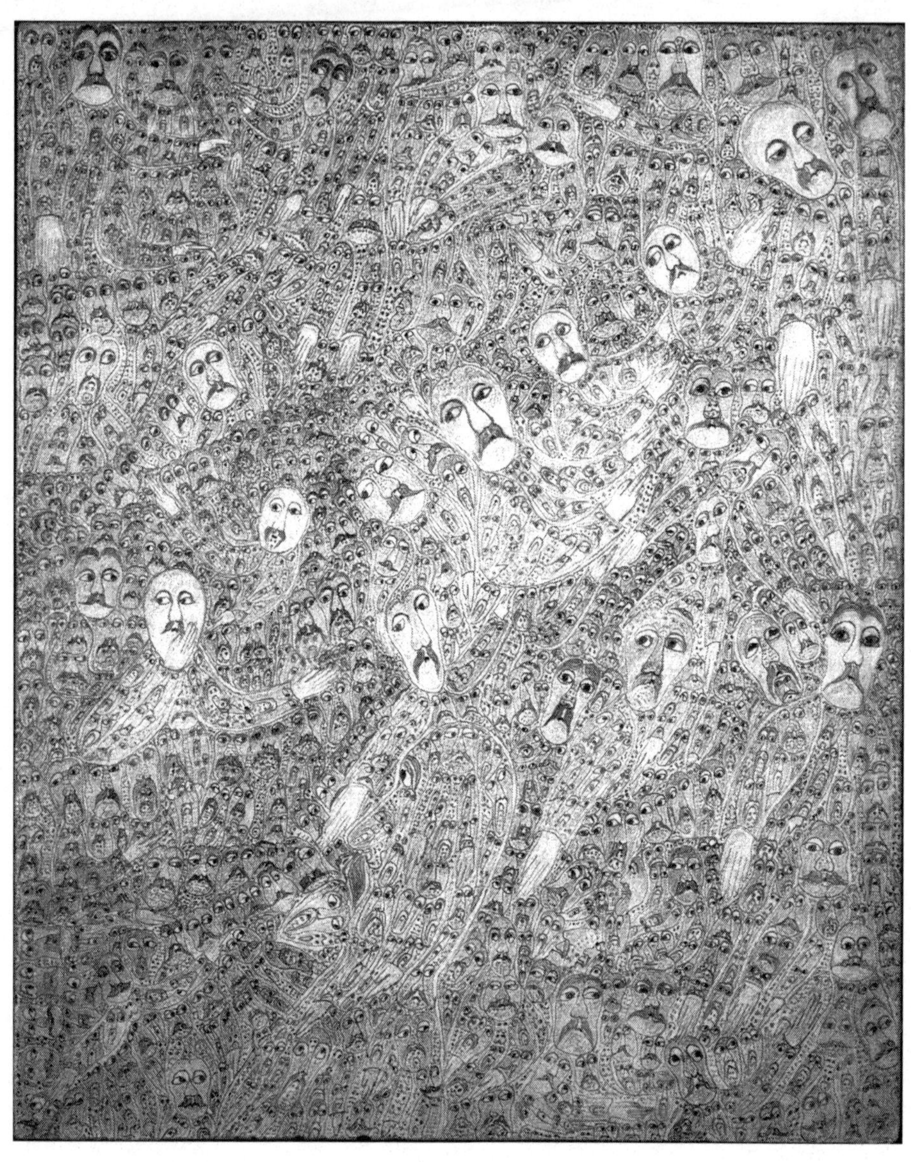

Edmund Monsiel *'Untitled'* c.1940 lead pencil on paper 8 x 6 ins
Collection de l'Art brut, Lausanne

Instead, it clutches at fresh and innovative solutions to the problem of expression, informed above all by intuition and spontaneous initiative, and draws on a precious assembly of private insights. Stylistically, Outsider Art varies enormously, since each creator will adopt his or her own strategies. When we analyze Outsider artworks, we often find that they exploit a deceptively modest stock of devices and motifs, though they may handle them in unusual ways. What is impressive is the way that the artist, driven by fierce emotions and sometimes obsessional ideas, projects an undeviating honesty and urgency into the artefact, constructing authentic meaning by way of an intimate dialogue with the materials and with his or her innermost self. To look deeply into works of Outsider Art is therefore to witness the shaping process at its most intense.

*

The work of Edmund Monsiel (1897-1962) is exemplary in this regard. This artist is known to have had no artistic training and minimal contact with the world of art: the most one can say is that he was exposed to popular and religious imagery in his early life. Monsiel ran a small shop in a Polish town until it was taken over in 1942 by the occupying German forces. He panicked and went into hiding in his brother's attic for the entire duration of the war, by which time he had developed a delusional mental system and probably experienced hallucinations: he is thought to have been schizophrenic, though he never received formal medical treatment. Only after his death in 1962 did it emerge that he had been making secret drawings dating back to the war years.

These works are remarkable demonstrations of unfettered proliferation. Typically they consist of faces within faces, with an almost exclusive insistence upon the same stereotyped male physiognomy, with a large nose and moustache. The outlines of each face become the containers of other, smaller faces; and indeed every corner of each sheet of paper is jampacked with further faces, in what Michel Thévoz has called "an anarchic generation of hyperactive, cell-like physiognomies". Some figures are easily identifiable from Christian iconography: Christ, the Virgin, the Devil; and the ostensible meaning of these insistent works is confirmed by Monsiel's occasional writings on the reverse side, which reveal him to be an avid Bible-reader who sees himself as God's emissary in a sinful world.

But if the religious allusions seem straightforward, there still remains a great mystery about the work. This inheres above all in the terrible density of the pencilled marks which have built up the imagery. So much repetition and embellishment, at once stark and delicate, creates a sense of high claustrophobia verging upon asphyxiation; so that the viewer feels obliged to draw back from the work to take a few breaths of fresh air. The very process of drawing – with an extremely sharp pencil and with the face close to the paper (perhaps even using a magnifying lens?) – seems redolent of a process of auto-hypnosis. The drawings establish a compelling and utterly private world, rigid yet infinite, an inner domain whose forms speak less of a shared belief-system than of something irreducibly personal and disconnected from everyday understanding.

In his pioneering study of psychotic art-making, *Bildnerei der Geisteskranken* (*Artistry of the Mentally Ill,* 1922), the psychiatrist and aesthetician Hans Prinzhorn discusses several cases of mental patients who evinced a spontaneous gift for artistic expression. Scanning the remarkable collection of works which he had built up in Heidelberg, Prinzhorn observes that the incidence of creative talent is probably no greater among schizophrenics than among any other group in the population. Perhaps, however, there is a case for supposing that permanent incarceration within the bounded space of an institution, along with the fact of having a lot of spare time, are factors conducive to the liberation of the creative impulse. Above all, of course, the fact that psychosis entails extreme distancing from the conventions of normal thought and behaviour means that new and outrageous precepts of understanding and expression will inform the resulting work, making it im-

mediately distinct from that of so-called sane artists.

While other psychiatrists were excited by the possibility of exploiting such art as a diagnostic tool, Prinzhorn's great merit was to have advanced beyond purely clinical terms of analysis and shown himself sensitive to aesthetic considerations. Reluctant to generalize about any such thing as a fixed schizophrenic style, he nevertheless observes that there are recurrent and recognizable effects of ambivalence and abstruseness which arise in the work of most psychotic artmakers[1]. Their artistry, he suggests, is governed not by normal logic but by a kind of solipsistic "magical thinking", which is in fact "less a thinking than a desiring" – a drive to expression which privileges subjectivity over objectivity and, manifesting a "meaningless consistency" (*pointenlose Konsequenz*), produces an impression of "fascinating strangeness" (*faszinierendes Fremdheitsgefühl*). Writing some forty years later, the Viennese psychiatrist Leo Navratil observes of schizophrenic expression that it can take the form of a striving for orderliness or consistency which, because it cannot handle the rational symbolic discourse which other people share, instead releases a distinctive air of hesitancy, ambivalence or enigmaticality: "The enigmatic is characteristic of a transitional phase between an original order and a new, higher order; it epitomizes the attitude of a person who is on the verge of entering a new order, but has not yet managed to take a step forward."

Many further instances of occultation could be cited. The work of Jean Mar (1831-1911) is a case in point. A patient in the Bel Air clinic in Geneva from 1900, he remains to all intents and purposes anonymous, in so far as hardly any details of his life or clinical profile have survived: even his name has come down to us only in the truncated form dictated by the medical protocol of the time ('Mar' being the first syllable of his surname.) First institutionalized at the age of forty, Mar spent the remaining four decades of his life in total retreat from normal human contact, spending his days mumbling to himself and scrounging paper and pencils on the wards. His work consists of tiny words and doodles inscribed on very small scraps of paper. He also made small collage-like documents out of paper, leaves and petals, which he sewed together with thread or glued with masticated bread.

The residue of his *oeuvre* — for we must assume that most of it was thrown out by the asylum staff as mere litter — is now carefully preserved in the *Collection de l'Art brut* in Lausanne. Mar's art of fragments is an example of resolutely private production, poignant in its inwardness and minimalism. The art-therapist and aesthetician David Maclagan reminds us that "at the invisible core of much creative work, there is something that lies beyond any question of addressing others". Mar's tiny scrawls, curls and glyphs, with their nervy ornamentations, remain esoteric and resistant to normal scrutiny, to the point that they resemble a set of coded messages abandoned by a spy.

Among the small number of recognizable elements in Mar's drawings are depictions of a palace with three gables, of a row of podgy round faces and of a regal couple whose faces and bodies are completely elided. Mar's doctor, Charles Ladame, quotes his patient as commenting on this latter image in the phrase: "MYSELF the KING strolling in his CASTLE with the QUEEN his wife", arguing that Mar suffered from a persecution complex and had accordingly retreated into a private fantasy of omnipotence. This might indicate that artmaking functioned as a compensatory defence-system against the nullity of Mar's actual existence. Yet since there is little chance of eliciting a sustained narrative, the work hovers only on the verge of meaning. We are drawn to it precisely because, as a human artefact, it challenges us to solve the puzzle and establish its human significance. Yet we feel embarrassed, for we know that it was never intended for our eyes.

Johann Fischer (1919-2008) is a member of a group of artists who form a community in the House of the Artists at the Gugging clinic outside Vienna. Fischer was one of the more disciplined of these undirected creators, working regularly to sustain an output of similar works, care-

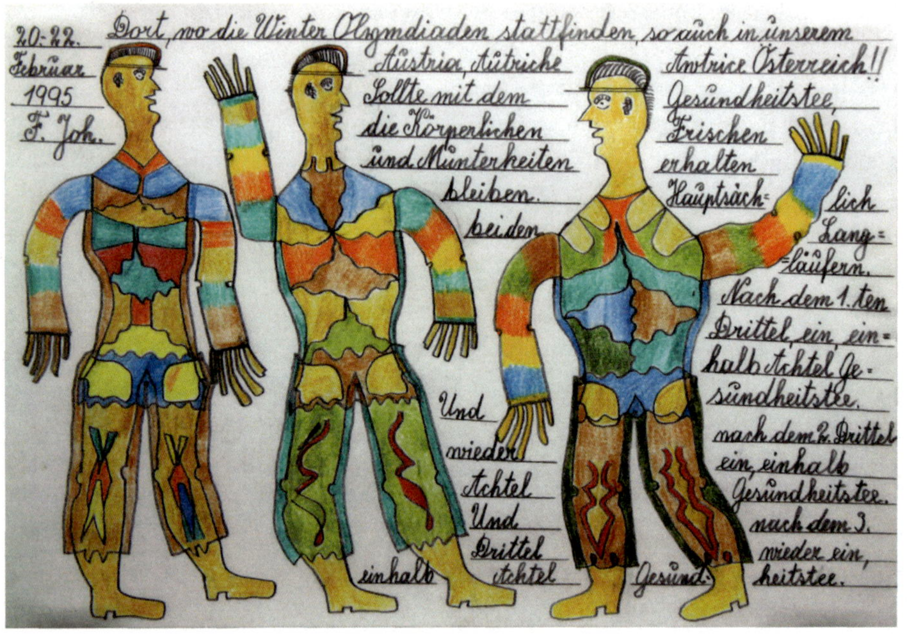

Johann Fischer *Untitled* 1995 crayon, watercolour and pencil 8 x 11.5 ins
image courtesy Henry Boxer Gallery

fully dated and signed, which appear to be growing into a kind of archival series. His works consist of painstaking texts, each statement carefully underlined, and interpolated colour illustrations, usually of human figures. Most texts harp upon Fischer's native land, its religion, its laws and customs. It could be said that each constitutes a kind of guidebook entry to the Austrian life-style, whereby a given topic or proposition – such as the wearing of hats, the composition of a family, folk-dancing, the feeding of swans, the preparation of dairy products – becomes the point of departure of a chatty essay. The text typically contains mock-pious references to Fischer's homeland, in one case with a bathetic shift of tone: "Our Sovereign Confederation of Austria and our Sovereign Republic of Austria!! Sparrows reproduce very fast and die off very fast."

The manifest content of these creations is not in itself obscure, for Fischer executed his calligraphy with ritualistic care and clarity, and his flatly rendered, semi-caricatural figures are easily identifiable. However, the naïve directness of his verbal-visual discourse is qualified by an eerie sense of irony, enough to suggest that – for all his seeming dependence on the staff of the Gugging institution and his acceptance of the role of docile mental patient – he was in fact capable of astonishing insights into his own social and psychological predicament. These form the sub-text of his artistic message, and the fact that they are more or less latent means that Fischer's surface fresco of country yokels and farm animals is yet another 'front' for deeper meaning. We may conclude that, behind a semblance of naive disorientation, Fischer is in fact totally responsible for what he is saying.

A sometimes baffling sphere of Outsider Art production is that associated with the practices of mediumism, whether directly or indirectly associated with the belief-system known as Spiritualism. Such work can be envisaged in two antithetical ways. For those who accept the notion that there exists a world beyond this one from which the dead communicate to the living, the mediumistic artwork is taken as a direct record of otherworldly circumstance, typically dictated by a spirit guide: the live person acting as medium is no more than a passive receiver and is not responsible for the message. For the sceptical, the creative expressions produced by the medium – strange ornamental formations which arise during trancelike states – are a record of unconscious or semi-conscious processes: although he or she may deny its attribution, there is a strong case for seeing the work as inseparable from the medium's controlling hand.

The bewildered female faces and giddy architectures produced by the London housewife Madge Gill (1882-1961) offer a locus of debate about intentionality and meaning. As a mediumistic artist, Gill herself was very reluctant to claim au-

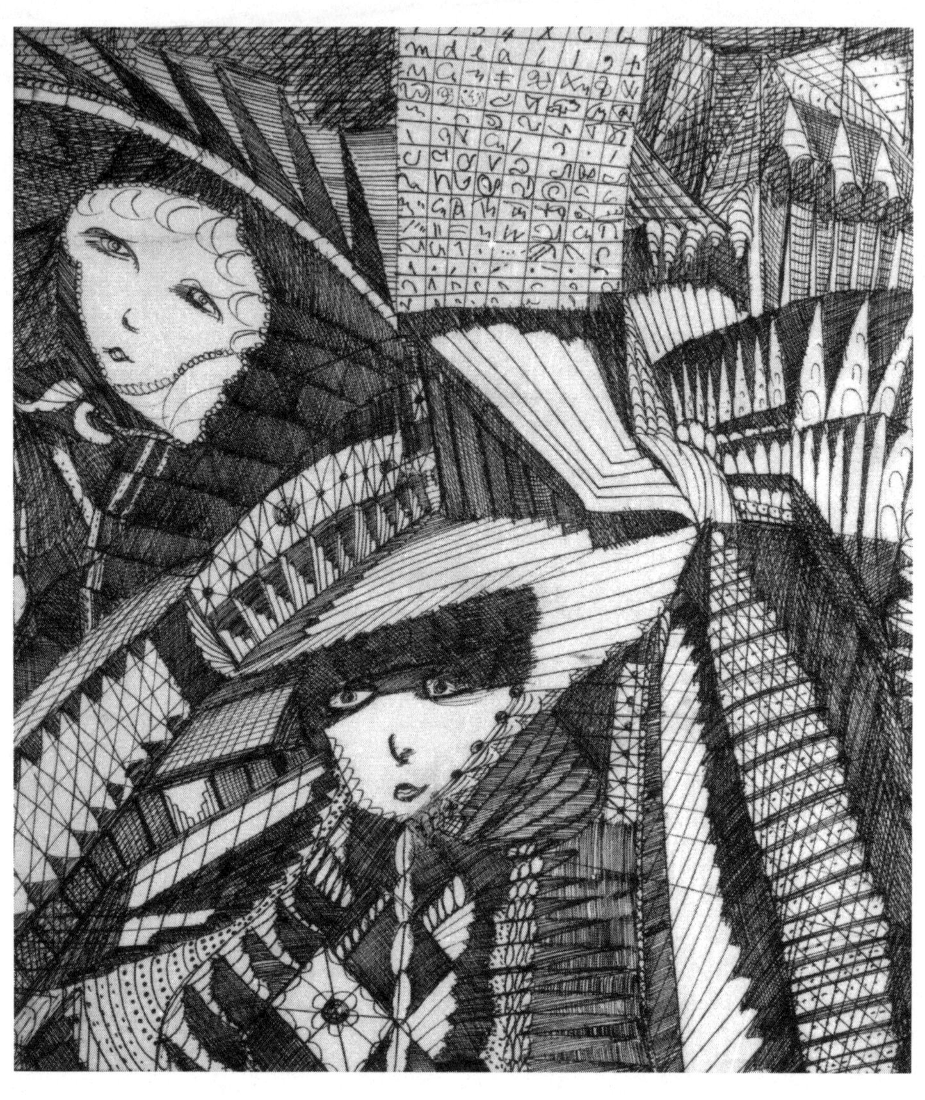

Madge Gill *'Untitled (Heads and Hieroglyphs)'* c.1920 ink on card
image copyright of London Borough of Newham

thorship even for her most ornate works, humbly crediting her spirit-guide Myrninerest with their inspiration. Although she did occasionally exhibit her art, it is said that she refused to sell any of it, since it was not her property. Brought to light only after her death in 1961, Gill's tireless improvizations, done in black or coloured inks upon paper or cardboard surfaces, with occasional ambitious undertakings on long rolls of calico, are immediately compelling. They are likely to seem uncanny in so far as they purport to spring from a dimension entirely foreign to the one we ordinarily inhabit. How should we react to pictures of a world we have never seen?

One reason why the images are so mesmerizing is that their composition is so intricate and optically provocative, in ways that anticipate the Op Art of the 1960s. Gill was a virtuoso of symmetrical and assymetrical design, combining a repertoire of rigid checkerboard patterns with fluid arabesques, as it were negotiating between orderliness and haphazardness. (An unfinished piece reveals that her method was to lay down a freehand spread of intersecting threadlike lines and then work over them to instil a more deliberate and regimented pattern.) Her art remains mysterious in so far as the spaces it summons up – nameless palatial interiors, mystic shrines, casements, colonnades and mosaic floors – seem wilfully to shun comparison with any known architecture; while the omnipresent female faces and figures which hover within these spaces appear at once anonymous and urgently in need of identity. Should we try to name them by reference to members of Gill's family – her mother, her aunts, her stillborn baby? Once in a while, a legible word or phrase finds its way into the composition, though Gill also invented her own deliberately unreadable ciphers. Our aesthetic response – qualified though it may be by our knowledge of her biography – can only remain imprecise, beyond reason. It will always, of necessity, be faltering: for the best we can say about her pictorial universe is that it is spectacularly at odds with our commonplace reality.

In similar fashion, another artist inspired by Spiritualism, the onetime French coalminer Augustin Lesage (1876-1954), produced from the outset an architectural world which, despite being patently theatrical and flimsy, and therefore entirely unreal, nevertheless exhibits a cogency and purposiveness that are amazingly persuasive. Lesage's adamant compositions are rigorously geometrical and symmetrical; and while they make occasional concessions to familiar iconography, as in the interpolation of the head of Nefertiti or the silhouette of a bird (motifs derived from Ancient Egypt, a favourite reference in Spiritualist lore), they are in the main non-referential, a kind of coloured mosaic of adroitly impressed dots, curls and segments – as it were an abstract painting designed to celebrate some sort of preternatural experience. As with Gill's

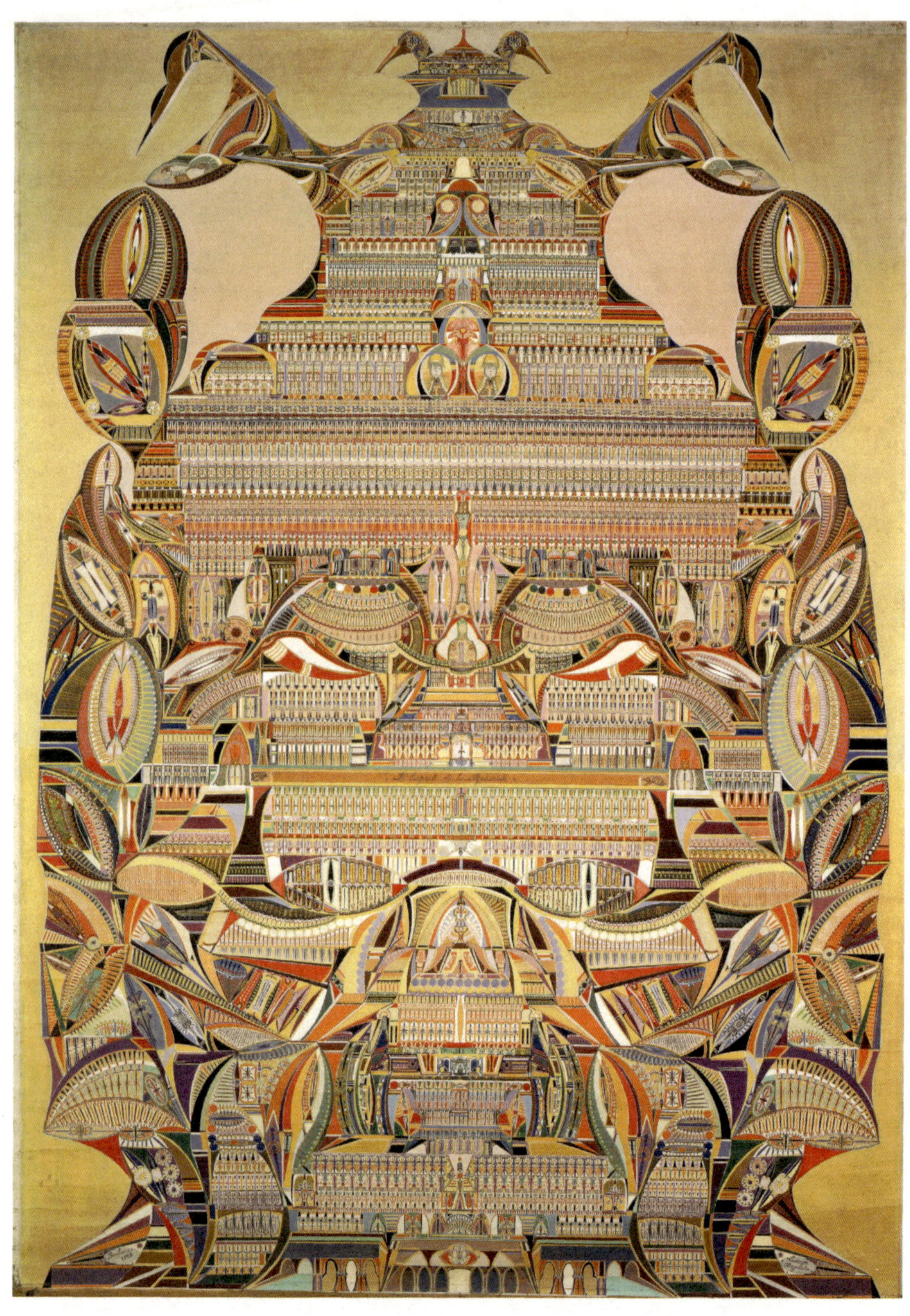

Augustin Lesage, '*L'Esprit de la Pyramide*' 1926 oil on canvas
image courtesy LaM, Lille Métropole Musée d'art moderne, d'art contemporain et d'art brut,
Villeneuve d'Ascq. Photograph by Claude Thériez Inv. : 2005.13.1

work, one may assume that an authentic spiritual belief motivated this mammoth endeavour of articulation. The fact that Lesage applied himself to his art over some four decades leaves us in no doubt as to his commitment; even so, it is hard to say just what it is that his images are supposed to represent. As a compromise, we may wish to say that these are depictions of the Otherworldly, and that the artist is attempting to capture the magnificence of a domain which – albeit real to him - lies beyond the reach of ordinary perception. But this is hardly a satisfying explanation for the impact of these grandiose solo performances, whose sheer obdurate *effortfulness* remains inexplicable[2].

Like that of so many Outsiders, the art of the reclusive Muscovite Rosa Zharkikh (b. 1930) seems to have arisen amid unhappy social and psychological conditions, as well as severe health problems: however, what most decisively characterizes it as genuine Outsider Art is its intrinsic strangeness and dynamism. Zharkikh has produced work in a variety of formats – drawings, paintings and fabric pieces, including garments and multimedia assemblages. There have been reports of a visionary impulse which prompts her to give shape to the images that flash convulsively through her mind, components of a continuing spiritual revelation. Be that as it may, the origins of her expressivity remain unspoken and are probably a mystery even to her. Her fibres, with their fluid hues and glittering spangles, establish a space of fantastical association, a fairytale domain in which figures may rise momentarily to the surface but are intrinsically more at home in the depths, hidden beneath the swirl of her multicoloured entanglements. There is nothing derivative or standardized about Zharkikh's creativity. Hers is a surreptitious, puzzled approach to making things: I am tempted to say that her art is a precise articulation of the very facts of hesitancy and uncertainty. In such work, ambivalence and obscurity seem integral to both process and meaning. One might draw a parallel with what the literary critic Malcolm Bowie says about the challenging style of the Symbolist poet Stéphane Mallarmé, when he writes of the "difficulties which are the product of an intended and scrupulous indecision on the poet's part". Zharkikh's art appears to drift in and out of focus: its very evasiveness seems to provoke a vibration, as if tuning us to a wavelength beyond the range of the ordinary.

An utopian realm of magnificent cathedrals, monuments and exhibition pavilions, featuring countless ornamented porticos, cupolas, steeples, flying buttresses, alcoves and finials, such is the creation of Achilles G. Rizzoli (1886-1981), the onetime junior draughtsman in a San Francisco architect's office. Here is a case of someone who took an orthodox system of representation, namely architectural drawing, and then exploited it as a foundation for the most outlandish mental

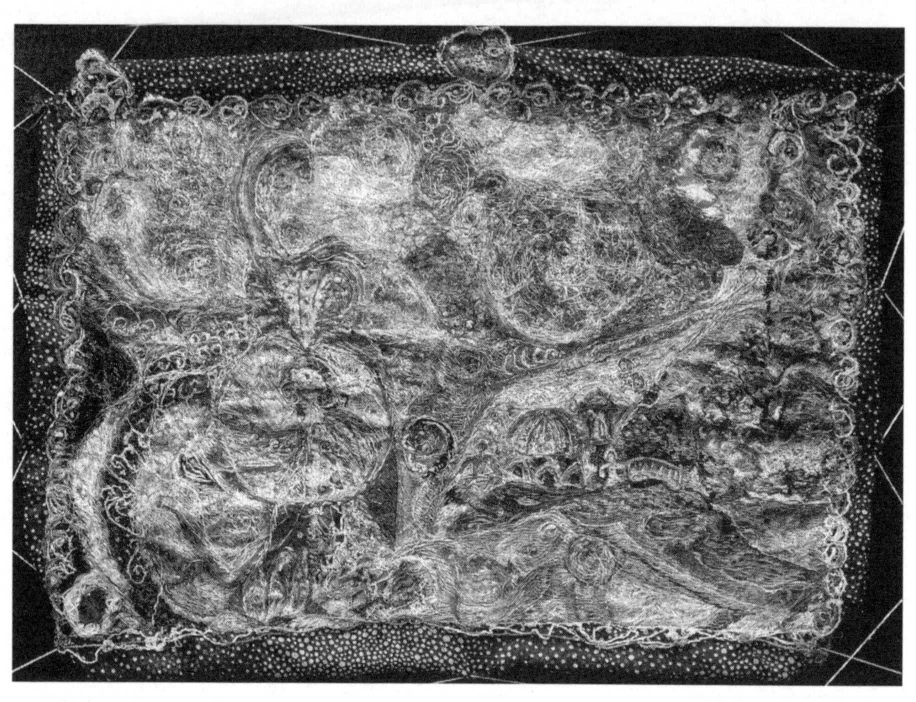

Rosa Zharkikh *Parallel World* 1995 embroidery
Outsider Art Museum, Moscow

fabrications. On a primary level, Rizzoli's extravaganzas adhere to a recognizable idiom – his cathedrals may not ever be built, but at least they do resemble real buildings. However, each of these conjectured structures secretes a secondary meaning, for a given cathedral is typically designated as the symbolic embodiment of a person, either his beloved mother, or one of Rizzoli's friends or neighbours. Yet even as Rizzoli's symbolic system is made explicit, it remains sufficiently bizarre as to baffle us, mainly because the draughtsman's passion for ornamentation creates an excess of iconographic completeness. These oblique 'portraits' are configured with such preciosity of detail as to create eddies of eerie emphasis, inducing in the viewer an almost sickening vertigo, akin to that evoked in some of my previous examples. A born pedagogue, Rizzoli excels in inserting little banners and labels into his drawings: their inscriptions are meant to explicate and rationalize what he has done, yet their actual effect is to make us feel that a crazy inventor is whispering insistently in our ear. In the end, the pedantry sabotages our credulity and confidence, as if Rizzoli were injecting anxiety into every crevice of his baroque façades. As if camouflaged by redundant inscriptions, his structures finally embody a sublime fantasy architecture as prolix and abstruse as that of Lesage. An intimation of enigma and insidious disorientation seems central to their impact[3].

Perhaps the most famous yet least fathomed artist in the Outsider canon is Adolf Wölfli (1864-1930), a Swiss schizophrenic who spent half his life in the Waldau asylum near Berne and, as if to refute the brute facts of physical incarceration and mental derangement, produced a private cosmology of unparalleled expansiveness and intricacy. Like so many self-taught creators, Wölfli made shift with minimal materials, cadging coloured pencils and cheap paper from his guardians and producing ornate images coupled with fervent textual commentaries. Many of his folio pages were sewn together to form bulky albums. The work is stunning in its formal complexity, for individual scenes are squeezed into tiny 'cells' – alcoves or niches fitted within vast architectural ensembles – while decorative elements cram the remaining spaces, creating the same claustrophobia as in Monsiel's work.

Wölfli's ornamentation is an irreducible feature of his art. His multiple frames, surrounds and fillers are made up of semi-decorative, semi-representational motifs – giant slugs, birdlike creatures (*Vögeli*), sets of bells, sections of brickwork, musical staves. These constitute a fixed permutational system which, strangely, never becomes monotonous. The rigour and trenchant drive to symmetry in the compositions follow an internal logic, establishing a coherent visual space, hypnotic and multidimensional, within which the work's autobiographical content can be staged – essentially the journeys and dramatic adventures of Saint Adolf II,

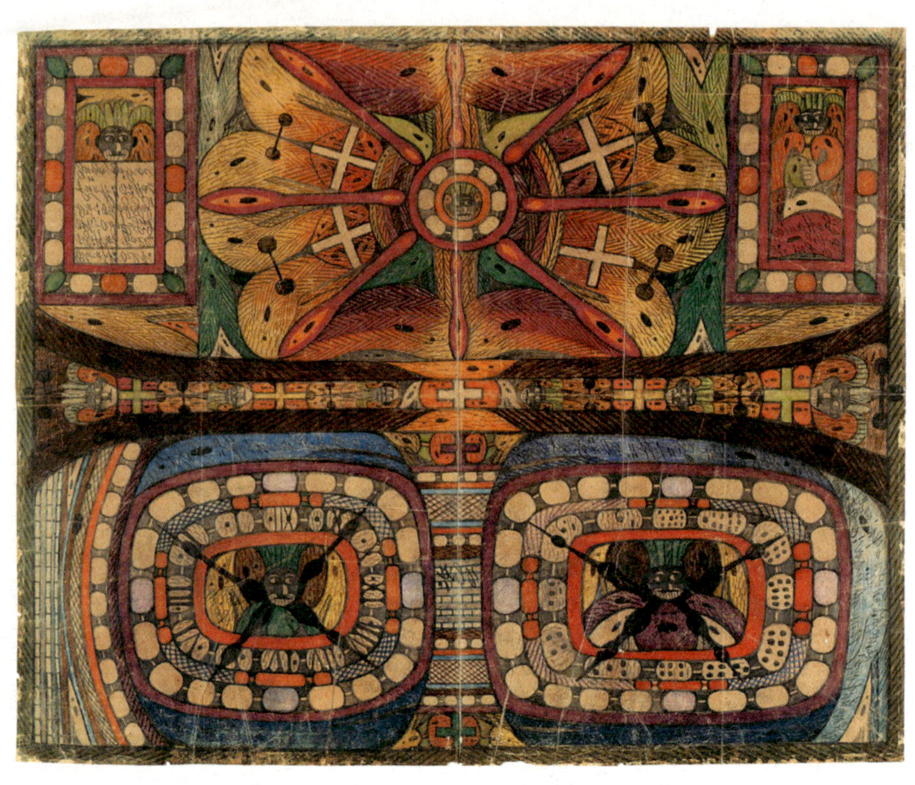

Adolf Wölfli, '*Bettania Gotttes*' 1926 Coloured pencil and graphite pencil on paper
image courtesy LaM, Lille Métropole Musée d'art moderne, d'art contemporain et d'art brut,
Villeneuve d'Ascq. Donated by the Aracine collection in 1999 Inv. : 999.7.1

the artist's *alter ego*. Wölfli's narrative is sustained through brief written labels and textual supplements which (much as with Fischer and Rizzoli) are all part of the work. Wölfli's genius was to step out of his banal everyday situation and enter a stupendous auto-fiction, travelling with the retinue he called his *"Giant-Travel-Avantt-Garde"* and asserting his authority as emperor of vast imaginary domains. As Louis A. Saas observes, "Wölfli's sense of elevation and exaltation extends beyond his feeling of kinship with what is titanic or immeasurable in external objects [...] to include his sense that these objects actually depend on him for their existence." Geographically, his "St Adolf Giant Creation" covers actual sites in the world, such as New York or the Gulf of Mexico, while cheerfully embracing other places whose status is entirely chimerical – the Island of Neveranger, the town of Angelear, the Saint-Adolf-Star-Giant-Glacier , the Celestial Sea of the North. In the end, everything coheres at the same level of implausibility, for the artist is a master of strangification and manages to inject an air of fantasticality even when he introduces photographic material of real ships and landscapes, snipped from the pages of popular travel magazines.

All of this represents nothing less than the creation of a private world, or what the novelist-artist Henry Darger (1892-1973) called "the realms of the unreal" – an autonomous, transcendent domain based on "magical thinking" and imper-vious to the conditions of our collectively acknowledged reality. The scholar John M. MacGregor insists that the authentic Outsider can almost always be identified as the creator (and, so to speak, the sole inhabitant) of a distinctive 'world' or self-defined cosmogony. Jean Dubuffet, the great collector and originating theorist of Art Brut, used to invoke as a criterion of authenticity what he called the "mental depth" (*profondeur mentale*) of his favourite practitioners. In an essay on one of these, the cement sculptor Henri Salingardes (1872-1947), he defines the Outsider as one who is capable of "inventing from scratch a totally new and original form of artistic output, one which implies – and provokes – an unprecedented mental posture"[4].

Referring generally to schizophrenic creators, Hans Prinzhorn speaks of the quasi-autistic withdrawal from reality which allows them to ignore normal environmental facts (apart from a select few which they are able to accommodate to their fantasy life), thereby forfeiting the commonality of experience which is the basis of normal social intercourse. For his part, Jean Dubuffet frequently speculated on the deliberate sabotage of dialogue on the part of the artists he most prized, even to the point of announcing in 1966 that "we firmly believe that there exists an irreducible antagonism between artistic creativity and the desire to communicate with a public". Another artist-collector, Arnulf Rainer, evokes the "autistic theatre" within which expressive acts might be performed before an audience identical with the performer: this self-sufficient circle of communication and reception fulfils itself in strictly hermetic conditions and entirely dispenses with an external public. Such 'non-communicative expression' may seem weird and unlikely, yet is not altogether hypothetical. Clearly it has relevance to cases of clinical autism, which can foster modes of artmaking whereby any hint of communication seems annulled by the individual's characteristic shunning of social contact. Nonetheless, pictorial expressions which can be physically witnessed by people other than the artist are still images susceptible to appreciation and interpretation, and several examples of masterly work have reached us from across the autistic divide[5].

*

In general, the integrity and value of works of Outsider Art need to be judged by the consistency and purposiveness of a distinctive style which remains independent of external sources (even though it may occasionally plunder them) and sustains a tireless momentum. Such "festivities and enchantments" result from repeated expressive acts that ultimately establish the imprint of an individual being, a human body and mind linked in an interdependent project – of which the goal is the inscription of a unique presence, reflected in a conjectural system which is tantamount to the creation of an alternative world. We may speculate that any given pictorial or three-dimensional construct is, at base, an emblematic representation of the fact of individuality, of exotic idiosyncrasy, of flamboyant selfhood. (We may also suppose that artistic assertiveness is sometimes a way of disguising psychic vulnerability.)

To suggest that, through their artmaking, Outsiders claim the right to be recognized as persons in all their astonishing singularity, is indeed to recognize them as architects of a private structure of meaning, a mental and spiritual formation linked to their innermost being, a formation whose coherence and necessity rest on its being an exposure of self-sufficient reasoning and understanding. As the record of a unique "superior life" carved out "within the humble and inevitable reality of the everyday", the painstaking expressions of the true Outsider are often full to the point of opacity, as it were saturated with an excess of meaning. We witness them as appearances which are necessarily distorted and illegible as they rise from the level of the "inhabited depth" to the flat surface of our apprehension. Yet they emerge imbued with an aura of mystery which can transfix our gaze and commit us to a posture of sustained absorption, bordering on trance. These messages may not have been addressed to us, nor couched in an idiom we recognize, yet we at once sense their commanding tone and allure.

Mystery, we may recall, is best handled with "a very light touch". For us even to glimpse such art – as third parties excluded from the intimacy of that primary dialogue between artifex and artefact – is something of an embarrassment, in so far as we are in fact blundering into an expressive field designed in accordance with another person's secret motives. We may imagine many reasons for the Outsider's discretion. Expressing oneself in code can imply a search for solutions to acute social and psychological problems, a way of coping with hurtful antagonisms within the sensibility or the weight of urgent metaphysical riddles. From our impertinent vantage point, we can as viewers only guess at the artist's meaning – by referring to our communal understanding of human affairs, our clumsy tribal ideology, and our precious small sum of personal insights into the human condition. There can be no light without shade. In principle, we can never be inducted into all the niceties of an Outsider's hieroglyphics, and are, accordingly, forever frustrated, never wholly in a position to proclaim what it is the artwork 'really' intends or portends. Given time, patience and long acquaintance with these elusive expressions, we may feel able to hazard some intelligent guesses. Yet more often than not – and most especially at the outset – our interpretative resources are dolefully inadequate, so that we tend to throw up our hands, despairing of ever teasing a pattern, a continuity, out of what seems a vexatious enigmaticality, a jumble of twisting paths without issue.

All the same, I contend that we should be pleased to encounter works which don't submit too easily: like strangers or awkward objects, they put us on our mettle. To confront what Colin Rhodes calls the "exquisite vistas" of Outsider Art is to meet a very special challenge. Throwing up our hands may be a reflex born of despair, yet it can also be a way of acknowledging that, for once, we are in the presence of something truly *different*, something irrefutably original, something which outstrips our familiar modes of reception and really forces us to look. Again, the justification for our quest for meaning in the aberrant and the alien lies in the premise of a shared humanity. There is much wisdom in a remark made by the surrealist painter Joan Miró: "I am convinced that the more individual something is, the more it becomes universal".

A short version of this otherwise unpublished text appeared in a Finnish translation as '*Toisen taiteen mysteeri*' ['Mystery and Meaning'], in the catalogue *Omissa Maailmoissa. Taidetta, terapiaa ja liiteripicassoja*, ed. Arja Elovirta, Helsinki: Maahenki Oy, 2005, 83-103

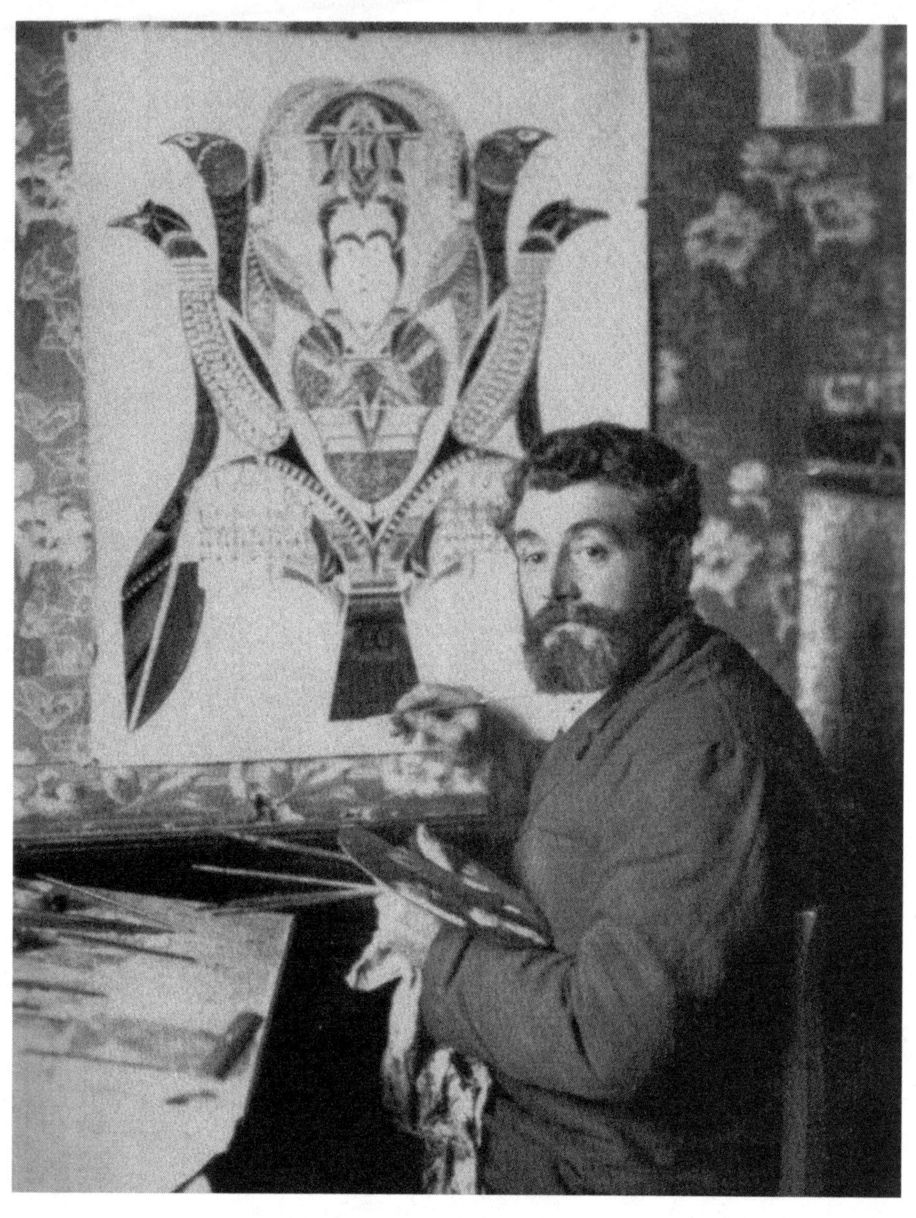

Augustin Lesage at his easel in the 1920s

Notes

1. For all that their work exhibits stylistic individuality – and even a fiercely adumbrated differentness from any other work – it is possible to follow Prinzhorn's lead and characterize a whole gamut of psychotic artists in terms of the common denominator of quirkiness, strangeness or enigmaticality. Mention may be made here of such masters as Aloïse Corbaz (1886-1964), Janko Domsic (1915-1983), Josef Grebing (dates unknown), August Natterer (1868-1933), Guillaume Pujolle (1893-1971), Martin Ramirez (1895-1963), Jeanne Tripier (1869-1944), Oskar Voll (1876-after 1935) and Carlo Zinelli (1916-1974).

2. Other notable practitioners of mediumistic art are Fleury-Joseph Crépin (1875-1948), Margarethe Held (1894-1981), Georgiana Houghton (1814-1884), Raphaël Lonné (1910-1989) and Hélène Smith (1861-1929). It has become customary to extend this sort of list to include visionary artists who may not be associated with spiritualist circles per se yet whose work is analogous, in the sense of being a compulsive and intricate production inspired by ecstatic, trance-like states. Such a list is likely to be dominated by the names of women artists, such as these: Consuelo González Amézcua (1903-1975), Eva Droppová (b. 1936), Minnie Evans (1892-1987), Séraphine Louis (1864-1942), Laure Pigeon (1882-1965) and Anna Zemánková (1908-1986).

3. The fabrication of "ideal palaces" on the part of the Outsider may be counted a recurrent, albeit never stereotyped, thematic option. Examples include the dreamlike early architectural sketches of Ferdinand Cheval (1836-1924), which were the basis of the three-dimensional Ideal Palace he built at Hauterives in France; and the majestic pictorial productions of such artists as Drago Jurak (1911-1994), Emanuel Navratil (1875-1956) and Marcel Storr (1911-1976).

4. Certainly the masters of Outsider Art tend to produce works which are not only visually startling and intriguing, but are also the manifestation of an idiosyncratic mental system of considerable stature and complexity. A list of such fertile system-builders might include Arturo Bispo de Rosario (c1909-1989), Frédéric Bruly Bouabré (b. 1923), Henry Darger (1892-1973), Willem van Genk (1927-2005), Emile Josome Hodinos (1853-1905), Bertus Jonkers (b. 1920), Armand Schulthess (1901-1972), Zbynek Semerák (1951-2003) and Joseph Yoakum (1890-1972).

5. Outstanding among autistic creators are James Castle (1900-1977), Nadia Chomyn (b.1967), Dwight Mackintosh (1906-1999) and Roy Wenzel (b.1959). Attracting notice within the context of creative workshops or art-therapy studios are those untutored artists whose pictorial expressions transcend the limitations on their daily lives imposed by certain neurological or physical deficits. Noteworthy are Aaltje Dammer (1907-?), Michael Hall (b. 1962), Jean-Marie Heyligen (b. 1961), Tobias Jessberger (b. 1969), Donald Mitchell (b. 1951) and Judith Scott (1943-2005).

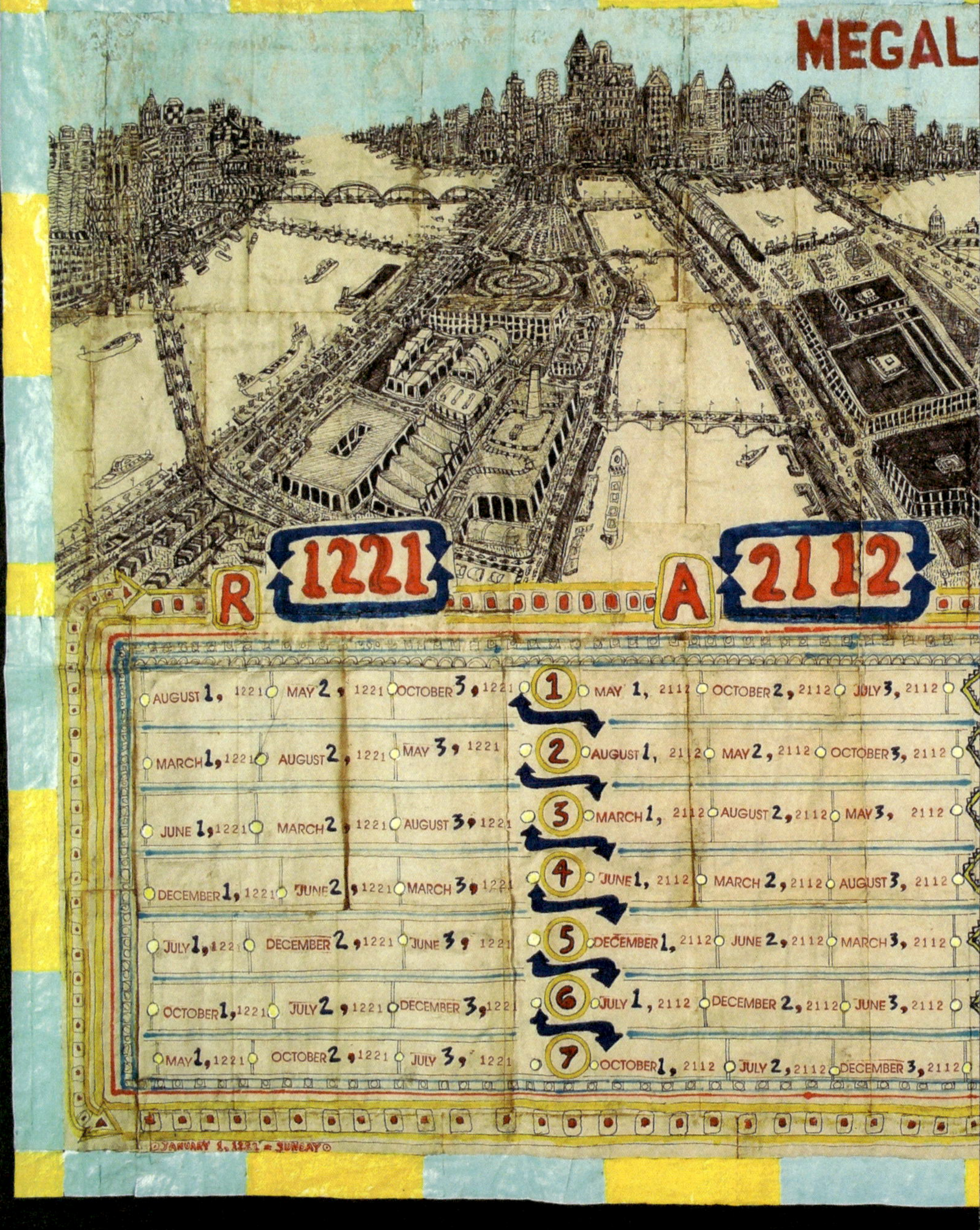

MEGAL
R 1221
A 2112
AUGUST 1, 1221   MAY 2, 1221   OCTOBER 3, 1221   1   MAY 1, 2112   OCTOBER 2, 2112   JULY 3, 2112
MARCH 1, 1221   AUGUST 2, 1221   MAY 3, 1221   2   AUGUST 1, 2112   MAY 2, 2112   OCTOBER 3, 2112
JUNE 1, 1221   MARCH 2, 1221   AUGUST 3, 1221   3   MARCH 1, 2112   AUGUST 2, 2112   MAY 3, 2112
DECEMBER 1, 1221   JUNE 2, 1221   MARCH 3, 1221   4   JUNE 1, 2112   MARCH 2, 2112   AUGUST 3, 2112
JULY 1, 1221   DECEMBER 2, 1221   JUNE 3, 1221   5   DECEMBER 1, 2112   JUNE 2, 2112   MARCH 3, 2112
OCTOBER 1, 1221   JULY 2, 1221   DECEMBER 3, 1221   6   JULY 1, 2112   DECEMBER 2, 2112   JUNE 3, 2112
MAY 1, 1221   OCTOBER 2, 1221   JULY 3, 1221   7   OCTOBER 1, 2112   JULY 2, 2112   DECEMBER 3, 2112
JANUARY 1, 1221 = SUNDAY

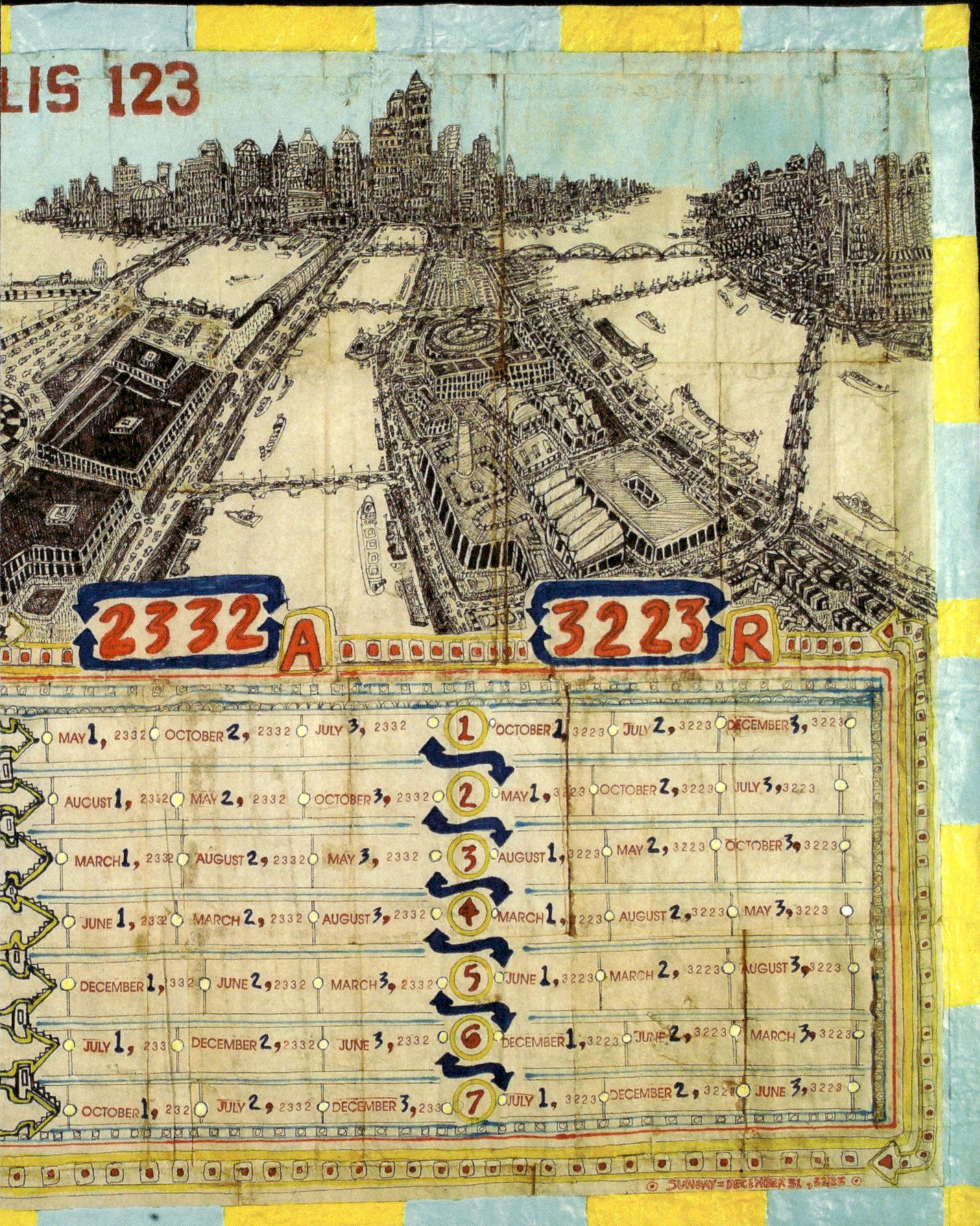

George Widener *'Megalopolis 123'* 2006 ink and posterpaint 27 x 40 ins
Cartin Collection, USA, image courtesy Henry Boxer Gallery

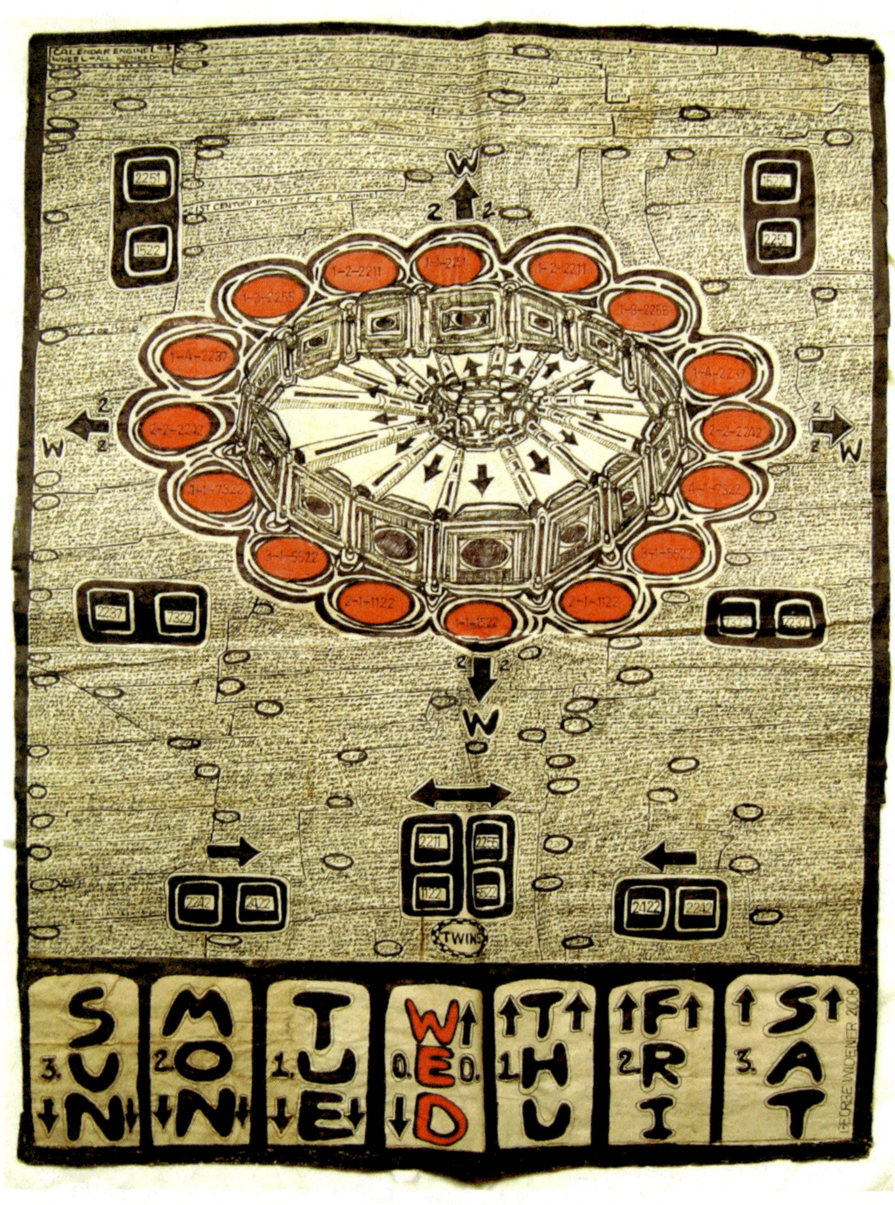

George Widener *'Calendar Engine Wheel'* 2008 ink on found paper 22 x 16 ins
image courtesy Henry Boxer Gallery

When I was an Outsider, I was outside The Outside. Because Outsider Art has of course become a label, a category of art. There are galleries, dealers, art fairs showing such work....

In my case, I have had specific interests all my life. I enjoy numbers, patterns. As a child I had definite talents with drawing and math that were recognized. My mother was an Appalachian woman who had gone to the inner city and was a barmaid, eventually became an alcoholic. But she was great person who did the best she could. I had joined the military at 17 and was a top secret photo technician within NATO's Cold War era.

Upon my discharge I determined to go to engineering school. Once near the top of my class, after several years at a top engineering university (despite having little prior preparation) something happened to me. I wasn't quite able to fit in and began to withdraw. It was devestating to me. Living on the streets, feeling alienated, lost, angry, I retreated to the drawing and patterns I had done as a child, out of a necessity. My investigations gave me comfort and meaning. I believe I would have ended up either dead or in prison without them. Later I was identified as a person with Asperger traits, but that too is a label. My brain has slightly different structure on left side that allows me con-

scious access to some inner calculations that doctors now believe exist inside everyone. I just do it, it's not something I dwell upon.

As an outsider, you don't know your own name of course. You're just doing your thing, your activity without real reference. I was discovering the calendar relationships, treating them as mechanical gears, and keeping them in my notebooks. I enjoyed it like some might enjoy a video game I suppose. At the shelter, they called me crazy and said I could only bring in so many papers so I simply threw them away sometimes. I began to hide them also and created a summarized 'master' code that I carried around and memorized. I began investigations blending Magic Squares and dates and coded all of that also, believing I was onto predictions. I was put in mental hospital 3 times because I would get so into these things I lost touch with reality, talking to myself with 'autistic' behaviors. Several times I worked odd jobs, saved up money, took more engineering classes (again a scholar) but couldn't stay long enough to graduate.

The THINGS I was doing with dates began to be so strong I finally decided to just live on the streets creatively and simply do my own things. At one point, I was given a test at a shelter and they

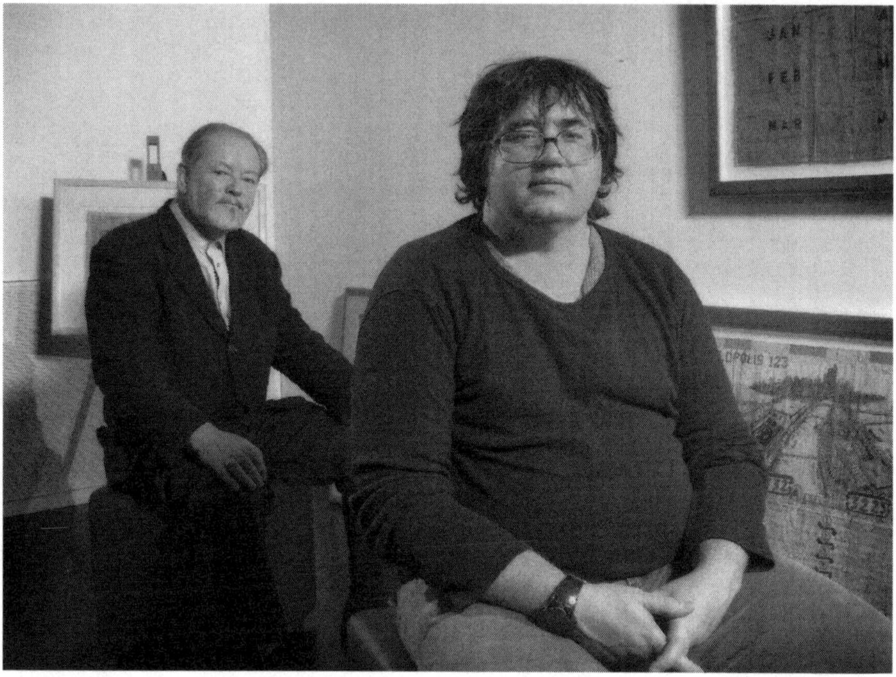

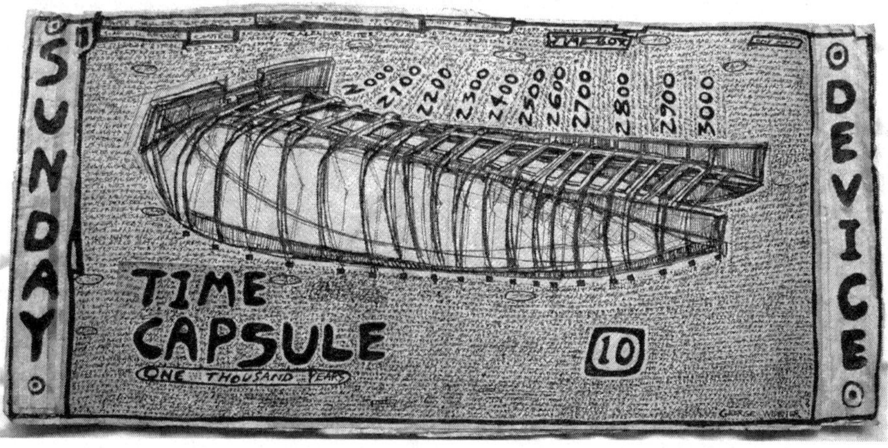

Top: George Widener (foreground) with Roger Cardinal
Bottom: George Widener *Time Capsule* 2008 ink on napkins 6 x 11 ins
images courtesy Henry Boxer Gallery

sent me on to university in a Rehab program, I finished with Honors in a general liberal arts program. I went back to the streets and did a short successful stint as a rare book and maps thief in Amsterdam (when I had lost passport and couldn't get any help from embassy or church). I lived in squat and continued my investigations into calendrical patterns. By the way, I have made thousands of other drawings of people and places but these are different, sometimes from memory, are all in my notebooks and have not been shown to audience. I was put into several medical studies, given tests, etc and they determined I was a high functioning type of savant. I was in several medical articles. I didn't care but did get free trips to Washington etc. Today I sometimes go on a medical science show but do not promote myself in this way. I have known several savants in my life. All were low functioning with difficulties living on their own. I'm not that way.

Then Henry Boxer of London saw some of my drawings and things and wanted to show my drawings. That was around 2004. I was shown at the Outsider Fair in 2005 for the first time and suddenly became an insider of The Outside. A few years later I became more aware of contemporary art and was self aware that I was outside The Inside. I have grown in my life. My work has grown. I may look at other artists' work now casually but dont really study them. I have met and chatted with other artists (the folks I used to believe were the ones who couldnt pass Differential Equations class). There's all kinds of artists I think and thats OK. It's ok to have 'success', sell a picture sometimes, 'cause poverty sucks.

Some might say I'm approaching the inside of The Inside these days. Interesting articles have been written by critics, saying things that make me think. I just keep doing my interest and if others also might find it interesting, I have learned to be flattered and grateful. At the end of the day, I'm simply doing my artwork, the same as I was when I was doing it for myself and could care less if anyone knew what I was doing. Artwork will need to speak for itself, regardless of what label it's been given or what some critic once said about it. That's what I think about it. Are there Outsiders out there right now? Of course there are but you don't know them and they're not on the radar.

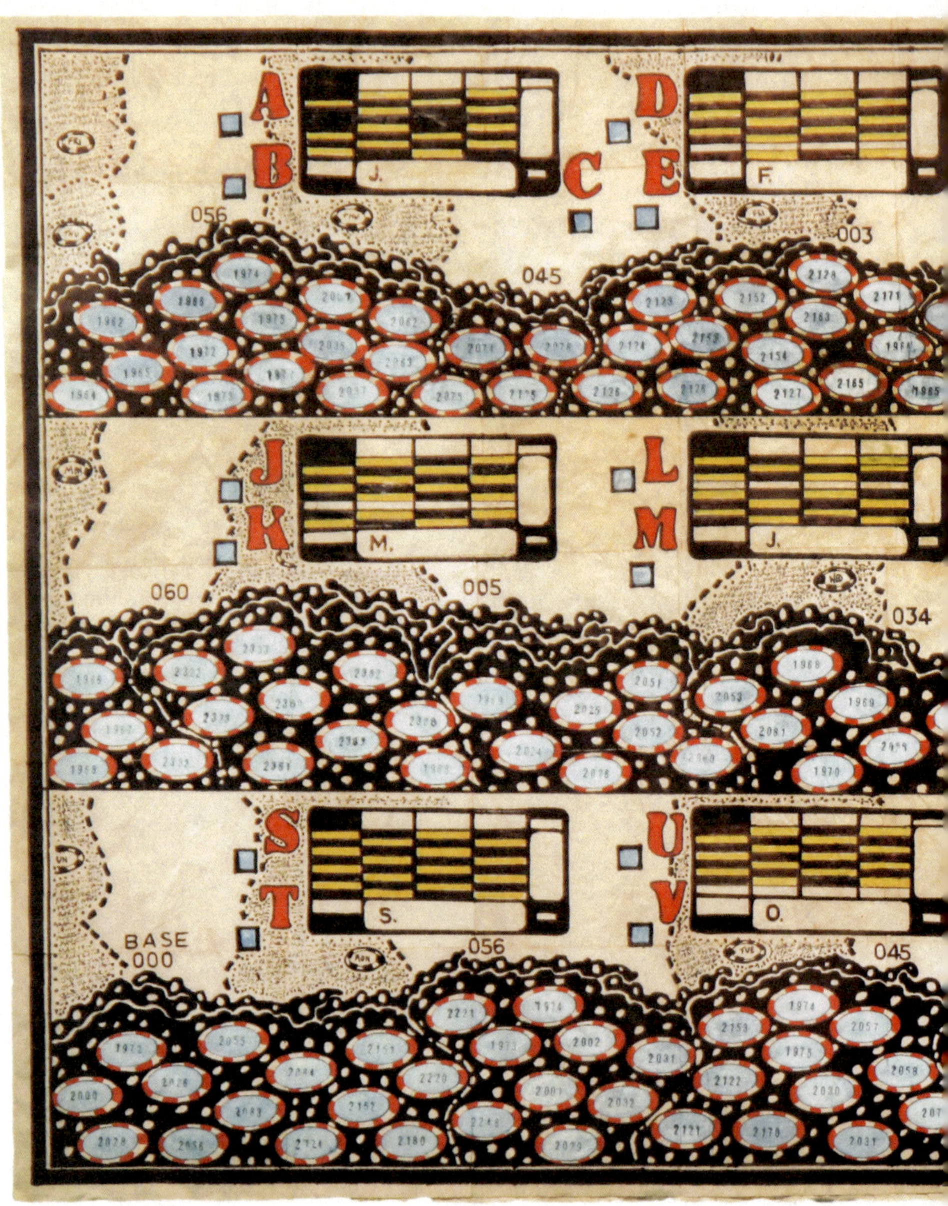

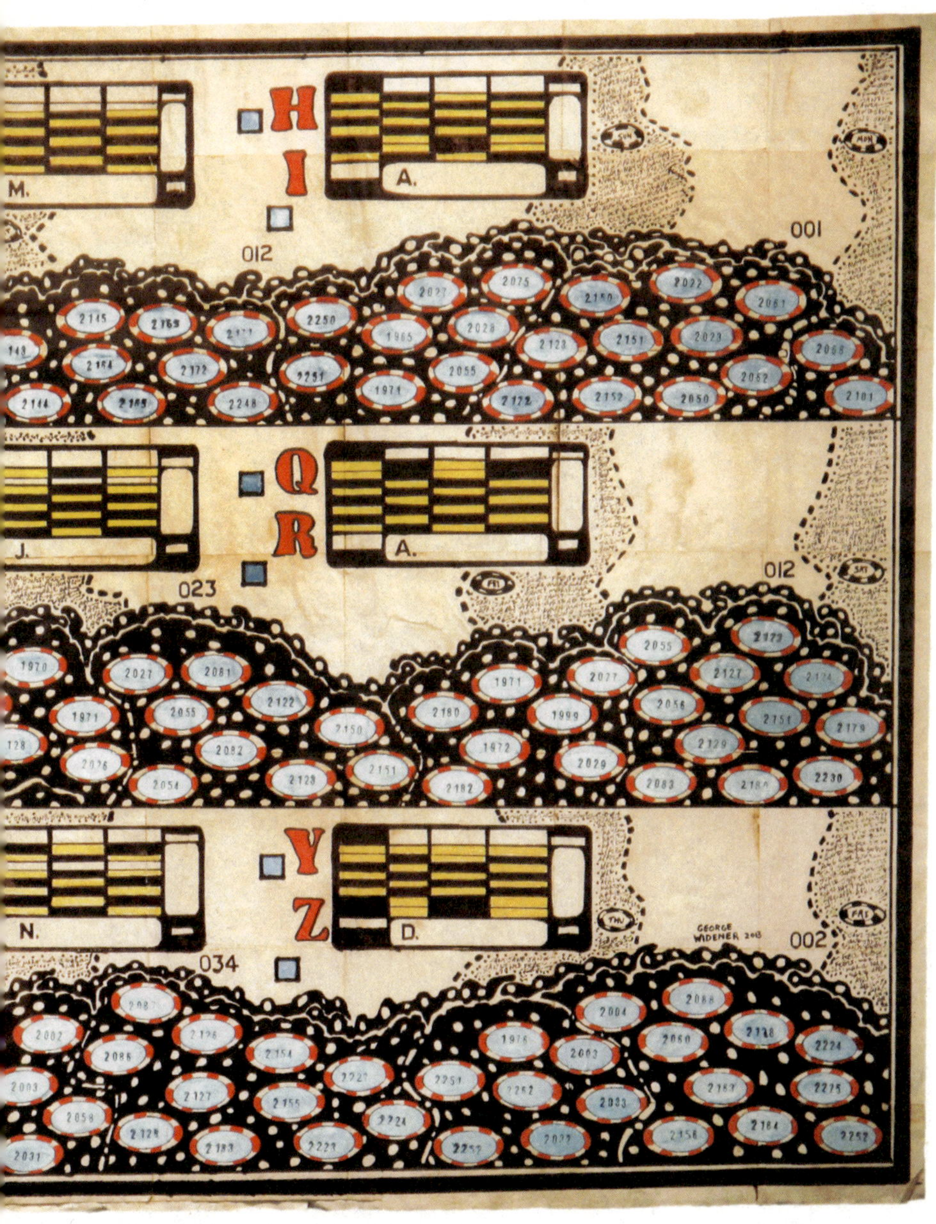

George Widener *'Cipher 1962'* 2013 mixed media on paper 28 ¼ x 48 ¾ ins
image courtesy Ricco/Maresca Gallery, New York

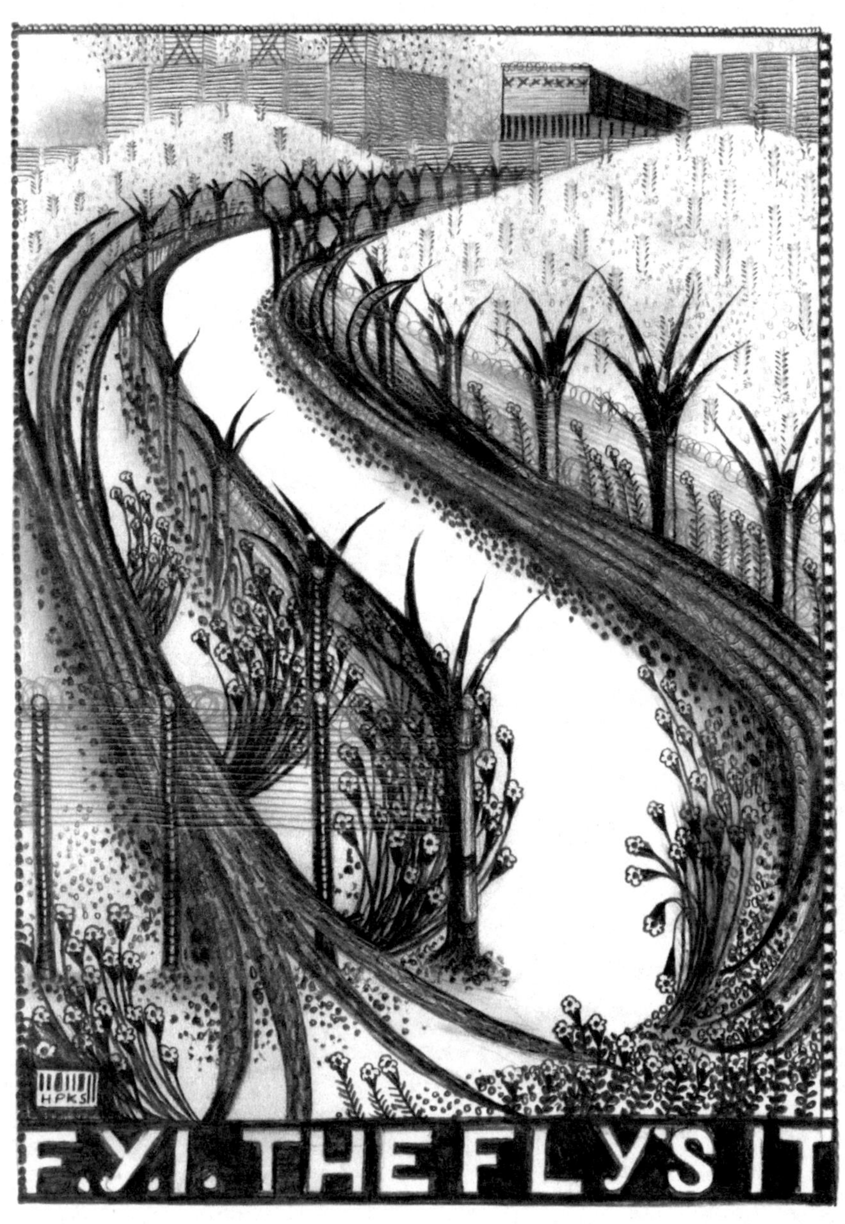

Chris Hipkiss *'FYI The Fly's It'* pencil, ink, metal leaf on paper 8 x 6 ins
image courtesy the artist

Outsider Art: An Inside View
Alpha Mason
The Alpha part of Chris Hipkiss

What is Outsider art?

It's a term that is sometimes bandied about in referring to the work of trained artists who adopt or appropriate a certain style; that style is – broadly speaking – infantile, 'doodle-esque' and usually intense, with more than a smidgen of horror vacui about it, whether expressed in two dimensions or three. However, in a general sense, Outsider art is identified by the biography (real or fictional) of the artist, with little-to-no definition in terms of style. In that respect, it is unusual in the context of art history.

Therefore, the more pertinent question may be: What makes someone an 'Outsider artist'? At this point, most cognoscenti of the field will wheel out a Dubuffet quote, words to the effect of '… an individual who has had no formal art training, does not view his/her creations as art, has no interest in selling the work and no connection to the gallery system…'. Often, a little corollary will be added, suggesting that one can find most such individuals in institutions of some kind. No mention of the art itself, then? It's at this point that those of us who've had a little too much experience on the inside of the Outsider art phenomenon realise that something is badly amiss.

A short disclaimer belongs here; there are some wonderful, genuine people amongst the arbiters and purveyors of Outsider art. We've had (and still have) the privilege and pleasure of working with several of them. They are drawn to the field by a weariness of art-school machinations, of what they view as the contrived nature of much of mainstream art's bite-sized concepts and projects, and of gallerists whose focus is on qualifications rather than quality. They are drawn to Hipkiss because the work amply demonstrates that freedom from the constraints of art schooling; it is perpetual, unselfconscious and the 'projects' (that most certainly exist within the perpetuity) can be reclassified as 'phases'. A lack of formal art training lends some kind of vindication to the label in our case, and – since a chance meeting with the editors of Raw Vision, during our search for a way into the art world back in 1992 – that's been enough for it to stick.

If it ended there – if it were just a nice little epithet to differentiate the manner of creating – why would we object? But, in more than two decades under this umbrella, we've discovered that it's very far from that.

The problem is that – once the work has been pigeonholed – the artist must be 'reframed' in order to fit the profile. For us, this has meant that: as two 1st Class graduates, our entire education is reduced to Chris having 'quit' school at sixteen; our thirty-year creative partnership, and the joint conception of the drawings, is omitted from any biography; and the work is portrayed as being the product of a male simpleton's fantasies of a female-dominated society. It's for this reason that, recently, we've overtly reframed our own biography by changing the pronoun to the plural; we are a feminine and feminist couple, and to have the female component of our partnership excised is an unconscionable irony. This we've done for our own sanity and self-esteem, but it is also a potent statement of opposition to our inclusion in the grouping.

In the course of researching for a forthcoming book, designed to allow so-called Outsider artists to speak for themselves, an obvious truth occurred to me: almost without exception, the artists are – or can be said to be – working class. The lack of education is key, as we discovered when a biography we used to feature on our website was routinely quoted only up to Chris leaving school and working in his father's factory. Reference to a brief stint as a lorry driver was also a regular aside. I then began to look, with new eyes, at the writings and quotes from some of the most vocal spokespeople over the years.

One of Britain's best-known names in the field is that of Albert Louden. Chris and I both spoke to him on the telephone a couple of years ago and found him to be a charming man who had fallen into the black hole of 'Outsiderness' for much the same reasons as we had. This is not clear from the literature, mostly drawn from the words of those who originally championed him; as with Hipkiss, the story goes that a funny little man approached them, arms outstretched in child-like fashion, loaded with wondrous, primitive creations. Choice adjectives, such as 'willingly' and 'gratefully' pepper these accounts, along with the notions of 'protection' and 'nurturing' on the part of the 'discoverers', as though to underline the hapless randomness of lost souls finding their way to sanctuary by pure chance. Like us, Louden was searching for people to promote his art, but what he found – friendly and ostensibly respectful attention – was not quite as it seemed.

A few years after his 'discovery', Louden committed the cardinal sin of accepting attention from mainstream galleries. The published reactions to this from his erstwhile friends were reminiscent of the parent of a fourteen-year-old girl who intends to go out wearing too much make-up and a short skirt. One quote reveals an attempt to understand Louden's motives, however, stating that most living Outsiders are poor, have no social life and want to make money. Apart from the glaring personal insult, such a view is interesting in two other senses; firstly, it directly asserts that Outsider artists are from the poorer, or lower, classes, and not well-connected; secondly, that it is possible to transcend (or be rejected from, depending on one's perspective) Outsider status once 'contaminated' with the commercial world and a realisation that the work can sell.

Taking the latter point first, it's a case of damned if you do, damned if you don't; one of the prime tenets of the 'Outsider' world is that the artist does not care about money (or, indeed, need to make a living, since they are 'protected'), so whilst certain pieces can attract a considerable price, the artist does not – and should not – benefit. However, once the hunt for 'living Outsiders' started, of course there were ordinary people caught up in it – and ordinary people resent the idea that others are profiting disproportionately from work they create. This is not a case, as the condescending words would imply, of being 'poor'; it is, rather, indicative of self-respect and the natural urge to be paid a respectable amount for one's labour. Whilst few artists ask to be labelled Outsider, for some, it is the only way in to the art world. So if one acquiesces to the label, one must expect paltry rewards for one's efforts, and if one rails against it, one must risk not being recognised at all…

As for the issue of class per se, again, there are noble exceptions, but an analysis of many publications and articles on Outsider art reveal a stark and uncomfortable truth: the subject permits well-off, mostly highly-educated and well-connected individuals, to publicly patronise – and, in extreme cases such as the one above – humiliate artists considered to have little social capital. In no other artistic sphere would this be tolerated, but another happy 'qualification' of this arbitrary set of artists is that they are not supposed to have a voice – or want one – so there is no comeback. It's hard enough for any lesser artist to gain the ear of the press; for those branded Outsiders, it's nigh on impossible. One must accept the defamation, or – as we have done – attempt to make one's protests via personal sites and blogs. Whatever the case, the 'Big Boys' win again.

So what happens to those who have the audacity to question the branding, assuming they escape an early, wrathful rejection, that is? We've been questioning it for years – since Day One, in fact – and, mostly, our objections are simply ignored. In recent years, we've managed – largely thanks to our exceptional galleries (Susanne Zander in Europe and Cavin-Morris in the US) – to garner wider attention; Hipkiss has been shown in mainstream places, and received good press with only passing reference to the 'O' word. But it's worth noting that there are two of us, that we are well-educated and not easily categorised as working class, and that we have persevered full-time for

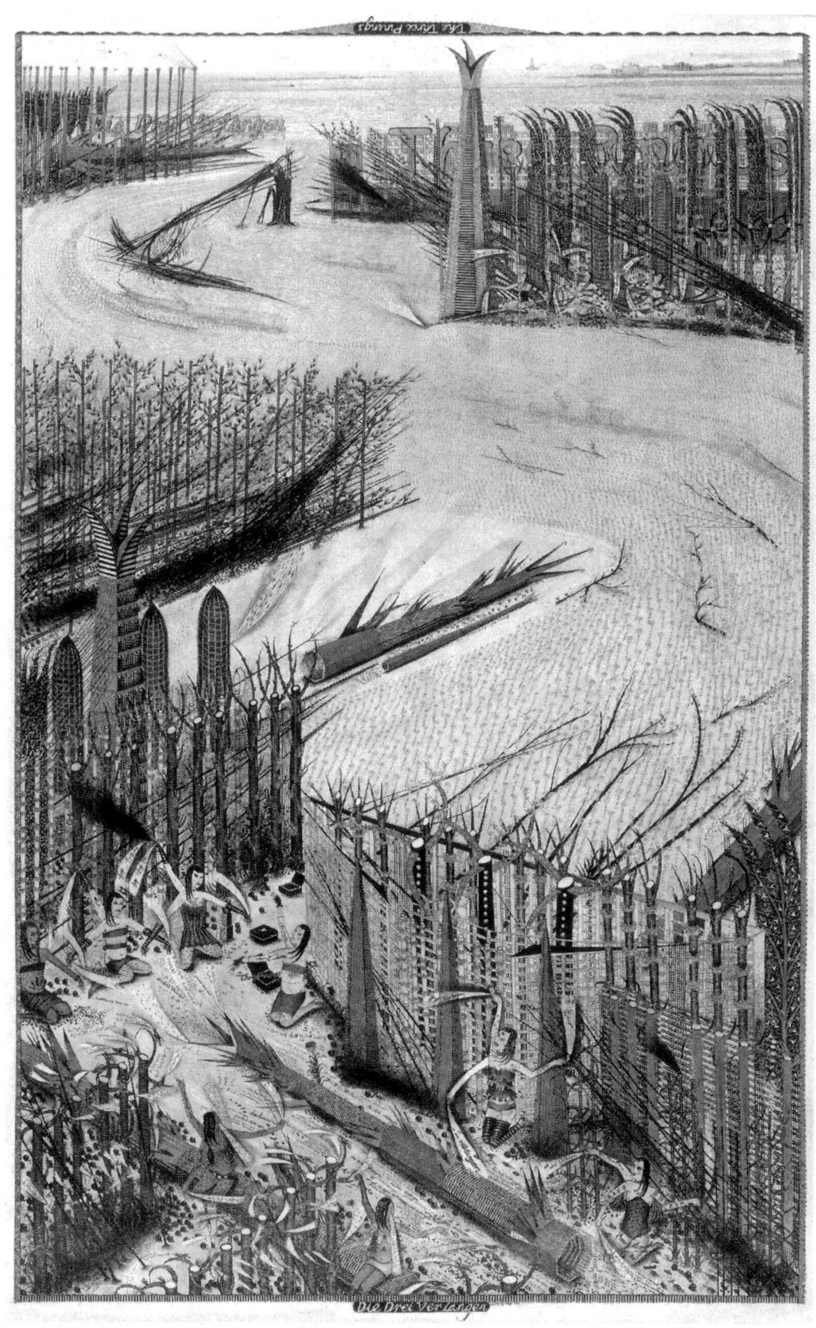

Chris Hipkiss *'Die Drei Verlangen'* pencil, ink, metal leaf on paper 71 x 44.5 ins
image courtesy the artist

many years, not just in creating the art, but in taking a keen interest in how we are portrayed. It's very time-consuming, and many just don't have that time or energy. One can be destroyed with a few choice words from the right people and thrown out of the fold, so the artist has to: either put up and shut up, give up on their aspirations, or continue to create for nothing. Stark choices…

A word, here, about 'genuine' Outsiders: Chris is fond of saying that the only true ones are dead, though, that, too, is questionable. I'm pleased to see that there is increasing debate concerning the myths built around Darger, Ramirez and other greats – artists some of whom, to my mind, have been subject to what would be actual libel had they been alive to contest it. Seeing, first-hand, how living artists can be so misrepresented, how do we know that these people were as isolated, single, uneducated, sexually perverted or 'insane' as they're made out to be? At the other end of the spectrum, in Traylor's case, there are issues of a genuinely harrowing story being rejigged to portray the 'happy slave'. Whatever it is, it feels uncomfortable to paint pictures of the dead with such a broad brush and scant evidence.

Those who worked with Dubuffet, at Gugging, and in other places where there was an official 'stamp' of mental health issues, can be classified more assuredly – and perhaps the label should have stopped there. Instead, that idea and these projects have led to a plethora of others, attempting to 'collect worlds' based on fabricated personal stories of an array of creators, which – ultimately – are grand installations credited to one party alone: the collector. Meanwhile, mainstream artists appropriate the styles and even compositions of so-called Outsiders, not feeling the need to credit them as they would a lesser-known, living art-school graduate. Once again, the power relationship is firmly in place.

Returning to the original question, for those who are living, Outsider art is simply a bucket into which untrained artists are thrown or forced. With several rare – if notable – exceptions, that lack of formal training means that there is literally no place for them in the art world. If someone pens a fine song, they're a musician; anyone can write a best-selling novel and be hailed as a great author. Amongst the creative arts, visual art stands alone in demanding a piece of paper as proof of one's eligibility for general recognition, even though one might have critical acclaim and a healthy throng of collectors queuing to buy one's work.

It's a double bind; when we move on from those who welcomed us into the folds of the 'Outside' world in search of a place in which we can hold our heads up as normal, intelligent human beings, their parting cries will almost invariably contain the phrase 'After all I've done for you!' The

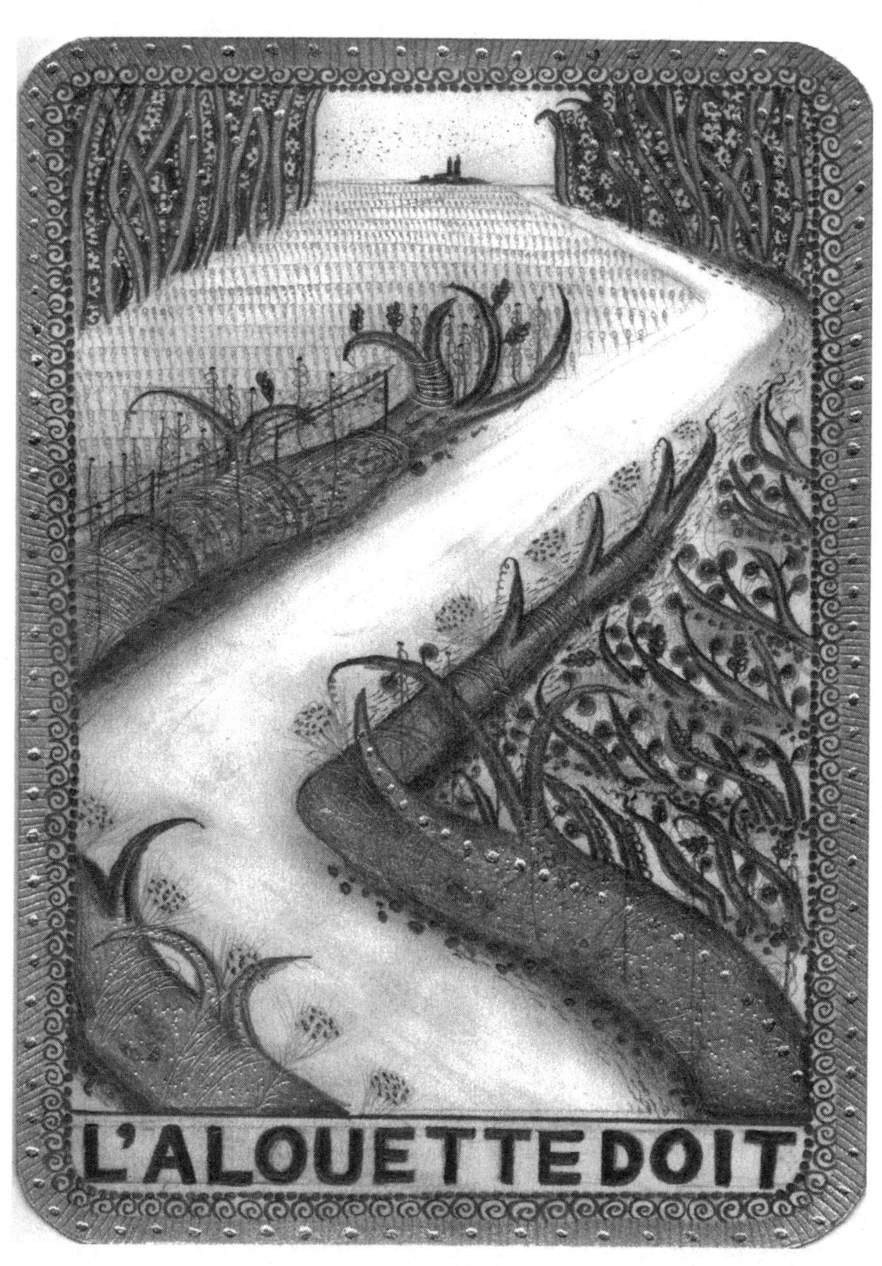

Chris Hipkiss *'L'Alouette Doit'* pencil, ink, metal leaf on paper 8 x 5 ins
image courtesy the artist

thoughts run through one's mind: 'Sold my work too cheaply? Paid me a pittance, then sold my work for a hefty profit? Allowed me to be utterly misrepresented, whilst posing as a friend...?' The worst thing is, in another sense, they're right. Without them, untrained artists might never get anywhere at all. But is it acceptable that the only available box is an entirely inappropriate one? Should anyone be forced to play the fool or the loon to get the attention their work deserves?

It's a fledgling project, but we have invented a new term, which we think neatly encapsulates those of us who find ourselves straddling the divide: Truant art. We chose not to go to art school, but we are just artists all the same. Our biographies are of no more import than those of any other.

There is much more to be written, and many omissions in this article, but I hope that the reader will question the label wherever they see it. Is that photograph a fair portrait, or – if the artist were mainstream – would it have been rejected on the grounds that the subject was momentarily staring into space, or sporting a manic grin after recounting an outrageous anecdote? Where is the evidence – the references, the in-depth interviews – to back up the writer's comments on an artist's private life? Who first called the artist an Outsider, and why?

I hope that the debate will gain momentum in more public spaces. Details of our blog etc., can be found at *chrishipkiss.org* do join the discussion!

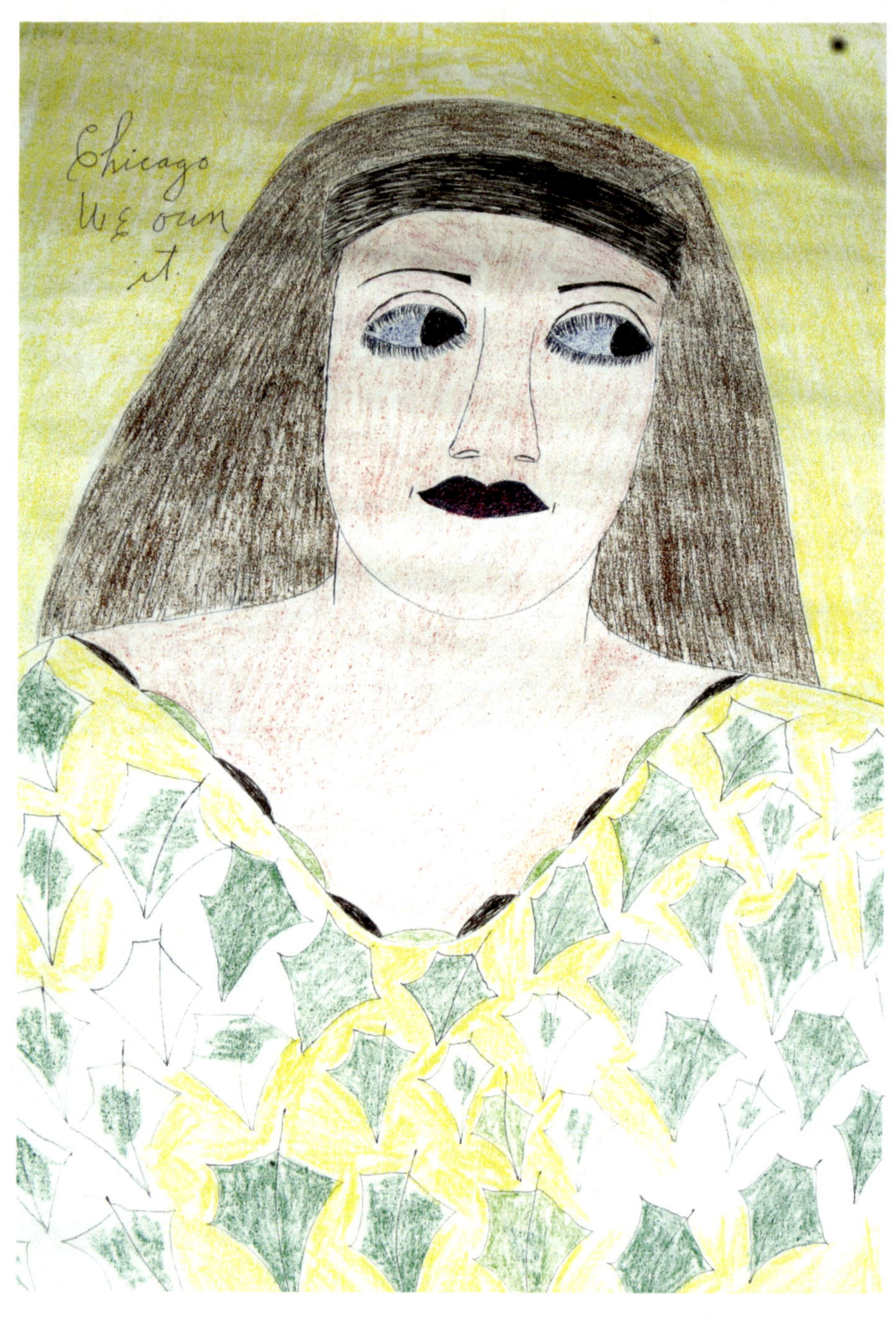

Lee Godie *'Chicago We Own It'* 1978 mixed media 23.25 x 31 ins
image courtesy the collection of Mike Pocius

You can learn quite a bit from outliers; anyway, you can learn all the things that really matter. Outliers are generally looked at suspiciously, associated with the word deviation and assigned a numerical value. Occasionally, outliers can be exploited for financial gain. Sometimes, outliers are the ones doing the exploiting. Outliers come from random coincidence, stupid mistakes, bureaucratic breakdown, deceitful conduct, contamination, failure and the freak show we called nature.

It is highly ill-advised to ever ignore outliers. The most valuable reflections are often derived from the more distant points. Snubbing outliers is the one serious flaw of all modern financial and investment theories, because you never can tell. You never can tell when profoundly consequential, rare events are going to happen. Outliers are non-computable and, in the long run, often turn out to be the most influential.

My strange attraction to word 'outlier' began with my study in the hideously boring field of statistics for human task analysis, but ended in my reading of the delightful book "Wrong Numbers," by Franklin Rosemont. Outliers are wrong numbers, wrong events and wrong people. Wrong because you never can tell what the outlier number will be, what the outlier event will bring and what the outlier people will do. Outliers may be unpredictable, unavoidable and wrong, but they are also the very core of creative authenticity and freedom.

To be an outlier is to emerge from the unstructured randomness found in life rather than the structured randomness of games, the system or the spectacle. All great historic events, scientific inventions and artistic accomplishments could be classified as outliers. While acknowledging the importance of outliers is a crucial key to unlocking the great mysteries of life, to be identified as an outlier oneself hurts.

The pain of being an outlier mixes freak show fame with significance via so called "failure." The sting of being an outlier hit me one day while sitting at a local bar where an inebriated artist was attacking the publisher of a magazine that I wrote for because his publication only included hipster, cliquish, mostly male, rich kids and art school elitists. The publisher stated his defense loudly with the sharp retort, "But we have Renay!"

I think he forgot that I was sitting there - drinking down at the end of the bar by myself. My head spun around as my eyes sprung wide open with the sting of his words. His eyes flashed over at me, realizing his blunder - the cat was out of the bag. He winced. I smiled, acting like it didn't matter even though it did.

That's right: unbeknownst to me, I was secretly viewed as some kind of outlier freak. Maybe because I was a woman, maybe because I was older, maybe because the rich art kids were looking down on me like I was a pathetic bag lady or maybe because of my affiliation with surrealists. I have always embraced my role as a black sheep, but there are difficult feelings that result from being stigmatized. For whatever reason, I was apparently viewed as the Lee Godie of the magazine staff. In many ways, this was more honor than insult.

Lee Godie was a well known outsider artist in Chicago. I remember Lee Godie sitting on the steps of The School of the Art Institute of Chicago when I first went to school there. She sold drawings of herself to students and faculty, also painting her face. She was eccentric, mysterious, feisty and pervasive. At one time almost everyone I knew had one of her drawings hanging on their refrigerator door.

A personal mythology developed around Lee Godie, including the rumor that she was secretly rich - just pretending to be homeless - now her art sells for quite a bit of money. She defied the usual description of "outsider artist" because she definitely was extremely aware of the art world. She sat on the steps of The Art Institute of Chicago for over twenty years. Sometimes she even went inside the building.

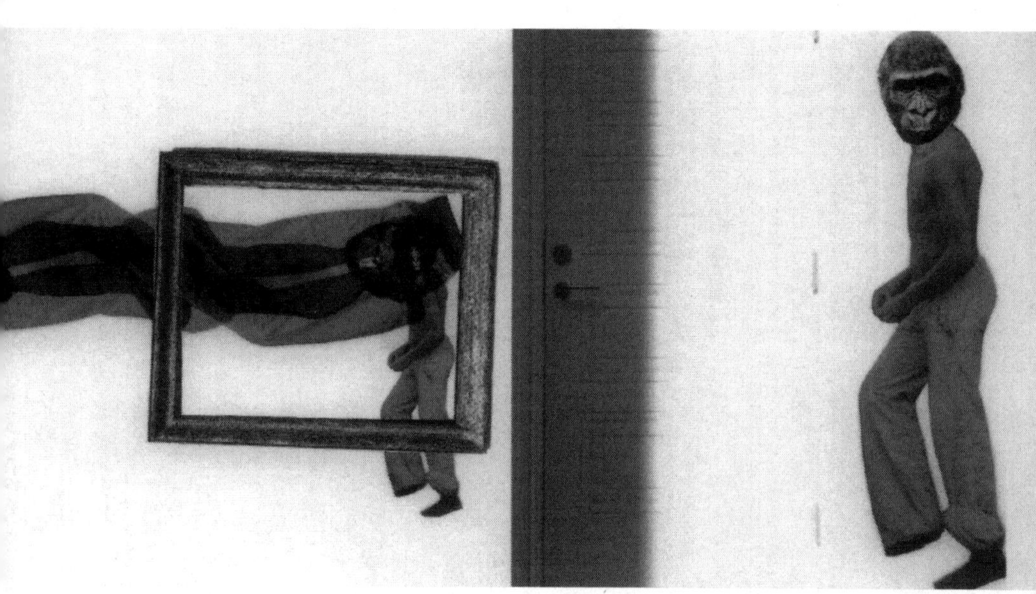

Lise Holm *'Funky Frame'* 2013

However, no matter how many trips she may have made inside the museum, her art did not seem to change at all.

Personal mythology is vital to validate the outsider artist as a true outlier. Some fetish ideas of "the pure and isolated" far-outside outlier may have caused the real stories of artists' lives to fit an art world script. I remember eating Indian food with Franklin Rosemont and a few Chicago surrealists, when Franklin told me about how he had come to meet Henry Darger's landlord, Nathan Lerner. Contrary to what some accounts might lead us to believe, Henry Darger may not have been a "pure" isolated artist. I asked Penelope Rosemont about Darger and she told me that even though he was isolated as he grew older, as many older people become, there were indications that he had traveled in his life much more than most people do and that he may very well have been quite sociable when he was young. Coincidently, the Rosemont's often ate at the same restaurant as Henry - *Roma's* - although they never met.

The inclusion of outsider art into the "inside" art world could be problematic for the artists. It is difficult to remain authentic and to resist institutions, corporate sponsors and corporate symbols. I was in an art show with Wesley Willis' brother, Richard Willis, and someone bought me a wooden block that Richard had made with a BP symbol glued to it. Frankly, I found this block of BP "art" to be extremely annoying. Maybe that was the point. I asked Penelope Rosemont what she thought of corporate symbols in outsider art and she pointed out to me that to someone experiencing the world from a whole different level, these symbols may hold another meaning. Perhaps it was an image he liked because it was familiar. I tried to talk to Richard about using corporate symbols, but he immediately changed the subject. He wanted to talk about the exact addresses and dimensions of specific buildings in Chicago—a topic on which he has an encyclopaedic knowledge.

Even if the art world could completely assimilate outsider artists, there will probably always be outliers that not only resist absorption but make being different into an art form. I first learned about being really different when I was ten years old. I was at a fair in Kansas and I went into the wrong door. I ended up at a sideshow. For some reason, this fair had about fifty trailers and tents full of "freaks." I stood in a group of about twenty people who were waiting anxiously for the entertainment to begin. I was fascinated by the paintings that decorated the tent. What was to happen next was one of the most profoundly influential experiences of my life.

A man was helped out onto the stage and was lifted up above the crowd on a perch. He had no arms or legs. He had a big head and his mouth formed a giant smile. He had a certain angry charm.

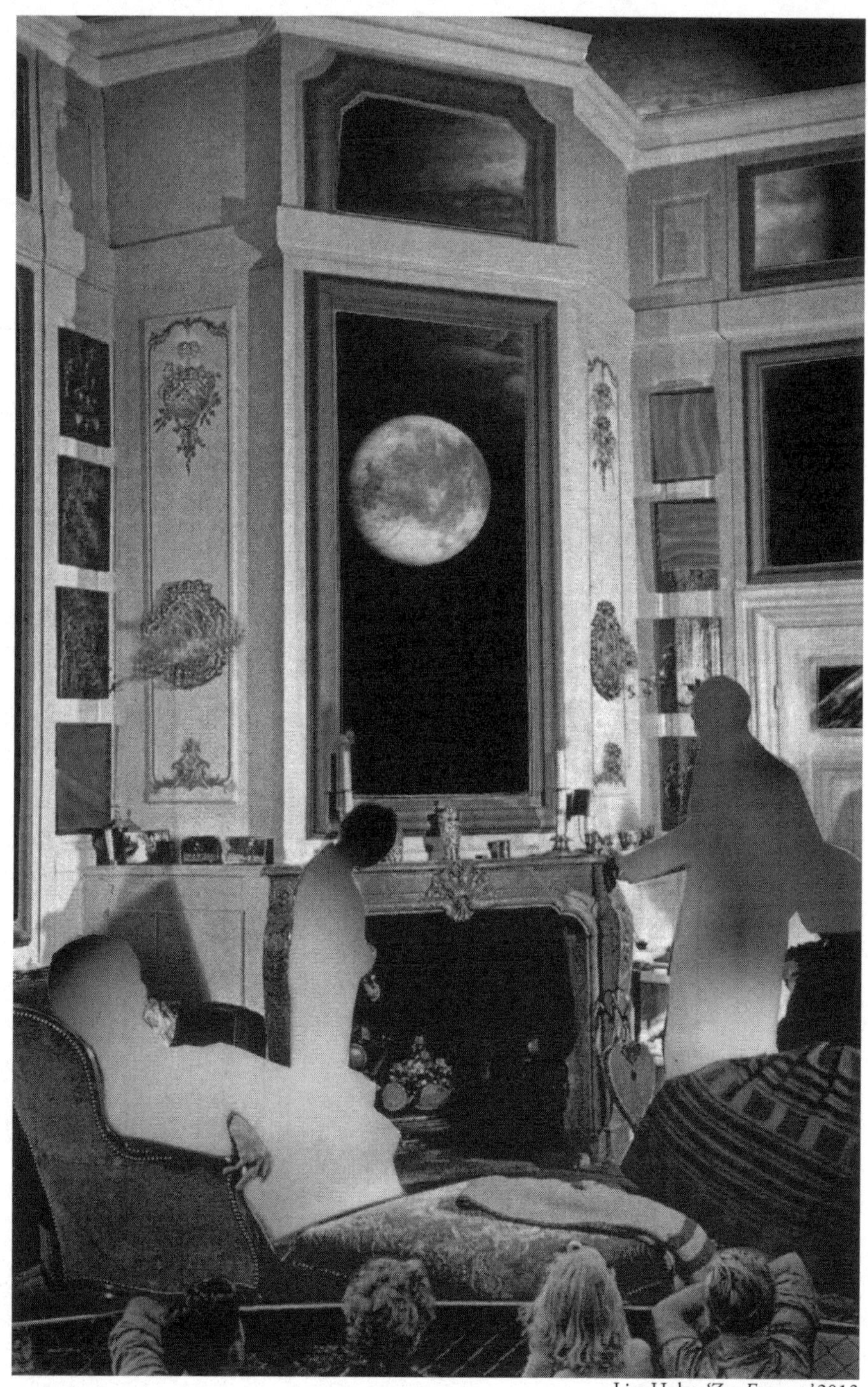

Lise Holm *'Zoo Entrants'* 2013

"Hello everybody and thanks for coming to our show. Don't feel bad, don't feel shame. We're glad you came. Thank you for giving us your money because otherwise we'd have to live in a goddamned institution."

That caught my attention right there, because I'd never before heard anyone say the word *"goddamned"* in public. *"They call me a Bucket Baby. I have no arms and I have no legs, but I can assure you I am not a baby. I am a man. A grown man—just like you sir and you sir and you."* Then, he was handed a bucket full of shaving lather and with his twisted hand that protruded out of his shoulder, he lathered his face and started shaving. He repeated the phrase, *"I am a man. I am a man. I am a man."* over and over and over. It did not seem to me that he was being exploited by anyone, it seemed to me that he was running the show. He was a performance artist and a teacher who was educating the public - not so much about disabilities but about prejudice and the human condition.

When the show was over, I did not follow the crowd into the next room to see the lobster boy. I had to go outside and sit under a tree by myself for awhile to think over the things that this man had said. I felt an unexpected mixture of pain, shame and enlightenment that only comes from a brush with rare outliers. This man may have been the person portrayed in Mat Fraser's one-man show, *"Sealboy: Freak"* although I don't remember him being called Sealboy. This particular sideshow was an outlier event in and of itself. No one could have predicted that going inside that door, they would have their entire belief system about people who are different exploded to bits.

Some outliers can crash your economy, some make the most profound scientific discoveries, some create the greatest art - some outliers change your life. If you walk into the wrong door, it may, in fact, be exactly the right door - you just never can tell.

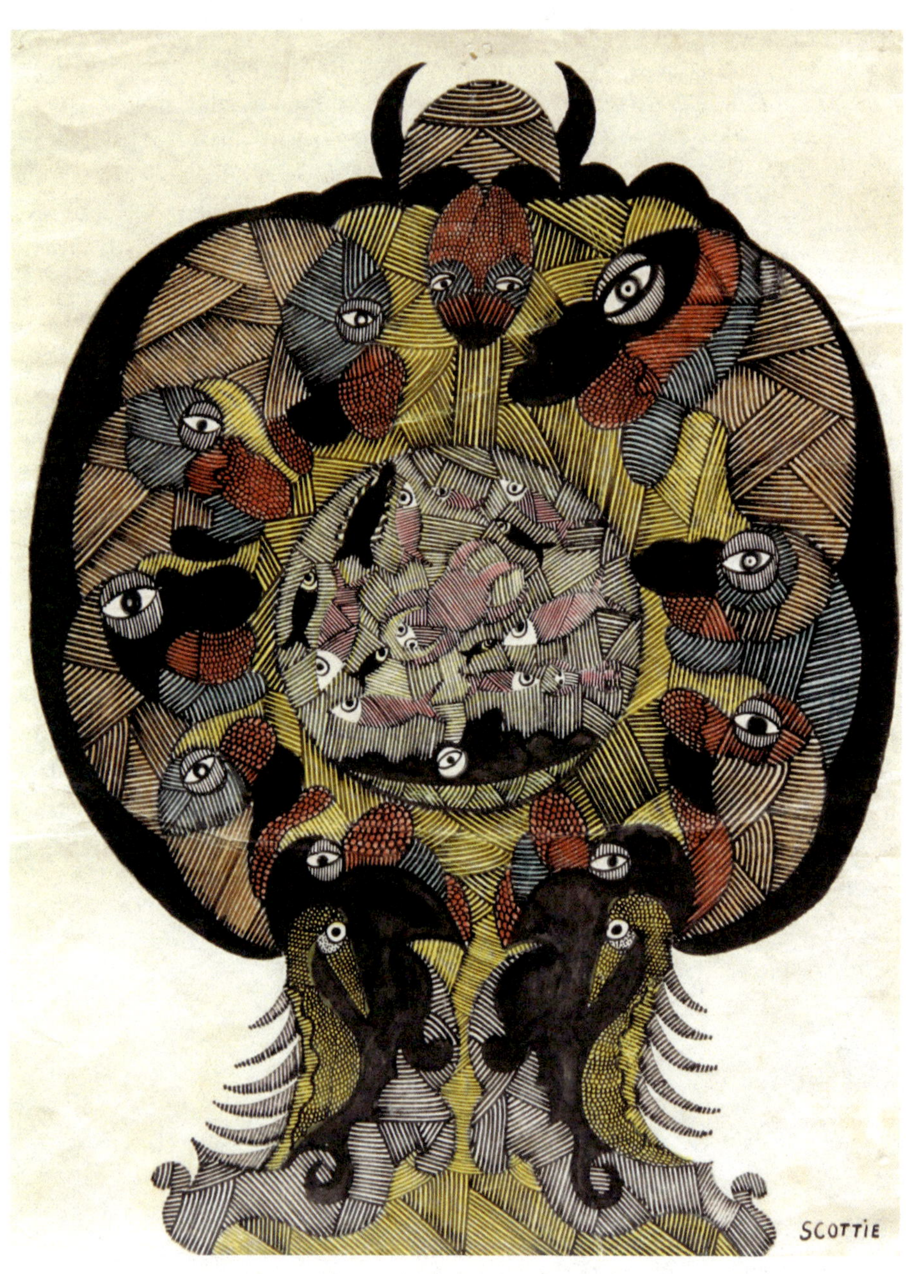

Scottie Wilson *'Untitled'* c.1946 ink & crayon 14.5 x 11 ins
image courtesy Henry Boxer Gallery

**The vibrancy of the subconscious:
"Scottie" Wilson's cross-hatchings**
A contribution to British surrealism

Michel Remy
University of Nice

The mystery of creation, the challenge of rationality, the secret of origins, the gold of time sought after and discovered, are secretions secreted by Scottie Wilson's works, haunted by the language of the birds. Whether in the facts of his life – all of them steeped in the shadows of doubt – or in his obsessional drawings, those words constitute paltry attempts at covering up our incapacity to fully comprehend what is at stake in his visionary works.

His life is brilliantly recounted by George Melly in his *Life and Work of Scottie Wilson* with the appropriate amount of precaution and hypothetical statements, especially as regards the earlier part of Wilson's life, before he came back to, and settled in England around 1945. Suffice it here, indeed, to recall the main stages of his youth and early adulthood. Born on June 6th 1888, unless it be in 1890, in Glasgow, unless it be in the East End of London, of Jewish Russian descent, unless his accent told of his Scottish Glaswegian origin, he went through a series of adventures which all fed his extraordinarily fertile imagination, taking on several jobs including a junk shop in the Caledonian market first, then in Leather Lane,

befriending no one except the shopkeepers and drunkards of those areas. His parents, immigrants from Lithuania, were given the name Freeman, when arriving in Hull, by the customs officer who couldn't decipher their Russian name but later on, Louis, one of their four sons, changed to the name Robert Wilson after either escaping from France, where he fought in the Scottish Rifles regiment in World War I, or deserting for humanitarian reasons from the Black and Tans regiment he was enlisted in in the twenties. Having (in either case!) taken refuge in Ireland, then Canada, he eventually opened a bric-à-brac shop in a back street of Toronto for which, as the anecdote has it, he had gathered an incredible variety of objects, among which a collection of hundreds of fountain pens. One of them was a particularly big one, with a wide and thick 14-carat gold nib, to which he gave the name "Bulldog". One day, leaning over an old table covered with a piece of cardboard and waiting for clients who never came, he automatically plunged the pen into black ink and started to draw on the table, distractedly and inattentive to what he was doing. The result, probably given its hypnotic quality, pleased him and egged him on to make others.

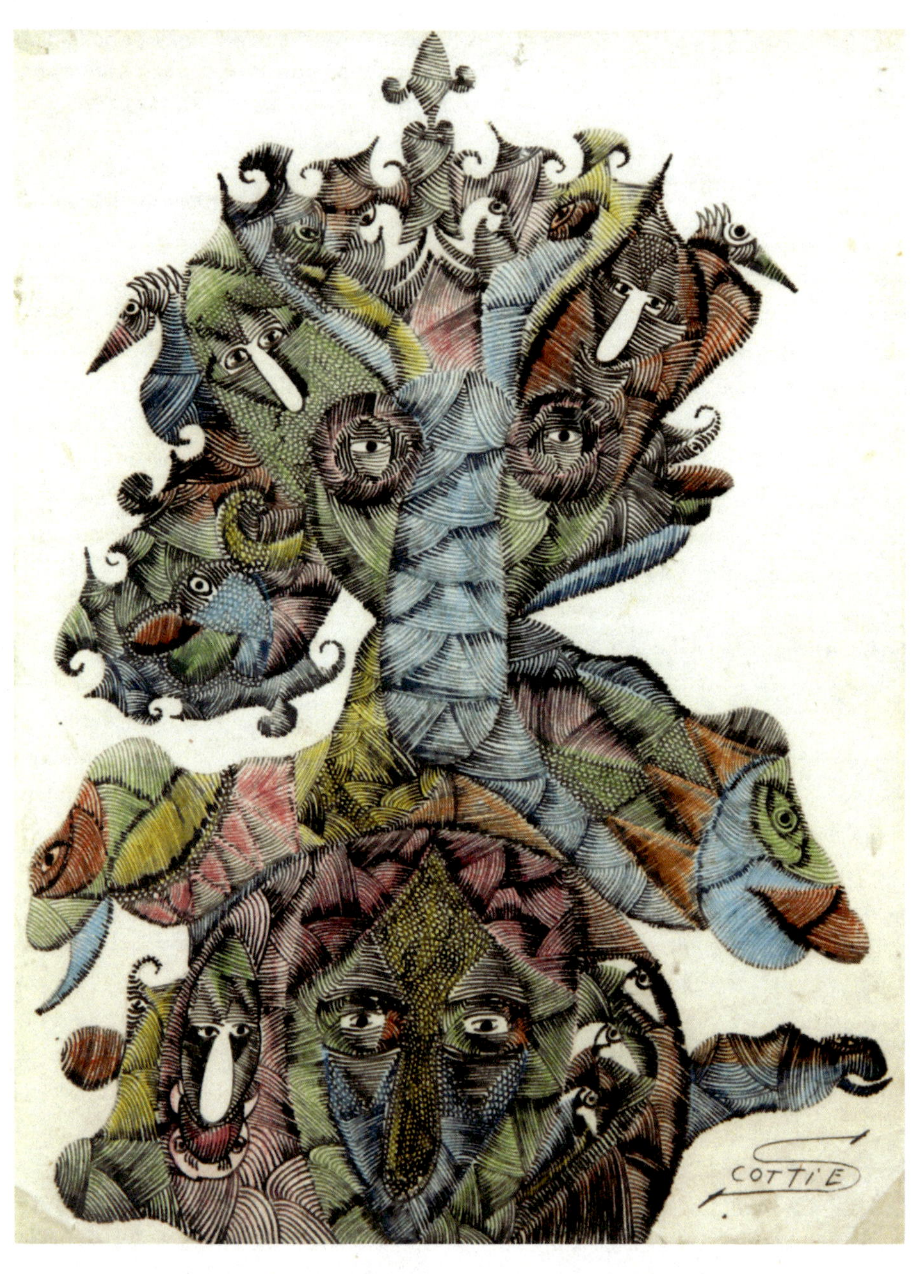

Scottie Wilson *Masquerade* c.1935 ink , crayon & watercolour 11.75 x 8.75 ins
image courtesy Henry Boxer Gallery

A few weeks later, he sold his shop, moved to Winnipeg and Vancouver but continued to draw the same kind of intriguing images, using his drawings to cover the walls of his new shop, "thus saving buying wallpaper", as he recalled. Then started a most prolific production of works on various kinds of paper or cardboard, of all sizes, using the same repetition over and over again of tiny lines conjuring up grotesque faces, stern or smiling personages, sinister, grinning monsters, joyful birds swimming around or fishes flying about - irrepressibly, as if those creatures *needed* to emerge from a timeless past, a hidden time-space to which he instinctively had discovered the secret entrance.

Critics have suggested that those faces or creatures were echoes of the Indian totems of the Canadian West coast or that they might soar up from the depths of his childhood, traces from the zoos and circuses he loved to visit at an early age or from the designs in the doilies, tablecloths and lace curtains of his childhood home. One may also detect resemblances with the carved designs of the ancient Celts, the triangular inscriptions of African sculptures or the irregular rhythms of South Seas carvings. Whatever that may be, it is obvious that Scottie Wilson's drawings point to the mysterious springs of the imaginative powers of the mind, between time and timelessness, where images are formed, grow and ripen until the moment when, transformed and awakened by subliminal impulses and the compulsion of creation, they come up and express *themselves*, a process he himself summed up when he said: " I enter into a trance and when I wake up, I see them all waiting for me, they are ready. A Chinaman does it all for me."

Scottie Wilson's vision is paroxystically poetical. Every drawing is different from the others and the successive stages we can distinguish in his dealing with specific themes and figures, are the result of an intensely existential experience deriving and emerging from the whirling turmoil of memory – stages of his life marked by spectres, enchanted cities, castles, vases, fountains, birds, fishes, human faces, houses and delirious architectures. Not two lines in his drawings have the same function, suggested Victor Musgrave, one of his few faithful friends and "promoters", with slight metaphorical exaggeration. Indeed, their parallel repetition forms triangles or rectangles which, in their turn, form a multitude of baroque shapes which, in their turn, form faces or bodies or buildings. It is a process based on the infinitesimal variation of texture, thickness and direction of the ink stroke, giving to static images a trembling dynamism of visionary delicacy and subtlety. Innocence and lack of planning are key words regarding what one must call his technique, for lack of a better word, constituting a thoroughgoing opening on to *surreality*, which André Breton acknowledged and celebrated in 1947 when he welcomed works by Scottie on the walls

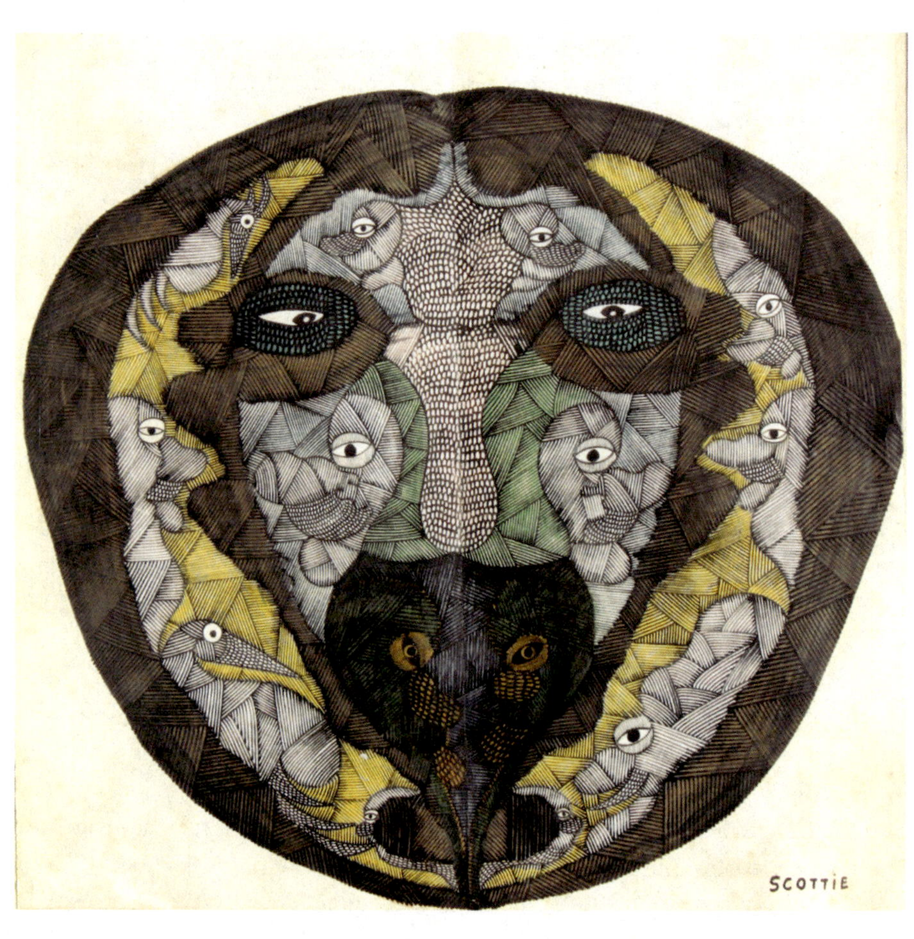

Scottie Wilson *'Untitled'* c.1947 ink & crayon 15 x 15.5 ins
image courtesy Henry Boxer Gallery

58

of the Galerie Maeght on the occasion of the International Surrealist Exhibition. Before him, E.L.T.Mesens, to whose attention Roland Penrose had brought Scottie's works in 1945, had declared in the *Horizon* issue of June 1946 that "he had never seen such prismatic interplay of cross-hatchings which creates light and volume" and "gives to the technique such eloquence and discretion. It is magic reached by the simplest means". He went on to stress that Scottie was " a man who has refused to be slave to our enchained civilization,…who has achieved his own liberation not in the light of the spirit nor through an intelligent interpretation of materialism, but through the discovery of drawing *for himself.*"

Indeed, Scottie Wilson's use of the line is by no means linked to, or dependent on, any specific goal. He doesn't tend *towards*, but sojourns *within* an extremely volatile interior space between presence and absence, between the infinite quality of the repeated inscription of the lines and the finite quality of the completed image, between the Same and the Other. The completedness of his images is the result of a never-completed, ceaselessly-repeated process, of a movement issuing from the depths of the mind but *arrested* and commenced again. From these obsessional cross-hatchings, there emerge various forms, prompted by an energy *of their own*. One cannot say that his flowers, birds, fishes are made of those lines but exactly the reverse, in a kind of in-

version of the representative process. In other words, those small lines are left free to go where they want, their repetition does not depend on any kind of intention on the part of the artist. The order to stop or change direction originates in the place where the secret they aim at conveying, is lodged, an unutterable, unreachable secret. Lines give birth to forms, forms are *delivered* by lines, lines acquire some kind of existence only in and from this process of delivery. Lines are differentiated from themselves by and into what they let escape, unwittingly, thus arresting the flow of the energy which underlies each stroke. The surrealist line will be ever-wandering, or will not be – the surrealist line is an errant line.

This kind of lateralization of the line is evidence that the question which Scottie Wilson raises, which is the central question of surrealism, is how to have access to the other side, to the reverse of reality but *within* reality, how to work one's way towards an inaccessible origin. It is in this passage, in this horizontal move – not a vertical move into some depths – in the gap we bridge from one tiny line to the next, from one form to the next, from one image to the next, that traditional dualisms (same/other, inside/outside, communicable/incommunicable) become suspended and collapse. What is given evidence of in these drawings is that the *same* lines, when repeated, necessarily give onto the *other, their other*, that is a form, and the forms once repeated, also give onto their other, other forms which contain them. The same begets the other, the same *is* the other, the same is, somewhere, what is *different* and categories are no longer separate. Compartmentalization (those little squares and triangles) are *exceeded*, annulled. *Surreality*, Scottie Wilson's drawings actually proclaim, is that third reality which sends us back to the origin of forms, before they are fully identified, an origin, we repeat, for ever inaccessible. Deprived of any fixed, identifiable origin or end, Scottie Wilson's lines automatically disseminate and open another space in the viewer's eyes, another space of dissemination, the addressee of which is the viewer, and for which he is totally, pleasurably and vertiginously responsible. The lesson of surrealism, as is repeated by Scottie Wilson, is that we must learn how to recognize all the accesses we are given here and now to an interior space which we must eventually acknowledge as *ours*, independently of any given so-called reality.

Hence, the radical anonymity of his drawings – a liberation of the drawing from him who has delivered it, a liberation of the name from the letters which compose it. Here we come across another fundamental principle of surrealism: a surrealist work has no author, no one, in other words, has any authority over it. It *is* itself its own authority, the result of the irruption of a pre-historic, a-temporal expression of what can never be fully expressed but keeps on wanting to be expressed, an unidentifiable force to which one can't possibly give a name unless one is a usurper. In no way is Scottie Wilson a usurper, and many declarations of his affirm this. Evidence of it is indeed given by his attitude outside the galleries which exhibited his works for sale at a high price: he would stand outside and sell drawings he would make on the spot for a negligible sum, just as he would do on the streets or piers of Scarborough or Margate from the back of his van, not selling his drawings but making people pay to see them and giving them one. "Scottie" is literally a man in the crowd, refusing to turn his name into a marketable object, a man "erased" so to speak by his drawings, anonymous, an author no longer the genitor of his offspring, an author who has lost his name and has wholeheartedly and definitively surrendered to the creative principle in him. Remember: "A Chinaman does it all for me" !!

However anecdotal it may be, a simple look at his signatures before and after 1944 reveals how they emblematize this unconscious refusal of authority. In the early part of his life, the letters which spell a fragment of his name, COTTIE, are cradled in the lower curve of a huge S; the first letter is overcapitalized as if it protected and sheltered the process of division of the name, trying to secure some of it. After 1943 or 1944, the name appears in its totality but de-capitalized, levelled down, uniformized in the succession of capital letters: SCOTTIE, no one being more important than the other. The capitalization of each and every letter, together with their separation one from the other, implies the refusal of the name as an authority, a process of self-erasure concomitant with the dis-organization of the subject. Indeed, the capitalization of a name indicates that the name is a *proper* noun, unrepeatable, unique of its kind and closed upon itself, all attitudes which Scottie Wilson refused. The drawings he made did not literally belong to him. They belonged to a Chinaman….

According to many of his declarations, Scottie Wilson was convinced he was working for the construction of a better world or at least for the development of people's awareness of the necessity to find a way to create a harmonious world. As Roger Cardinal wrote: " (he believed) in the regeneration of mankind, an entry into a new order of things in which a wise simplicity will obtain in human relations, and 'a true civilization' will emerge". In other words, Scottie Wilson's drawings have to be considered as experiences of what is central to man, his fundamental, radical humanity or human-ness, what makes him good as well as evil, a blending of contraries and contradictions.

Going as far back into time and man's subconscious as possible, it is not surprising that Scottie Wilson should have somehow gone beyond "the gates of horn and ivory" (Nerval) and that this "sensation of primal wonder" (Cardinal) links up with, and opens onto, the subconscious forces at work in all men, especially at the very moment of creation, when desire is confronted with its accomplishment in a never-solved tension, the former always aiming at short-circuiting and overcoming the latter. In that respect, repetition proves to be sublimely regressive. In his attempt to erase differences through repetition and come in sight of an Edenic world, Scottie Wilson works his way towards the birthplace of our fears, complexes and haunting images of our infancy, surrendering then to the authority of the Other. Evidence of this is clearly given by the many phallic shapes, the flaccid bulbous noses, the limp extended tongues, the vagina-like mouths and the testicle-like forms but also by the symbolic images of an intense, avowed albeit repressed, sexuality, such as the masculine spires, fishes, towers, cones and chimneys and the feminine circles, orifices, fishbowls and ovals of all kinds. They are a cry of the mind, the mind's screaming for liberation – a recognition by Scottie Wilson of the workings of the collective unconscious whose deep activity underlies and haunts our "awakened life" and has underlain and haunted it from time immemorial, the time-dimension of Scottie's peaceful, serene, although merciless, struggle with himself.

André Breton pleaded for, and advocated, confidence in the "interior model" and asked the artist or poet to turn to it blindly. Well, here is that interior model, passing from one drawing to the

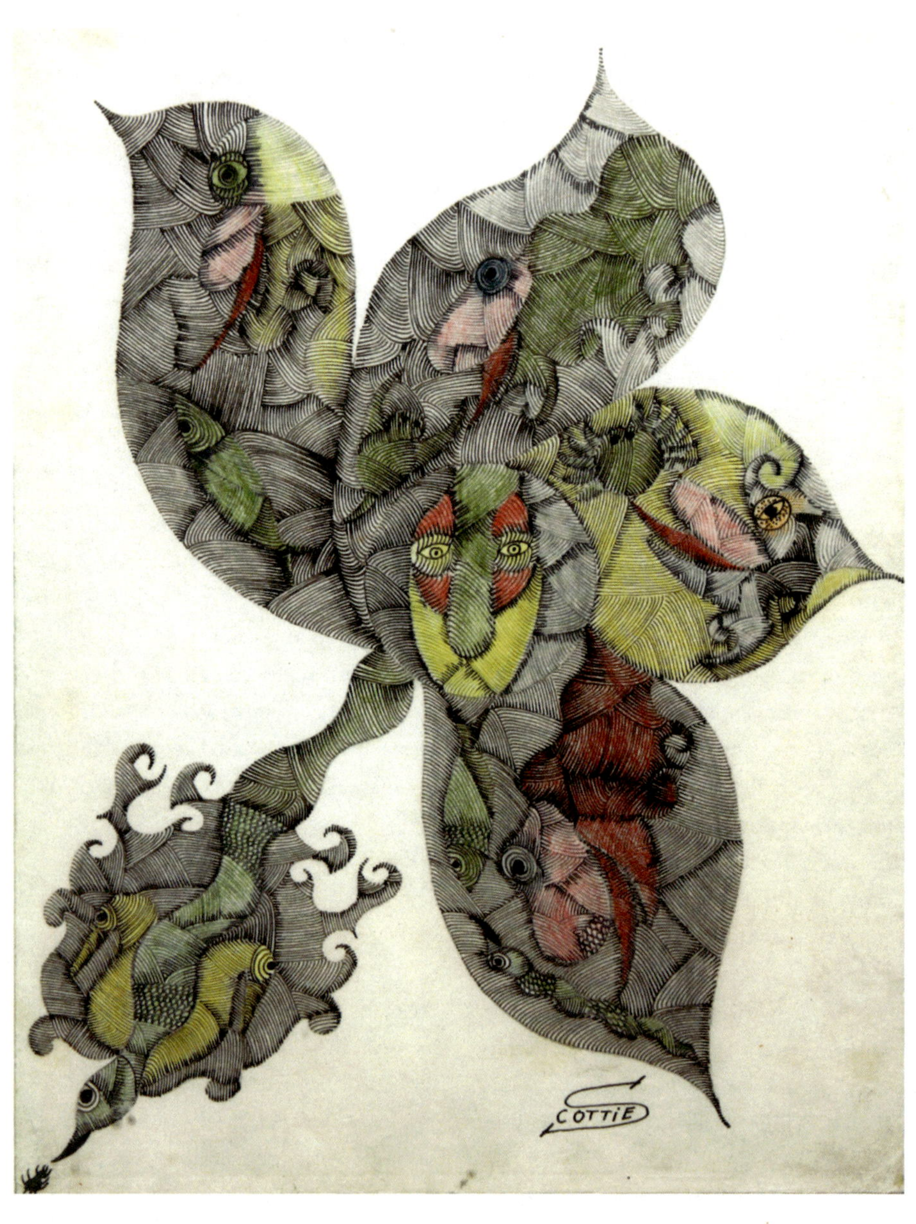

Scottie Wilson *'Curiosity'* 1941 ink & crayon 14.5 x 11 ins
image courtesy Henry Boxer Gallery
previously reproduced in: *'Outsider Art'*, Roger Cardinal, 1972.

next unstoppably, always the same and always different, ordering the production as well as the suspension of all those tiny lines, creating shapes autonomous in themselves but functional when they, in their turn, create other shapes and force us to invert our vision, haunting us with presences-to-come in a language which speaks before words are uttered. These drawings are the frontal presentation of the oneiric, imaginary and perfectly real beings in us. They are the archetypal echoes of the primitive scene inseparable from their own repetition, an original, or rather ab-original, scene, always lacking, always missing and missed, which the saturation of the drawing surface cannot ever reach nor exhaust.

Between lack and excess, between completeness and fragmentation, between desire and accomplishment, we attend the struggle and passion of the dismemberment of the body and the simultaneous re-membering of the mind. Scottie Wilson's drawings breathe, play, dance and vibrate at a threshold which it remains for us to face as if we were facing a burning tyger…

This article is an homage to Michel Thévoz, Victor Musgrave, Monica Kinley, Roger Cardinal and Mervyn Levy, who, among others, devotedly helped bring Scottie Wilson's works to public knowledge.

Bibliography

Cardinal, Roger, *Outsider Art*, London, Studio Vista, 1972.

Cardinal, Roger, "The Art of Scottie Wilson", preface to the catalogue of the exhibition of Scottie Wilson's works at Picturebrokers, London, 26 February-25 March 1986.

Dubuffet, Jean, in coll. with Victor Musgrave and Edward De Maine, "Scottie Wilson", in *L'Art Brut,* n°4, Paris, 1965 : 5-31.

Melly, George, *It's All Writ Out For You, the Life and Work of Scottie Wilson*, London, Thames and Hudson, 1986.

Mesens, E.L.T., "Scottie Wilson", *Horizon*, 13, 78 (June 1946).

Remy, Michel, "Seul le trait monstrueux montre…Problématique du trait surréaliste", in *Le Trait: de la lettre à la figure* (ed.Béatrice Bonhomme et al.), Paris, L'Harmattan, 2007 : 305-314.

Schreiner, Gérard A., *Scottie*, Bâle, Galerie Schreiner, 1979.

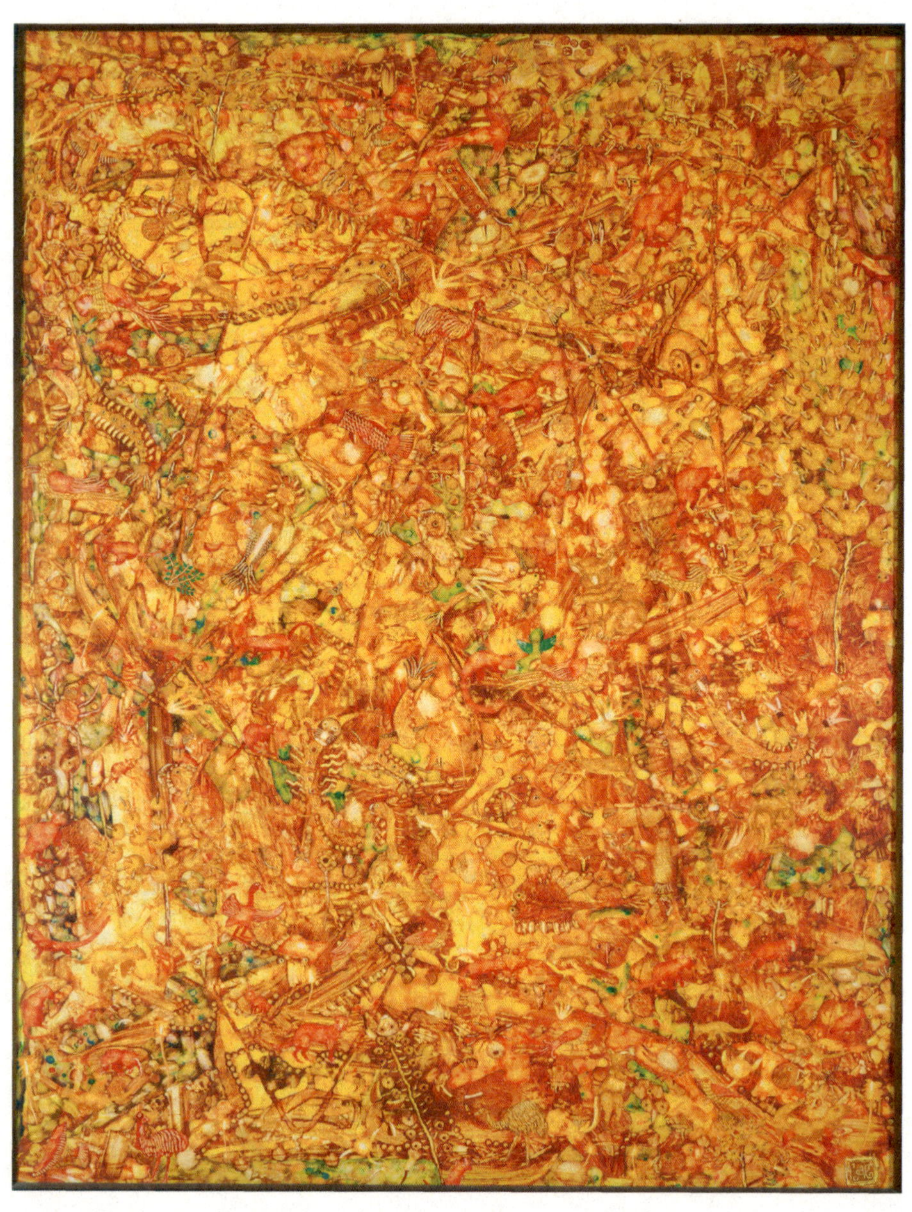

Tony Convey *'Terra Australis'* 1978 acrylic on board 48 x 36 ins
image courtesy the artist, photograph by David Pang

Since Roger Cardinal's book *Outsider Art* was published in 1972 things have changed. Outsider art has spawned a new academy with it's own Popes, Bishops and Gate keepers. Dubuffet's rigorous diagnostics about Art Brut have been collapsed by the spate of artists from all over the globe who have been exhibited, celebrated and denigrated under the Outsider Art banner. The term has become so elastic that verbal gymnastics are required to sustain the Outsider art paradigm.

I would like to examine a case history which might provide some insight into what constitutes an Outsider artist. My own. I was born in Prahran in inner Melbourne in 1946 and my early years still sparkle in my memory. However when I started school at the age of five my world fell apart. I had what I can only describe as an allergic reaction to school from my first day. Just being in the classroom made me physically ill. I would get headaches and lose control of my bodily functions. After awhile the teachers would let me go out to the playground and I would be alright but as soon as I returned to the classroom it started again. My life became a nightmare and for a couple of years I 'wagged' school and wandered through the streets and parks of Prahran and South Yarra pursued by truant officers. Eventually the Education Department exerted 'pressure' on my parents and I underwent an examination by a psychiatrist. He advised the Department that there was nothing wrong with me I just did not want to attend school so the best option was to send me to a boarding school. I was then incarcerated in St. Anthony of Padua's run by Presentation nuns on the Mornington peninsular. The first thing that confronted me was a statue of St. Sebastian, riddled with arrows, in the foyer. The school was full of dark hued paintings of pain and suffering and what followed was a season in hell. After my first attempt at escape I became fascinated by the only positive image I could see in the place a small picture of Stella Maris the Star of the sea. Somehow this radiant vision in various shades of blue calmed me and in some way opened a psychic window into the beautiful landscape the school was situated in. There was a wooded headland above a beach adjacent to the school and freesias and other bulbs glowed in the undergrowth. I loved being on the beach and I began shaping boats, vehicles and companions out of materials found on the beach. At the time I was being bombarded by a continual stream, visual and verbal, of biblical imagery. The stories of Daniel, Jonah and the men in the fiery furnace evoked strong feelings probably because, with the self absorbed eye of childhood, I identified with their imprisonment. My response was to summon up my own images of escape and transcendence.

One of my clearest memories is of a voyage undertaken with a raven and a bull. We sailed over glassy ultramarine seas alive with fantastically hued fish and serpents. The vessel was made out of driftwood, flattened food cans with wisps of faded labels still attached and a torn rag for a sail. This voyage was more successful than my attempts at physical escape from the school and in a sense is still in progress.

It was here that my love of music and it's transformative power was born. Each time I heard the bells my spirit soared. On saturday mornings we had singing lessons in the courtyard looking over the headland. We stood on little wooden steps and sang old songs like 'Westering Home'. Our conductor was a relentlessly cheerful man who rode a battered bike and played a clarinet. He wore what seemed to me odd clothes and as he conducted he threw little packages of lollies to those whose voices were most pleasing. This experience of communal singing was overwhelming. I was a voice and I was every voice and we seemed to be suspended on a shining cloud high above the mundane world.

I made one more attempt to escape from the school and I was being pursued by a couple of the nuns and a caretaker. I had run out onto a cliff and was standing on the edge contemplating the breakers crashing over the rocks far below. I was weighing oblivion against returning to the hated institution when I heard a rustling at my side. A large fiery red fox was staring at me from a tangle of scrub. His huge golden eyes drained me of destructive thoughts and I walked back to my pursuers and allowed them to lead me away. I had 'got my mind right' and I was allowed to return home. Sitting in my favourite chair with my beloved comic collection at my feet and surrounded by all the familiar and long missed sights of home I experienced another epiphany. The walls and urban surroundings dissolved and I was seated on a beautifully speckled lichen encrusted boulder in a luminous landscape. The songs of exotic birds tickled my ears as my eyes devoured this new radiant world. Many years later as a painter I returned again and again to this visionary landscape.

My last school years were spent at a Christian Brothers' college in East St. Kilda where I counted the days until I could leave school. My first job was as a Customs officer on the Melbourne waterfront. It was well paid and I was able to pursue my passions for music and literature and became immersed in Melbourne's vibrant underground culture. I wrote reviews and articles for a couple of magazines and tried to write creatively. In early 1967 I met the person who would become the single most influential person in my life Sylvia Pastars. We developed a close friendship initially based on our shared love of music, literature and cinema. We became lovers and in 1971 we moved with our young family to Canberra. Sylvia had been an artist since childhood and I was excited by her vibrant images and thought perhaps that I might be able to paint too. Sylvia gave me a small canvas board and one saturday afternoon I did my first painting. Although the finished picture was clumsy and crude I became obsessed with painting and knew that I had found what the Brothers and Nuns had called a vocation.

At that time in Canberra there were numerous opportunities to exhibit. This was a time before the dead hand of academia had closed most doors for 'amateur' painters and I began exhibiting my work in local shows. After I had been painting for about three years I won an art prize. At the opening the judge, who was then the art critic for the Canberra Times, almost apologized for awarding the prize to a 'primitive painter'. Up till then my interests had been in other fields and I had no knowledge of art history or schools of painting. Afterwards I asked Sylvia what a 'primitive painter' was and she did not know either. Not long afterwards we saw the book *Modern Primitives* by Oto Bihalji-Merin and I immediately felt a kinship with these artists.

In my first five years of painting my imagery was mostly of my inner world of dreams and visions and I had only completed a couple of landscapes of special places. We were now both fully immersed in painting and we decided to move to a more isolated rural setting to develop our work. We moved to the Upper Murray district in North East Victoria where the landscape was overwhelming. For the first year I worked in a fever and painted a large format series of paintings inspired both by the sublime landscapes we were embedded in and the folklore of the area. These clotted pictures were layered with traces of the ground underfoot, the mountains above and the patterns of weather and the new way of life we were experiencing. On a trip to Melbourne we arranged an exhibition with a gallery and six months later had our first show in a 'proper' gallery. This exhibition attracted some interest and we then hired a gallery in Sydney and this time we sold a reasonable number of paintings which gave us added confidence. Of course what we made from the sale of our work was not enough to provide a living for our family of four children so we moved to the Mitta Mitta valley where the Dartmouth Dam was being constructed and there was a chance of getting a job on the project. I did not get a job on the dam but I met a geologist who offered me a job working for a mining exploration company who had a base metals lease in the Gibbo river/Wombat creek part of the Mitta catchment. I had always had an interest in mining history as some of my ancestors had been miners in the early Victorian gold rushes of the 1850's. Having the opportunity to explore ghost towns and old mine workings in these rugged, spectacular landscapes was an incredible stimulus for my visual imagination and I was especially attracted by the stories of the eccentrics and hermits who had lived in these wild places. I eventually painted a number of pictures about these forgotten gold fields and their rough and ready inhabitants however these images were in no way illustrations of what they may have been or looked like rather they were attempts to capture the excitement they triggered in my imagination. Each picture only emerged when the stimulus could not be ignored and I had to start painting.

Another deep inspiration at this time was the lingering legacy of the first people who had inhabited these hills and valleys since the ice age but had been driven out by the pastoralists and miners. On walks I would observe their artefacts eroding out of banks and tracks and it coloured my appreciation of these beautiful landscapes and more broadly the whole country. I experienced the privilege of seeing their rock art in granite rock shelters and the effect of this unearthly imagery was profound and it has influenced my image making more than any other visual stimulus although not in a direct way rather it created a bench mark for me of what art could aspire to. That is the bringing into physical form of my deepest feelings about life and the cosmos.

We moved back to Canberra in the early 80's and for some time my paintings reflected the stimuli I had received in those sublime landscapes. Another aspect of my image making that had echoed my 'magical thinking' artefacts from my boarding school days had blossomed in our time in the Victorian high country, making use of found objects and painting on unorthodox surfaces. In Canberra these activities became more central to my image making adventures. I had been walking and drawing around the environs of the lower Molonglo river for some time and I began noticing odd pieces of scrap which had reached the end of their useful existence. Debris from man's force field they were scattered seemingly at random but probably in some coded pattern of rejection. They seemed to have some residue of life attached to them and called out to be reassembled in new shapes. My earliest pieces were simply creatures cut out of rusted metal. I affixed them to my garden fence or mounted them on lichen covered branches among bulbs and ferns. I also assembled pieces with wood and metal cut outs some of which I painted. Many pieces were also constructed and left on site attached to a stump or fence line.

I had now had a number of exhibitions and my work had gained some recognition which resulted in my being one of the Australian artists chosen to be included in the *World Encyclopedia of Naive Art* edited by Oto Bihalji-Merin. A change in my painting processes occurred around this time as previously I had either attempted to give form to images from my inner world or create narratives based on our life experiences or mining history and folklore. Now however I began painting without preconceived ideas and just applied paint to the surface and brought out the figures and landscapes which the paint revealed.

In 1988 I was included in the publication *Outsider Art in Australia* edited by Ulli Beier and Philip Hammial, the first study devoted to the subject in Australia. Since then my work has been, with rare exceptions, only exhibited in surveys of outsider art here in Australia, Germany, France and the United States. This has not been by choice however. Australia is an affluent country but with this affluence a creeping conservatism has overtaken many aspects of Australian society and culture in the last couple of decades.

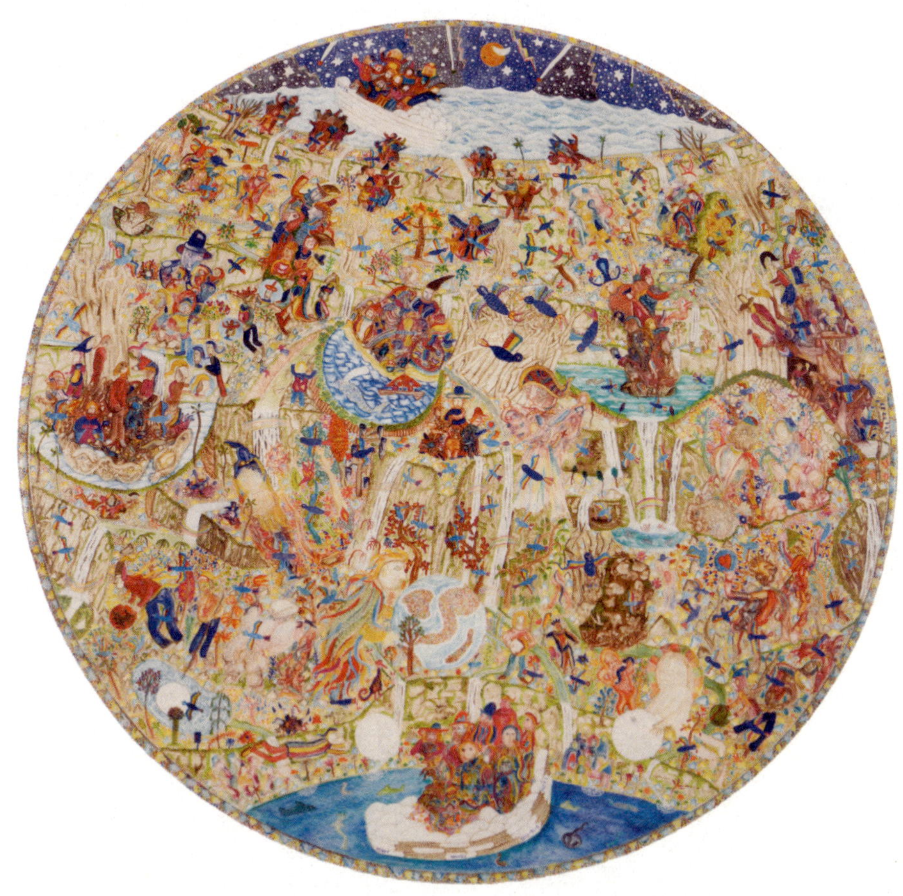

Tony Convey *'Hope'* 2012 oil on wood 45 ins diameter
image courtesy the artist, photograph by David Pang

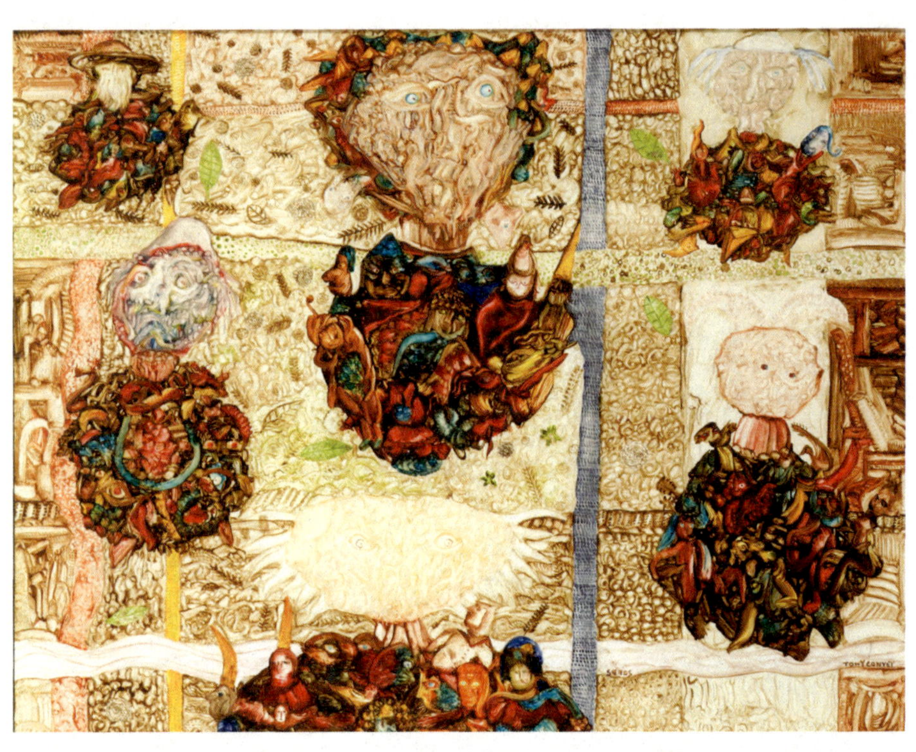

Tony Convey *'Seeds'* 2011 oil on board 30 x 20 ins
image courtesy the artist, photograph by David Pang

This is seen at it's most abhorrent in the political sphere where both major parties have demonized refugees fleeing from wars that our country has been involved in. It has been very marked in the visual arts where the institutions have become increasingly resistant to any kind of art from the margins unless, like graffiti art, it has enjoyed wide popular acceptance. The poet and artist Philip Hammial has battered his head against institutional doors to little avail for decades trying to gain a foothold for outsider art. At one stage in the late 80's it seemed as if there might be the possibility of establishing a permanent museum for Australian outsider art but that mirage has long since vanished and there is now virtually no curatorial support for art of this nature.

As an artist I always believed in showing my art as much as possible but opportunities for me to do so have become increasingly rare. I was once invited to participate in an exhibition *The Boundary Riders* at the publicly funded Canberra Contemporary Art Space. When I asked the curator about the show I became uneasy about it and declined the invitation.

When I saw the catalogue for the exhibition I was glad that I had. The curator railed against the labels that have been used to identify art outside the academic boundaries, such as naive and outsider art, and castigated writers Roger Cardinal and Ulli Beier for further marginalizing these artists by using such categories. Instead she asked that they be treated just like mainstream artists and judged on their individual merits and welcomed into the academic 'tent'. This of course reveals a truly breathtaking duplicity as it is only because of the efforts of such writers and their predecessors that so much of this art has survived. The academy has never, and will never, embrace the works of these art makers except in the most selective and patronizing way as they are fully aware that such art stands in opposition and stark contrast to the lifeless art cultivated in their institutions.

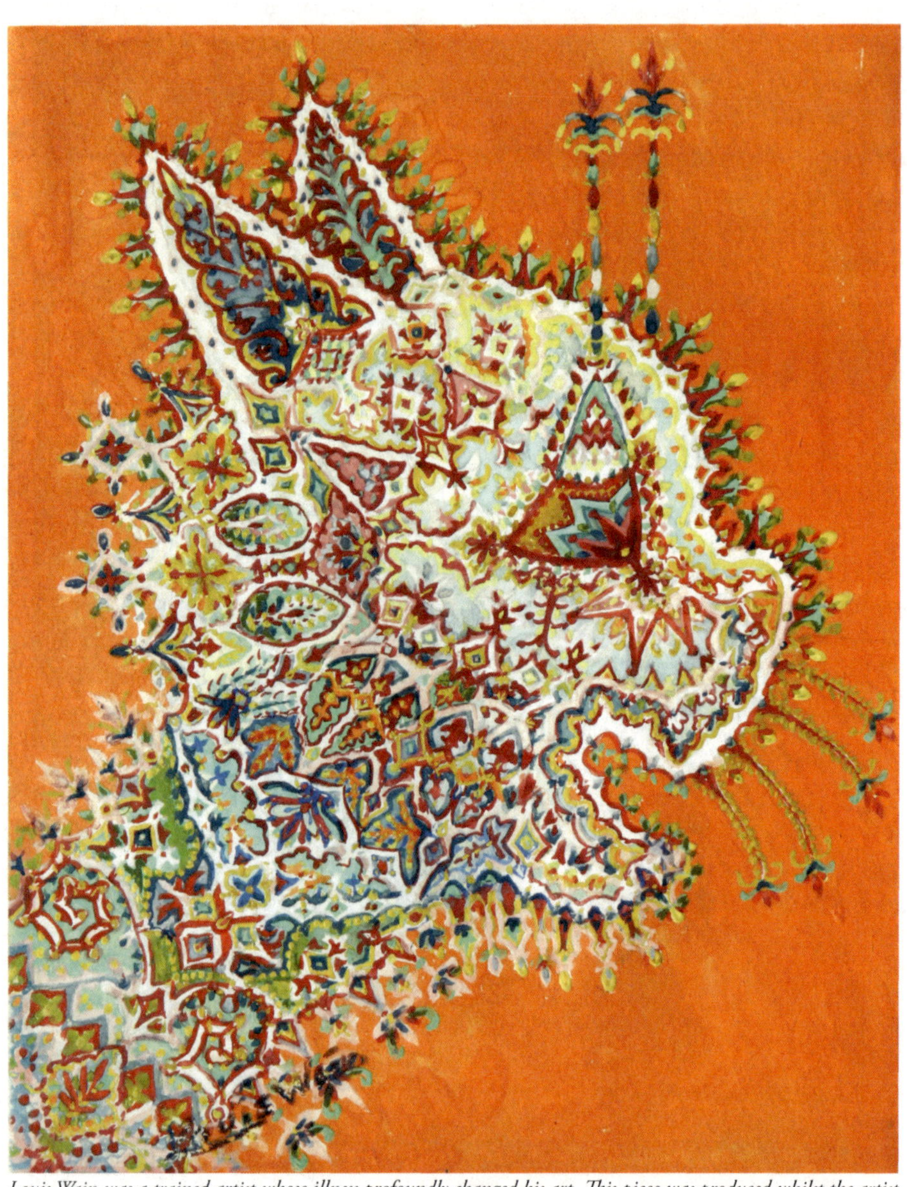

Louis Wain was a trained artist whose illness profoundly changed his art. This piece was produced whilst the artist was at Napsbury asylum, he died in 1939.

Louis Wain *'Untitled'* c.1933 gouache 9 x 7 ins
image courtesy Henry Boxer Gallery

Henry Boxer is a British collector and connoisseur of Outsider Art. He has dealt in Outsider and Visionary Art since the 1970s, specialising in the work of European Art Brut masters, including Adolf Wölfli, Edmund Monsiel, Scottie Wilson, Madge Gill and Johann Hauser. He also represents American artists Malcolm McKesson, Joe Coleman, Alex Grey, Charles Benefiel and George Widener. For over 35 years the Henry Boxer Gallery has exhibited and sold works by individuals who were often marginalised and unrecognised as artists, many of whom have now achieved renown thanks to Henry Boxer's passion and expertise. He was interviewed in April 2013 by Neil Coombs for this issue of Patricide, the interview below is followed by brief profiles of some of the artists that he has worked with.

When did you first become aware of Outsider Art and what drew you to it initially?

The first time that I was aware of it (although I wasn't aware of it being called Outsider Art because it was before Roger Cardinal's 1972 book) was in 1968 at an exhibition of 'Psychotic Art' at the Commonwealth Institute in London. I was seventeen at the time and I went to this show and had my mind blown by the work on display. There was one particular work by August Natterer called *The Witch's Head* that deeply affected me and I must have spent at least an hour looking at it. Also the works on show by Louis Wain struck me as extraordinary – there was a progression of Wain's cat drawings through which he seems to demonstrate the disintegration of the self or the ego.

The portraits progress from an initial illustration of a relaxed, smiling cat that, over a series of eight images, becomes progressively stylized until it develops into a fragmented, kaleidoscopic abstraction. They are totally extraordinary.

Do you have working definition of outsider art?

There are two things that are fairly essential for an outsider artist. The artist is usually (though not always) working for himself, he's not working for an outside audience and that's a very pure definition, perhaps closer to the definition of an Art Brut artist. The definition of an outsider is becoming rather blurred now but I feel there is a certain honesty in outsider art that is missing from much contemporary art.

I suppose that raises the question as to what extent recognition or critical success changes the nature of an artist's work.

There is sometimes a danger of that but more often with authentic outsiders, even though they have become discovered, if they are an authentic creator, then their art doesn't change. If the artist is just doing it to make money within the art market then it is no longer Outsider Art or Art Brut and it is possible that the art can become polluted. One of the things that draws me to outsider art is its honesty in comparison to much contemporary work produced for the art establishment. Outsider artists are often producing totally original work – for example artists with psychiatric issues are often coming from a place that is completely different to that of any other artist and that leads them to create things that are totally new or original.

John Holt has written that "creativity is the immune system of the mind". Do you think that this is an interesting way to approach Outsider Art?

I think that it really goes far beyond that. Outsider artists are often making contact with things that are deep inside themselves, within their own psyche, that they are not even aware of and that they don't know how to express, yet they are trying to express it in a way that goes beyond language. There is a great depth to much of the work that I am interested in.

What do you think of the way that groups such as the surrealists embraced outsider art?

The first artists that I believe really engaged with outsider art were those initially involved with the German Expressionist movement. Artists such as Max Ernst and Paul Klee, who were later associated with the Surrealist movement, were inspired by art produced in institutions. Both groups would have been aware of Hans Prinzhorn's groundbreaking book *Artistry of the Mentally Ill* (1922) which must have been influential for a number of modernist artists. You can see in some of their paintings that they used classic outsider imagery in their work. Dubuffet was a champion of Scottie Wilson but he also used some of Scottie Wilson's images in his own work. You would only know that if you knew both artists' work intimately - you can see there are certain figures Dubuffet used in his paintings that are exactly like Scottie's early figures.

Are there any Outsider Artists that you believe deserve to be better known?

There are many outsider artists who have yet to be properly recognized, the one that comes to mind first is Malcolm McKesson - although he is not a classic outsider. He fits more into the category of what the *Collection D'Art Brut* in Lausanne consider *Neuve Invention* or New Invention. Many of the artists that are now emerging are not pure outsiders, as it is rare for them now to be untouched by a broader cultural awareness. This has much to do with access to the media and so forth. It was very different in the 1930s, 40s or 50s - but now it is much more difficult to be truly outside. What is exciting about outsider artists is that they are gaining access to areas of human experience through their work that mainstream art doesn't touch and that's why it has such a power. Mainstream artists tend to be concerned with the idea of being seen and being well-known, whereas outsider artists tend to desire exactly the opposite: when Henry Darger's work was discovered, he was asked what he wanted done with it and he said "burn it".

How would you describe the importance of Outsider art?

Outsider art provides an experience that allows the viewer to develop an empathy with the art work in a way that goes beyond language and intellect and that is why it can be difficult to talk about. I have been dealing in outsider art now for over 35 years and I am as passionate today as when I first began. For me outsider art is really defined by a purity and honesty that transcends the usual experience of the art world and I feel really grateful to be involved with it.

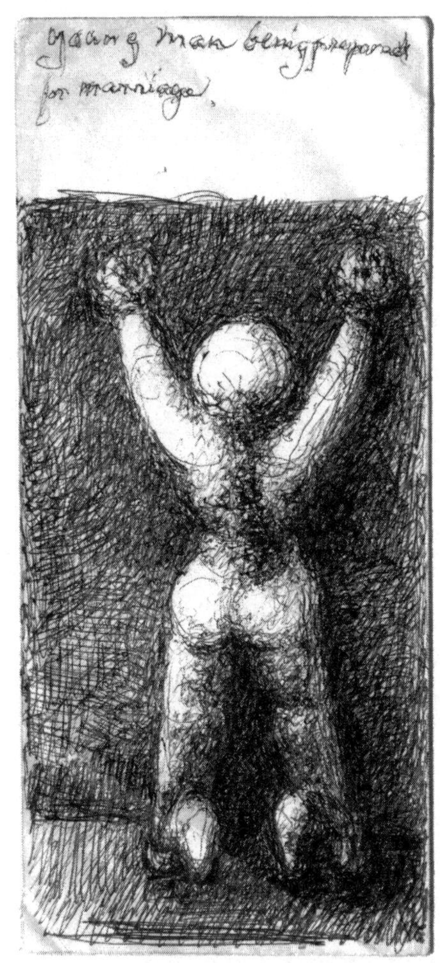

Malcolm McKesson *'Young Man Being Prepared for Marriage'*
c.1975 ink on found envelope 9.5 x 4.25 ins
image courtesy Henry Boxer Gallery

Ionel Talpazan

Talpazan is a self-taught visionary artist, who has created more than one thousand works of art inspired by his often traumatic and transformative experiences. One childhood incident in particular, an encounter with a swirling blue energy, seems to have been the trigger for his life-long fascination with UFOs. Ionel considers these works (paintings, drawings and sculpture) to have a scientific as well as artistic value; his ultimate goal is to reveal to the world the mysterious technology and hidden meaning of UFOs.

Nick Blinko

Blinko is a British artist who has, at times, been hospitalised due to mental health issues. Prescribed therapeutic drugs adversely affect his ability to work. His pictures, constructed from interconnecting figures and faces, are made when he is not taking medication and reflect the psychic torment that drugs supress.

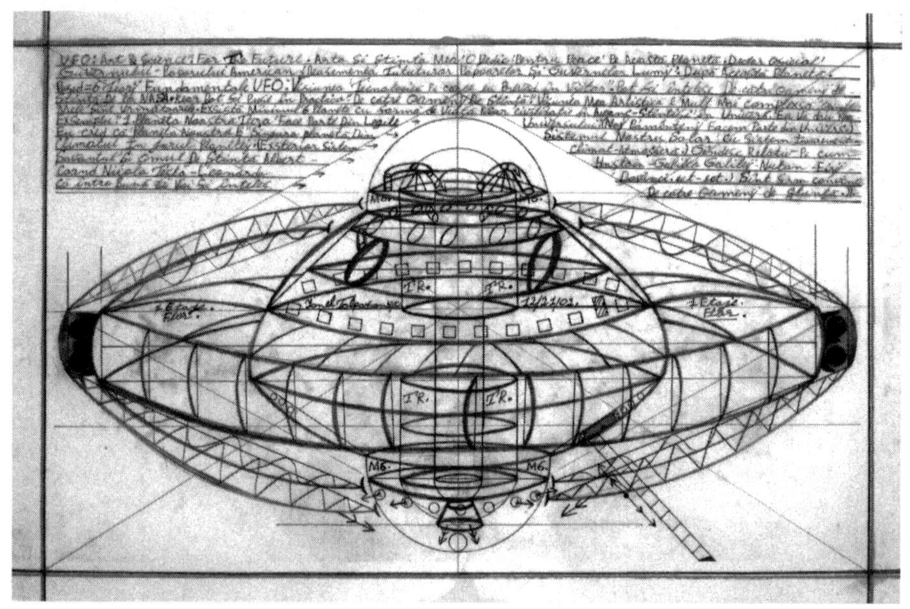

Ionel Talpazan *'UFO: Art & Science'* c.2004 pencil & crayon on paper 20 x 30 ins
image courtesy Henry Boxer Gallery

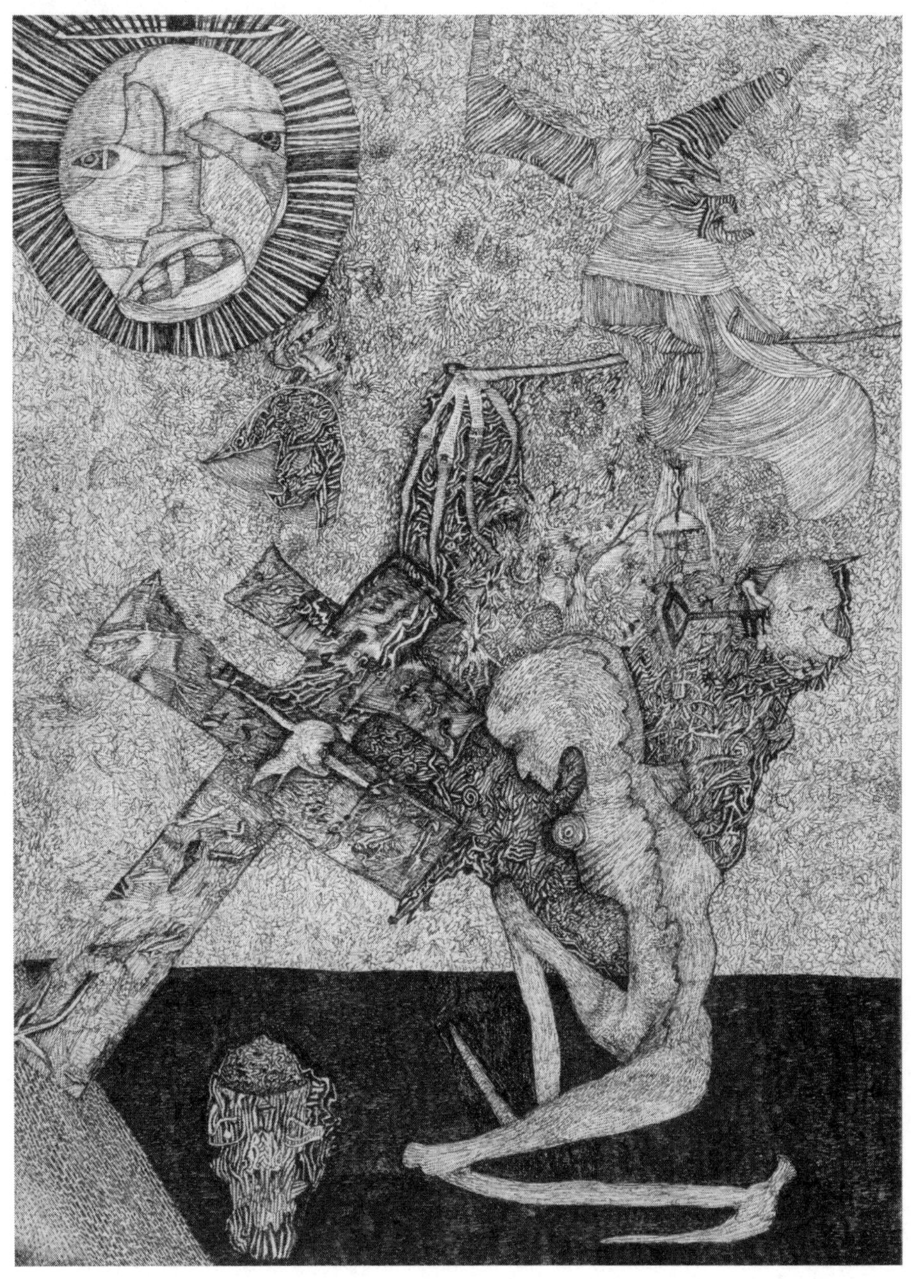

Nick Blinko *'Untitled'* c.1985 ink on card 11.5 x 8.25 ins
image courtesy Henry Boxer Gallery

David Abisror

Abisror was born the 22nd of June 1957 in Paris. When he was 8 years old, he lost his mother to whom he was extremely close. Immediately after the funeral he was sent to an orphanage, separated from his brothers and sisters. At the orphanage he became withdrawn and immersed himself in a world of the imagination. Only later, as an adolescent, did he start to paint and draw, eventually leaving his native home and traveling to Tibet and India looking for some sort of remedy for the pain he had carried around since his unhappy childhood.

Being unable to attach himself to anyone or anything, it is only now, after many years of therapy, that he has at last found himself able to exorcise his deepest feelings through the obsessive use of his pencil work. His works allow him to transcend the traumas of his childhood.

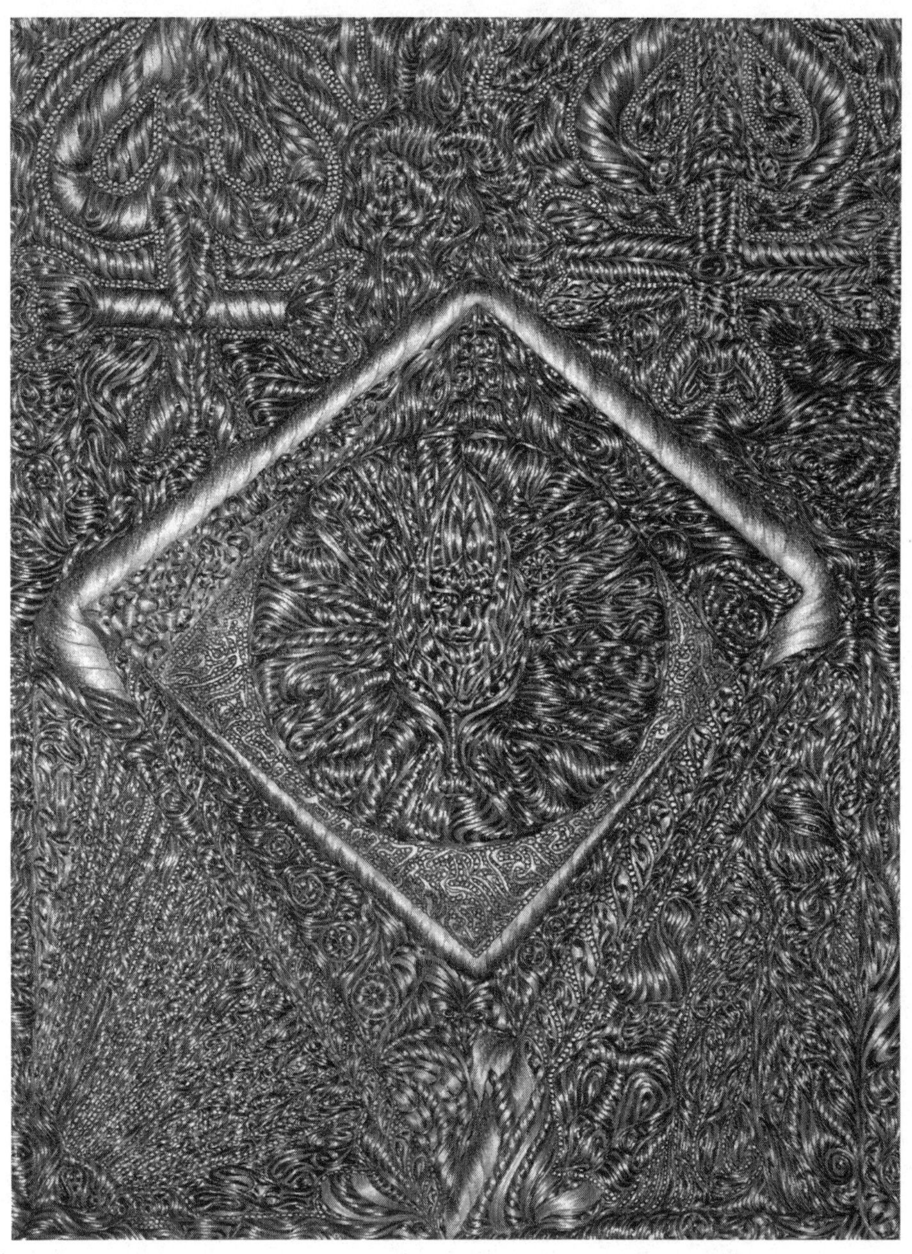

David Abisror *'Untitled'* 2010 pencil on card 13 x 9 ins
image courtesy Henry Boxer Gallery

Madge Gill

The tremendous creative outpourings of
the mediumistic artist Madge Gill began
after her only daughter died at birth in
1919 and a subsequent illness during
which she lost the sight in one eye. Her
early life had been no less traumatic. Born
in london to an unmarried mother, at the
age of nine she was placed in an orphanage and subsequently sent to Canada as a
farm servant.

Gill returned to london when she was
nineteen and before her marriage lived
with an aunt, who introduced her Spiritualism. Gill's discovery of drawing was
a direct result of attempts to contact her
daughter and one of her sons, who had
died during the influenza epidemic of
1918, the other side.

She maintained that she was guided by
a spirit she called Myrninerest and often
signed works in that name. Her oeuvre
ranges from postcards, produced one after another in all-night sittings, to drawings covering immense rolls of calico,
which she finished incrementally, earlier
parts of the drawing becoming hidden as
the fabric was rolled to reveal a new blank
surface. At times Gill exhibited work at
amateur art exhibitions in the East End
of london, but rarely sold her creations,
insisting that they belonged to her spirit
guide.

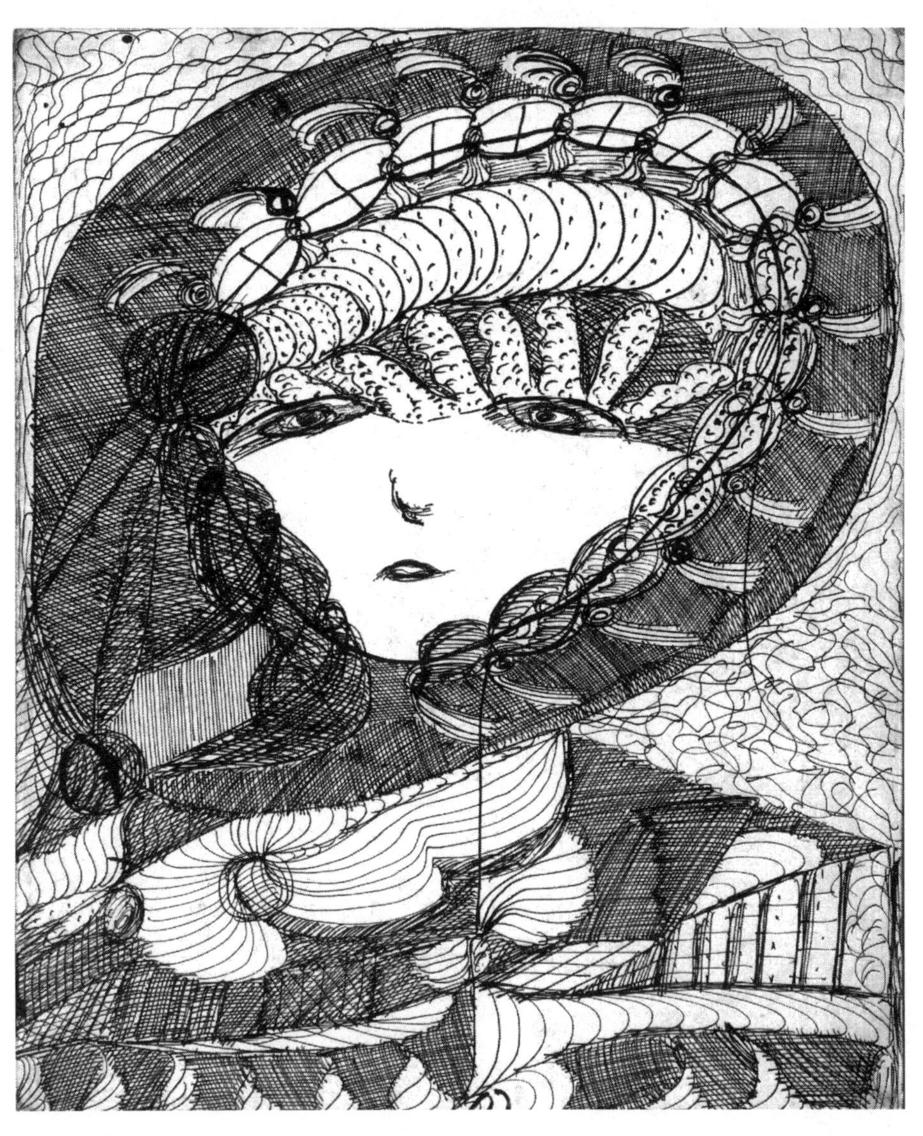

Madge Gill *'Untitled'* c.1955 ink on card 12 x 10 ins
image courtesy Henry Boxer Gallery

Mehrdad Rashidi

Mehrdad Rashidi was born in the town of Sari in Northern Iran in 1963. At the age of 20 he fled Iran because of his strongly held political views and settled in Germany.

In 2006, for no particular reason, he began to draw. He found it relaxed him and made him feel happy, he also thought of his homeland, his childhood and easier times in his life whilst he doodled on any piece of paper that came to hand. Using old notebooks, envelopes, shopping receipts and discarded advertising pamphlets, he gradually, in what seems to be an obsessive and compulsive surge of creativity, began to produce an extraordinary, and hauntingly beautiful body of work. This creative outpouring has continued to this day, the momentum, and the joy it has given the artist have not ceased.

'I was not interested in advises (sic), how to work, nor did I copy anyone elses work. I was happy that I had started and I'm still curios how it develops and grows. All I draw comes from me, my own feelings. With my pictures, where you find different animals, human beings and all sorts of creatures, I feel happy and free. The subject "Love", "Men and Women" and "Nostalghia" are the most important to me. I can draw for hours, day after day. I have to care for my two sons, so I do my drawings whenever I can in my sparetime. It makes me happy and I hope it makes other people happy as well.'

Mehrdad Rashidi.

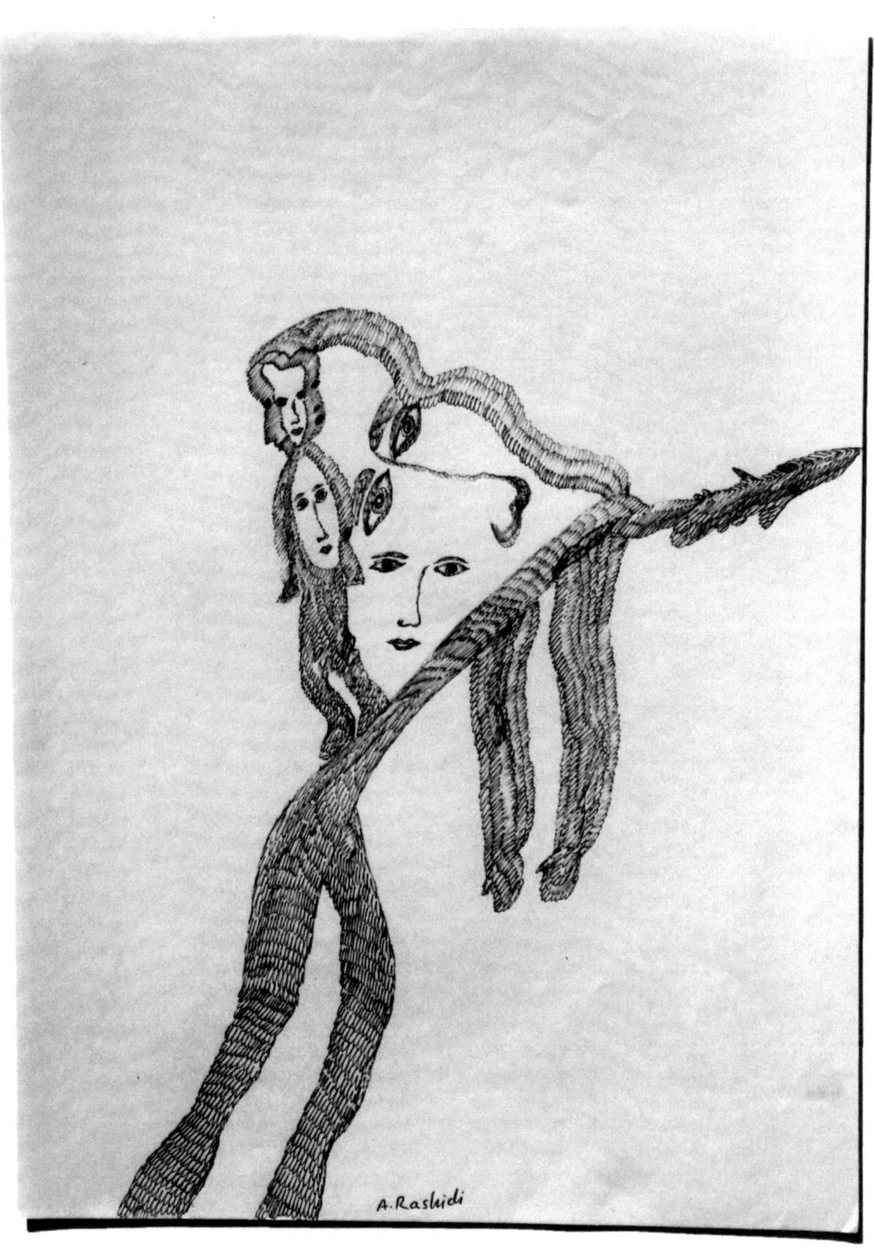

Mehrdad Rashidi *Untitled* 2007 ink on paper 11 x 8 ins
image courtesy Henry Boxer Gallery

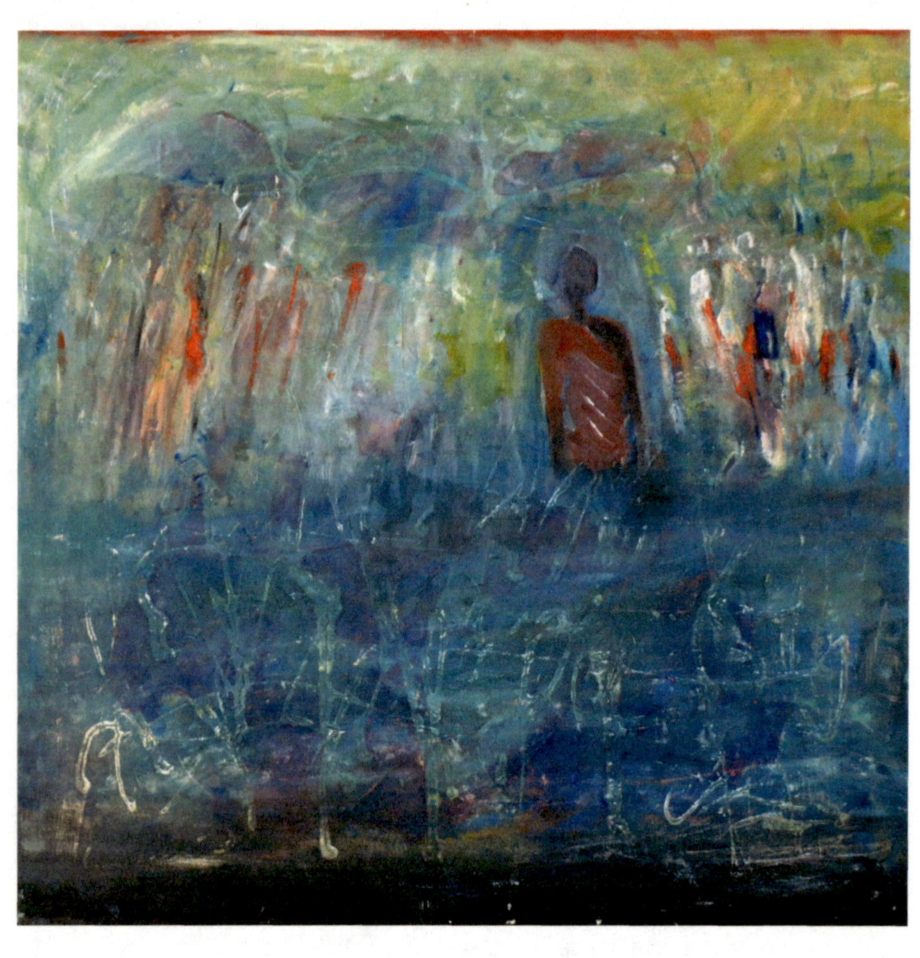

Manon Wyn Owen *'Shangrila'* 2013 acrylic on canvas 24 x 24 ins
image courtesy the artist

My name is Manon Wyn Owen. At the moment I am unemployed as I have been having mental health problems since 2000. I have been diagnosed as a paranoid schizophrenic and have had treatment in a psychiatric hospital. I am now living in a council flat in a vandalised and litter-thrown part of Caernarfon town in North Wales. The flat was recently improved with a new kitchen and bathroom.

I used to be employed before I realised that it was futile. During my employed years I travelled through South America in 1997 visiting Bolivia, Peru, Chile, and Argentina. I can ski very well as I also went to the Alps about five times and the Andes in Chile. But now I get government support and I am trying to recover from my illness. I am trying to move on from a bad psychosis. I was run over by a car when I was 7 years old in 1981 and had visions of an afterlife. I am influenced by religions such as Christianity, Buddhism, Hinduism, Islam. I am also interested in Tai Chi and Feng Shui.

I have always loved art, especially art by the Impressionists where they use a lot of bright colour. I started art around the same time as I was admitted to a psychiatric hospital. I found I had a lot of time and I wanted to be an artist. The first drawings I made were pencil and charcoal sketches. I went to art college about 2001 off and on and made a lot of drawings but I couldn't finish until 2011. I wanted to paint canvases and experiment with colour, but the college process hindered this process I found. So it was after I decided not to go back to college, and do my own thing that I think I painted my first canvas properly.

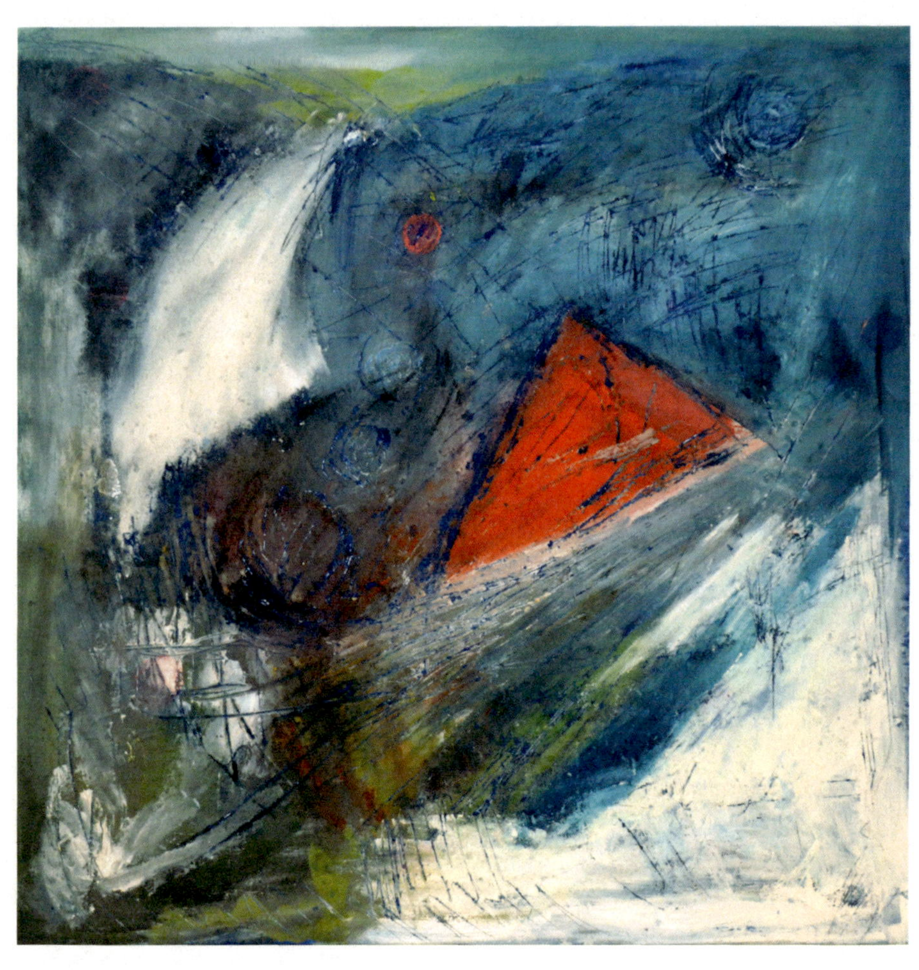

Manon Wyn Owen *'Y Goron Drifflyg'* 2013 acrylic on canvas 24 x 24 ins
image courtesy the artist

I researched Outsider Art on Wikipedia. I don't know much about it, but I think it is art that has not been tainted by institution and is a reflection of pure life. It makes the artist who paints it feel better. I don't know if my art is Outsider Art because I have been to college. I think the term is misinterpreted because it covers a lot of different artist types.

I have used a lot of different media. Most recently I bought some square canvases and acrylic paint. I wait until it is a sunny morning and paint on my knees in the living room. I don't paint often and I don't sell anything because I haven't framed anything yet.

Last year I had visions of another afterlife called 'SHANGRILA'. Everyone is made of water, everyone is happy and colourful, like it is in India. This made me paint a few colourful canvases so I could try and communicate my visions. I found out that a lot of meditations on Shangrila are already available to everyone on Youtube. I call my first painting *Shangrila*, the second is called *Y Goron Drifflyg* (The Triple Crown) because it was painted the same day that Wales won the triple crown last year 2012. The third is called *Bywyd Glöyn Byw* (Butterfly Life) (Machu Pichu) - it is a sun gate in Machu Pichu, Peru and the one thousand steps that you have to climb to get to it.

I made the paintings because I was in a depression. I was angry and insane and looking for some kind of balance.

The paintings made me feel better.

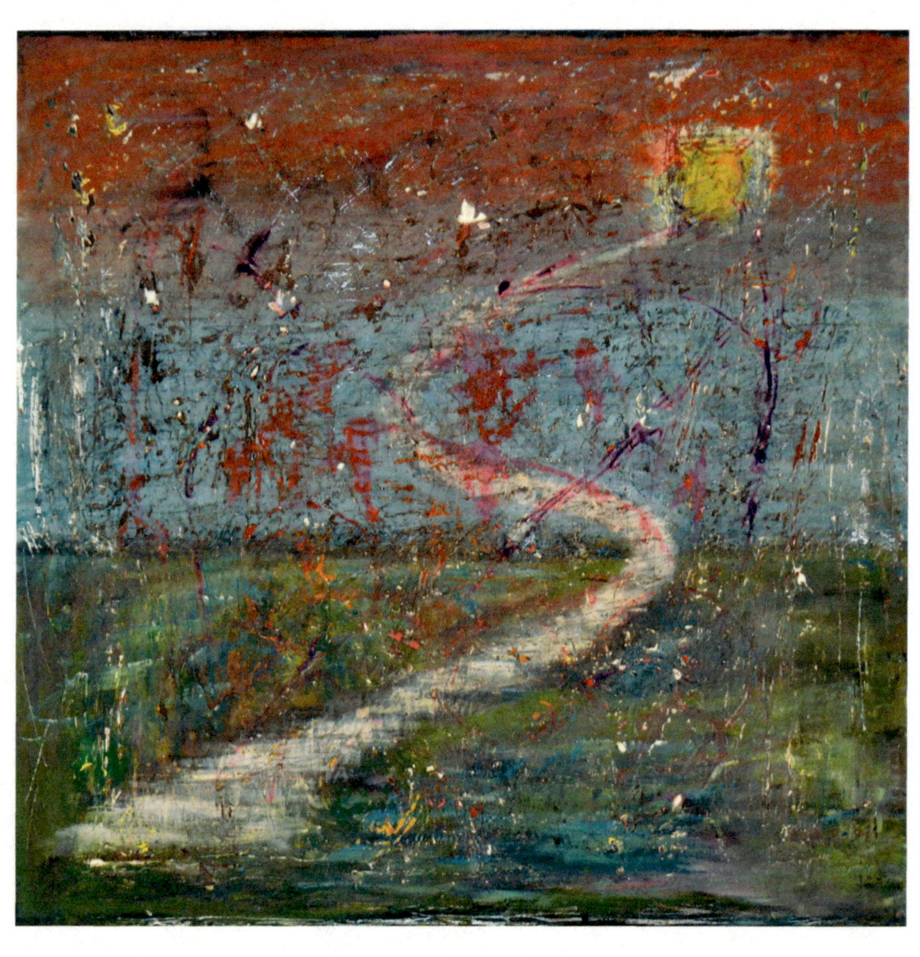

Manon Wyn Owen *'Bywyd Glöyn Byw (Machu Pichu)'* 2013 acrylic on canvas 24 x 24 ins
image courtesy the artist

Mark A. Murphy

To utter is to alter. - Niyi Osundare

Reviled is the man that sits down with beggars
and dares to speak of freedom
whilst sharing his evening meal with whores.
Reviled is the man that seeks neither place or fortune,
nor pays heed unto the lives of the rich,
nor gives credence unto celebrity -
when all around the congregation are looking for alibis.

*Reviled is the man that would rather die than surrender
        his own speculative reason.*

Oh we know the blood-letting must begin somewhere,
(speaking the truth is nowhere an inalienable right)
that Party neophyte and chauvinist hack
share the same bed, walk in the same shoes,
guardians of the historical taboo,
denouncing the rebellion, silencing the weary
for the good of the many, always for the good of the many.

*Reviled is the man that would rather die than surrender
        his own speculative reason.*

Poor Poets Sing

Mark A. Murphy

We shall not sing of 'defence of the realm'
or 'nation',
nor of Harlan Ullman,
(whose name shall ever evince annihilation)
nor Prime Ministers and Presidents, system-makers,
gangsters, bloodsuckers,
the henchmen of pound and dollar.

We poor poets would rather tear out our hearts
than give song
to the extraordinary lives of the rich.
We sing not of the dreams forgotten
in a century of wars,
but of the hard fought freedoms of our forebears.
For all those who have toiled, we shall fight,
and we shall learn to sing the truth.

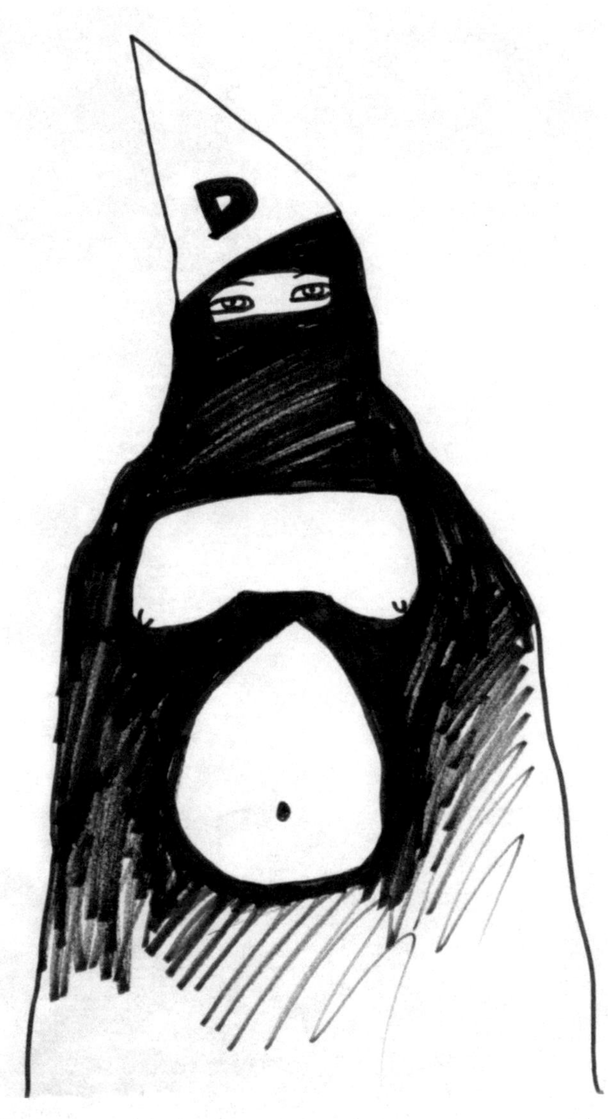

Stella Keen *'The Holy Fool'* c.1988

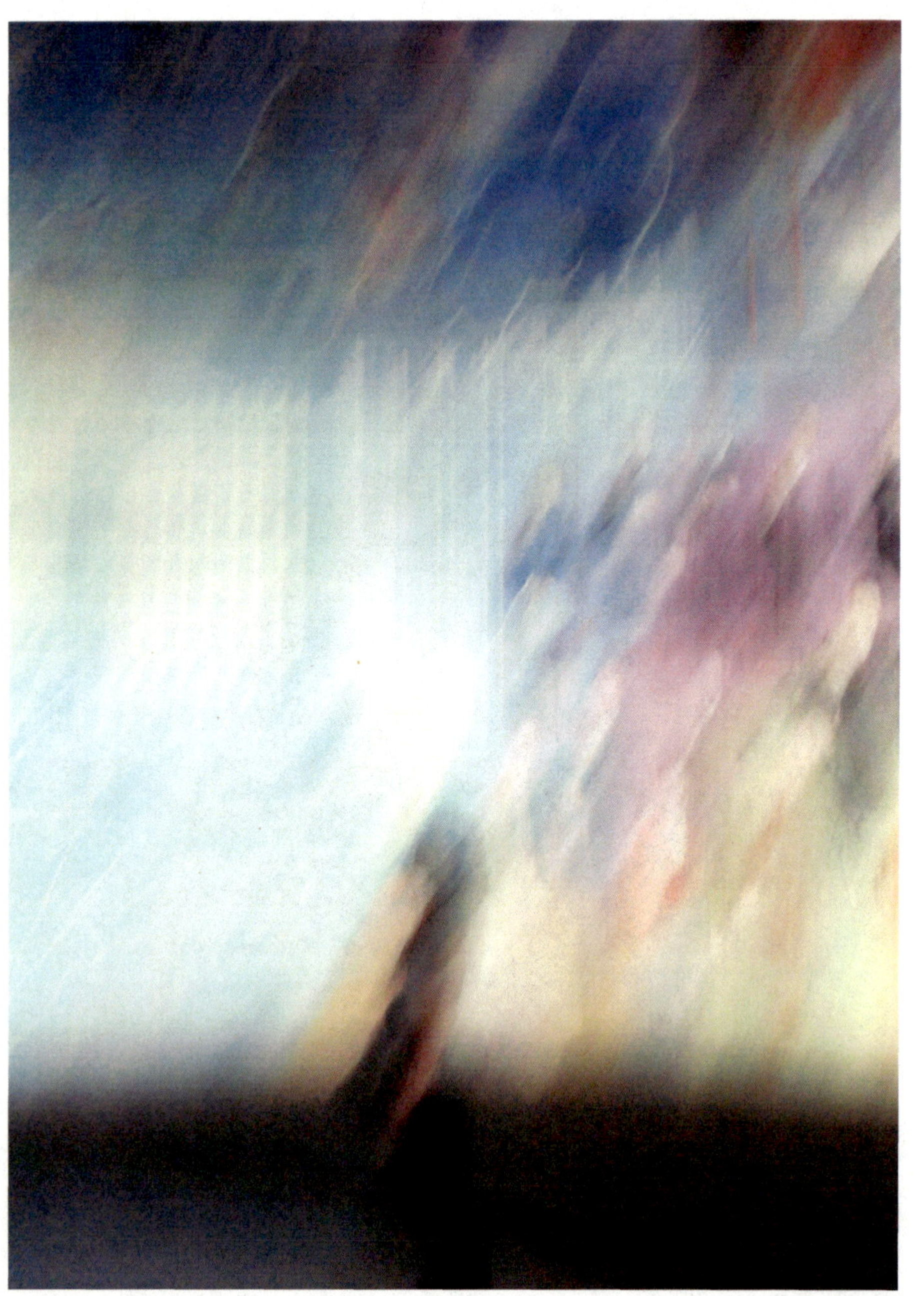

The Idea That Would Not Die

Brace yourself. You take for granted things that may be rattled a little loose or detached here. Certainly, timelines are going to be running parallel with each other in this text.

It was the early 1980's. I found a paperback in a Liverpool bookstore, one of many arranged in a row in front of the main desk, located dead centre of the shop as you entered. The paperback was *The Terminal Beach* (1964), a collection of short stories by J G Ballard. I had been raiding the shop for classic science fiction titles: Niven, Heinleinn, Clarke and Asimov. I had never read Ballard although I knew of him.

I was living a certain kind of life then. I'd get diagnosed with Asperger's Syndrome (a snob expression to allow you look like you are not autistic) thirty years later. But then I was calmly accepting my alienated lifestyle, my constant detachment from the people who wanted to be close to me. Performing in play after play where the relationships and experiences were realer than off stage. Ballard, who had realized the post-war dystopia of the Western world. Who lived in Shepperton, outer London with his children, his bottle and his unique experiences in Lungua airfield during WW2. What had we in common? In 2009 I made the album *The Terminal Beach*[1]. I had not in any way attempted to do so before then. It had only existed as wishful thinking. An idea that would not die.

Timeline

The eponymous short story dominated the collection. A tale of a man who had marooned himself on a pacific atoll, modelled on one of the chain that the Americans forcibly took from the inhabitants. (Legally and without force but otherwise coerced against their will. They paid huge amounts of compensation to these people forty years later). A black and white film of the 50/60's caught the whole experience. A man who discovers he has been marooned on one such island, and a bomb is about to go off. I wonder if James saw it?

Already we are simultaneously in the early 1980's, the nuclear testing sites of the 1940/50's, in and out of a film and living around Shepperton through the last part of the 20th century, through the end of the cold war, arriving at Ballard's death in 2009. This was the year I completed a task that I'd set myself nearly 40 years before. A promise kept. A life remembered.

Ordinary Ruins

Ballard had seen death and detailed it in a book I read five years later, his autobiographical *Empire of the Sun* (1984). Finally the sources of his perspectives were revealed to his readers. A world in which people would casually die or watch others travel towards death. A civilized ex-pat world turned into a surreal realm where the unconscious belief that death was avoidable or came with old age, accidents or sickness was gone. It was replaced with daily murder, illness or simply the passing of life right in front of a teenage boy's eyes.

In *The Terminal Beach*, the marooned central character, Traven, does not at first reveal his motives for being on the island. Rather, he travels around its structures and contours, discovering what was left behind after the bombs had gone off, oblivious to any irradiation that will have left the space toxic over time. A fact that is worth considering as you read the story, if you ever do in your lifetime. Ballard never once hints at radiation poisoning affecting Traven. But the tests have been too recent. No one lives on the island except him. They all visit.

People have come and gone from the atoll, erecting spaces and structures specifically relevant to atomic and hydrogen bombs being detonated, and nothing else. Then they have abandoned them. What else were they supposed to do with them?

Traven relates to it all the only way he knows how, as if it was an ordinary place for a human to be. But it is not. Like the film sets and their components he would find abandoned around Shepperton, the whole thing was brought into being and existed within tangible reality but was not permanent. Like people - hundreds of thousands of whom could easily be killed by the weapons tested upon the islands. James G Ballard witnessed the Hiroshima atomic bomb, *Little Boy*, flash overhead at the time.

Death by Ambience.

As I would walk the streets of the centre of my home city, taking everything in but disconnected from it, so too Traven walked the spaces, ponds and beaches of the atoll. He comes to find thousands of huge blocks arranged in a circle so great it becomes a sort of maze he gets lost in, I too walked in spaces that had no pragmatic relevancy for me.

Shops became pointlessly adorned caves full of objects. People walking around me, did not realize I was often killing time, riding huge amounts of euphoric energy. The trick is to look like you have somewhere really important to go to. Somewhere where you will be well-received and come away glad you went there. For me, that place was in the future. For Traven, it was at the end of the story, when madness brings his wife and son back to him.

As time moves on, Traven makes discoveries that he uses to make sense of it all as he interact with the space. Towards the end he discovers the dead body of a Japanese man. He explores block houses and bunkers, test ponds and abandoned aircraft. As he physically decays, so his mind does too, bringing him what he really wants. Towards the end Ballard hints that Traven may be feeding himself better. But then we realize that his imagination is taking over, and the atoll comes to make sense in itself as a canvas he has committed the end of his life to drawing upon.

Eniwetok as the birthplace of homo hydrogenesis, the post hydrogen bomb man.

The Death of the Cold War

All the way through the last part of the 20th century, the spectre of thermonuclear annihilation haunted everyone. You name the country and they had no illusions of escaping nuclear war. If it happened anywhere - it affected everywhere.

In America, a vogue grew for nuclear blast proof housing. Ballard would have seen the cast concrete buildings being born in the UK. The Barbican centre, where you can still find the patterning in the walls made by the wooden boards used to contain the aggregates. Shopping precincts around the country. Tower blocks erected quickly to house people in *villages in the sky*. Dead-ends in architectural evolution,

with only a few decades to live before demolition claimed many of them.

Ballard spent a lot of time alone at home with a whisky, relating the bleakness of post-war Britain, hungover from the excitement of WW2, awaiting the dropping of the bomb, with all the time in the world to consider the statements made on film about what could be. What will be. What may not be avoidable. Traven, searching the terminal beach, the world after the bombs had gone off. I am now in the year 2012. I know what happened. But I don't know what it will all lead to tomorrow.

Singing Machines

How did I make the album then? How did it escape from my head and into your ears?

When I first read *The Terminal Beach*, I owned a synthesizer called a Wasp. It was a simple machine, but was used in many key albums of the period. People tended to hide its involvement but its effects and voices were noted. I am still not and may never be a musician. This despite making three albums worth of songs under the name *The Model Aircraft Museum*, so far.

I abandoned synthesizers at that time. Later in 1990 I purchased a Juno-6 keyboard and had it for a year. I kept it in a tower block overlooking a motorway in the east end of London, and would play

the machine whilst admiring the view. Very Ballardian.

Night would fall and the cars would traverse the linear concrete structures, ascending flyovers at speed. Life, energy and motion perpetually there, but never personally connecting to me. The perpetual observer. I sold it and bought a bass guitar. I could not play it and gave it away. Then I did not bother for decades.

In 2003 I started making music with a friend. By 2007 I'd bought several synthesizers and started making my own. It took me all that time to develop a technique of realizing my ideas outside of myself. I called it externalization rather than composing. This since I don't see myself in any way as a musician. More someone who uses machines to realize feelings and experiences. The dream is to convey a pure-hit of my experience. Whether or not that was in any way valid to anyone but myself, is up to you to decide.

Folk Synthesizers

Having grown up a bit, I wanted to use synthesizers in a way that related my feelings and experiences honestly. It is all too easy to use presets on these machines. By the time I got back to using them, synth music was a bit of a pariah. Clichés ruled the genre. Dance music had claimed certain easily recognizable factory preset voices. Arpeggiators had made things a bit too easy to get a catchy beat and tune

going with very little effort or originality. Sequencers had become so sophisticated, they could play everything. Computers had started to impersonate classic machines, to the point that people no longer needed hardware at all. Just one computer with enough memory to contain all the simulations of the gear I had really loved.

So I got together a hardware collection, using a Tascam DP02 Portastudio to record it all. A minimum of mixing, using only added delay effects. All I had was an Access Virus TI Polar, and Moog Voyager (rack) and an Alesis midiverb III effects unit. An Akai MPC 1000 sequencer was occasionally used.

The rules were ones that John Foxx endorsed. As few tracks as possible. As little mixing save volume and appropriate delay effects. Some cut n' boost of bass and treble and that was it. Raw. D.I. (Direct Injection - trendy early 80's bands would bypass the mixing desk and send instruments straight onto the tape machine).

I listened to Ani Difranco, an acoustic and soulful artist, in order to find inspiration. I looked to her to counterbalance my early years of intense study of Kraftwerk/The Human League/Depeche Mode and my main inspiration: John Foxx. He released his Metamatic album in 1980 and it has never ceased to inspire and fascinate me. Only a few years ago in an interview he admitted that at the time he recorded it he read far too much J G Ballard.[2]

A recent documentary about the early 80's synth bands[3], made direct connections between all of them and Ballard's work. The waves lap the beach of the atoll, the sand frozen at the instant of the nuclear flash. People await thermonuclear world death, and the singing machines play their cold systematic signals as they are filtered and shaped and attenuated at the hands of both my heroes and now myself. Moog, Roland, Access. The same equipment.

Trap and Zoid – the Puritan

Constantine was a friend I made on MySpace, an environment once very successful on the internet. Like Ballard's decaying island, it is now seen as abandoned and a shadow of its former self. The Belgium artist had taken two antique RMS suitcase synthesizers and produced a series of tracks under the name Trap and Zoid.

They were simple, basic monosynth sounds. Square waves, modulated and filtered. Some soared and others meandered. They spoke of the soundtracks of 1950's science fiction films; of old Doctor Who adventures and of when using synths in this way was seen as radical, mysterious and weird. Moving atmospheres made with cold electronic circuits. Exactly what I was trying to do, only more basic. Back to the raw source. The heart of my heartless vision. The endless early 80's experiments with a friend's bank of Korgs, several Wasps and the Odd Yamaha. Stripped of the tyranny of verse/chorus, Trap & Zoid simply celebrated the machines in a way that I am still coming to terms with.

He captured the essence of what I loved in the early synth musicians, and in Metamatic. Monosynths, capable of only one note at a time, wailing strangely into delay lines and effects units. The cold predictability of the machine, the hum of the engine, the bleep of the indicator of so many gadgets we take for granted now. Square waves, sine waves, saw tooth. Who but a few like me know this vocabulary? Homo hydrogenenesis. The pre-third. Ballard had his own language too. Constantine's site was taken down years ago, and I have not been able to contact him. Although now, when this album is released, I will try and send it to him, with thanks.

Cold Singing Machines

Thank you for reading this somewhat self-centred and individuated document. I certainly don't represent everyone with autism, but I think you will find that somewhere within all this, is a world to itself that others can share. Experiences deeply personal to myself that have relevance and resonance to others who are the same.

Humans as synthesizers. People as the ruined dummies that Traven hides with to avoid being found by a search party. The blocks as civilization, that Traven runs around and around. He finds a door in each one, but never a key to open them. Ultimately he is consumed by his own mind, which gives him his family back, at the cost of his sanity. Perhaps the terminal beach, his suicide, had enough residual humanity soaked into it to share his experience kindly.

Or did it just act as a mirror? Why did the Japanese man come to die there? Was it as Ballard appears to intend, that he had the same experience, urges and motives as Traven? The ultimate development of man's machines, a gadget that in a flash could kill everyone? Is Ballard outlining the innate urge in people to end themselves, just as Foxx took his Metamatic title from a 1960's artist[4] who build a mechanical installation with the sole intention of destroying itself - his 'meta-machines'?

I found many ways out of this nihilistic world of the early 80's. But it left me with a great deal to express, and for me the only way to do it was with musical instruments cold and mechanical enough to do it.

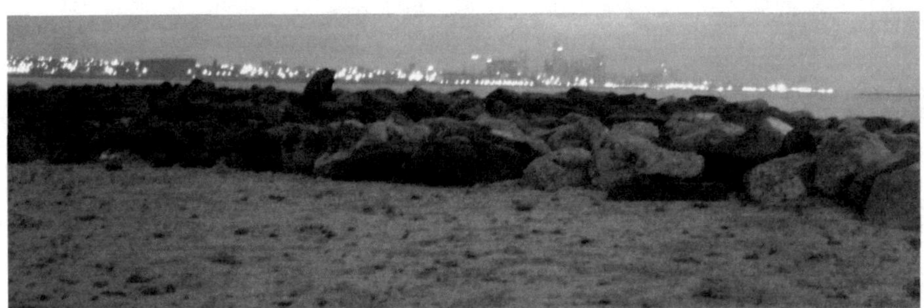

Notes

1. Paul Wady's album *The Terminal Beach* is available as a digital download from Linear Obsessional Recordings: (http://linearobsessional.bandcamp.com/album/the-terminal-beach)
2. See Simon Sellars's interview with John Foxx on the Ballardian website (http://www.ballardian.com/john-foxx-interview). Foxx wrote in the Sleeve notes for his 1992 album *Assembly*, "I was in retreat from bands, mightily convinced that electronics were the future, and reading too much J.G. Ballard. I lived alone in Finsbury Park, spent my spare time walking the disused train lines, cycled to the studio every day and wobbled back at dawn, imagining I was the Marcel Duchamp of electropop. Metamatic was the result. It was the first British electronic pop album. It was minimal, primitive technopunk. Car-crash music tailored by Burtons".
3. BBC4's 2010 television documentary series *Synth Britannia* (http://www.bbc.co.uk/programmes/b00n93c4).
4. Jean Tinguely's kinetic sculptures included machines for drawing and creating music.

Photographs by Paul Wady

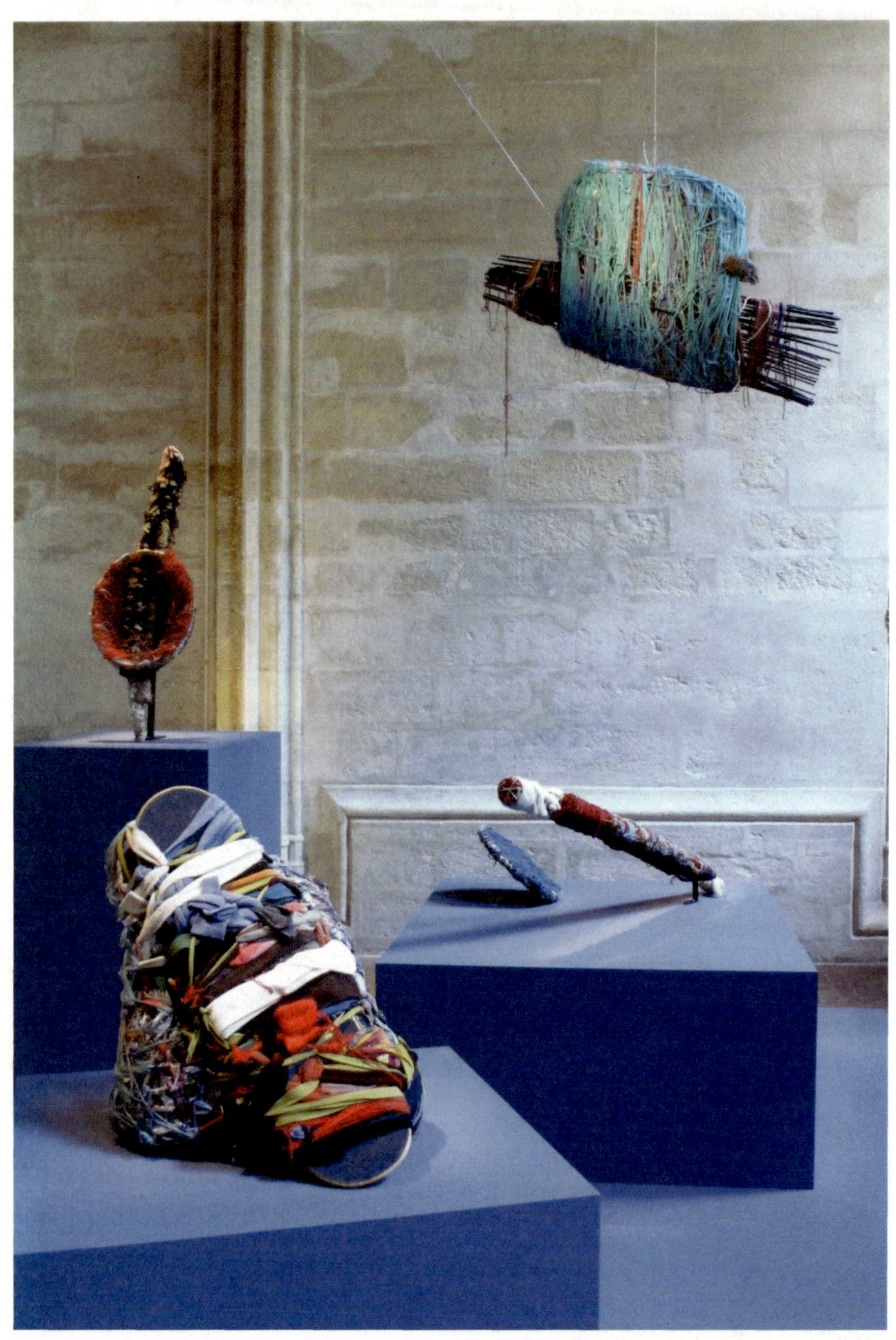

mixed media work by Judith Scott
image courtesy Joyce Scott

And yet real Art Brut, that is to say individualistic creation against the force of winds and of tides and even at the cost of one's own life, one's health, one's mental equilibrium, or which occurs as the consequence of previous disasters: the two sometimes being indivisible. The visceral art of these self-taught creators, often illiterate or on the edge of sanity, occasionally continues to surprise us.

Laurent Danchin. 1988. *Raw Vision* Issue 1. 1989

The first inkling of the existence of the artistic category Outsider Art emerged from the work of a few psychiatrists in the mid and late nineteenth century when it became clear that some psychiatric patients were spontaneously producing artworks - often on found scraps of paper - of unusual quality and power. In 1922 the German psychiatrist Dr Hans Prinzhorn published the first serious study of artworks by psychiatric patients, *Bildnerei der Geisteskranken* (*The Artistry of the Insane*), after amassing a collection of several thousand examples from European institutions. Both book and collection received considerable attention from the inter-war avant-garde and influenced artists such as Franz Marc, Paul Klee, Max Ernst and Jean Dubuffet. They were fascinated and inspired by an art that was produced seemingly without any influences from the modern art world yet which appeared highly original, compelling and contemporary.

It was Jean Dubuffet who realised that spontaneous, original and uninfluenced creation was not just the preserve of the mentally ill. Together with others, including André Breton, he formed the *Compagnie de l'Art Brut* in 1948 and strove to seek out and collect works of extreme individuality and inventiveness by creators who were not only untrained artists but often had little concept of an art gallery or even any other forms of art other than their own. None were professional artists or had contact with the art world and all were completely untrained. They included mediums, isolates and fierce individualists as well as psychiatric patients.

I was at an oversubscribed Outsider Art symposium at Tate Modern some years ago where the appeal and fascination with Outsider Art was clearly evident. Speaker after speaker revealed their "finds", their "discoveries" of the "primitive artist devoid of cultural influence who dwelt amongst us". Alarm bells rang for me as to exactly what was being defined, how the designation outsider had been arrived

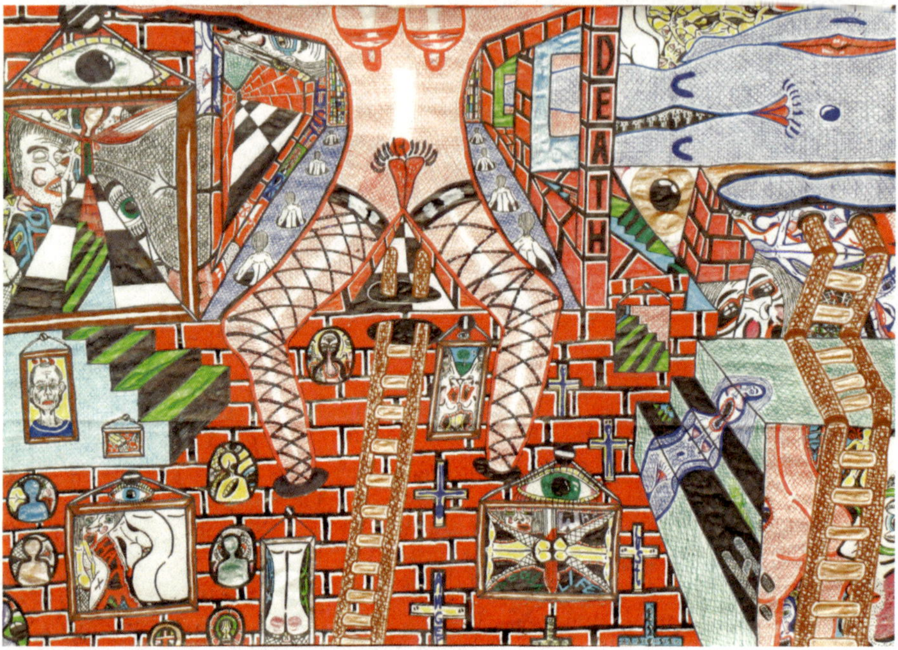

Sebastian Wilbur '*Pictures Within Pictures*' biro and felt tip pen on paper

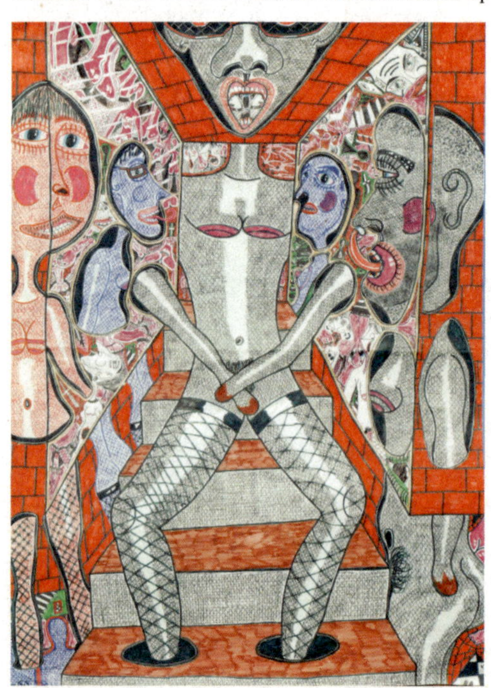

Sebastian Wilbur '*On the Steps*' biro and felt tip pen on paper   (images courtesy Matthew Meadows)

at, how was it being perpetuated and by what criteria? The question of authenticity in relation to outsiders intrigued me and still does - what criteria are being applied to authenticate the outsider and who validates the outcomes? There is much conjecture and debate as to who gets the outsider label, as I was to find out in practice as a consequence of my work with artist/patients within a high secure psychiatric hospital over a number of years. Putting forward the absorbing work of an artist/patient Sebastian Wilbur (not his real name) who I was working with at the time within at a high secure hospital to an Outsider Art patron/collector I was told that, because he had attended art lessons within the hospital (in which he was entirely free to develop his own work) that as such he could not be an outsider artist. The artist/patient had had no formal training and had only begun to make art, initially in secret, when he was incarcerated in a high secure forensic hospital (he called this his "Secret Garden Work"). This talented patient was clearly un-acculturated as he had only had a few cursory sessions in art (albeit by an inspirational and committed patient-centred teacher) and most of his more engaging work was produced in secret in his room on the ward alone. He said of his work:

As for their iconography: I made symbols to express and communicate my feelings. There were quite a lot of genitalia. This is because I don't understand relationships, what happens between men and women. As far as the brick walls, they express the closed off environment I was in for so long, the fact that I could not go anywhere. The crosses are obvious, they represent my suffering, and as for the eyes, also the faceless figures, they both represented my paranoia, just feeling watched and observed all the time, particularly in hospital.[1]

Another artist/patient who I worked with in a high secure psychiatric setting when presented with the term outsider said that he would never want to be labelled an outsider, that he just wanted to belong, to be accepted by a society whose prejudice towards the mentally ill was enough of a burden or stigma, let alone the demonisation meted out by aspects of the media to patients in forensic high secure hospitals. In my article *Anthropologists of the Mind* I wrote:

I have to be honest; I too have an inclination towards the radical, the subversive gaze. It challenges the stasis of mediocrity and the illusory foreground of a reality not, it seems revealed by the dominant paradigm, the prevailing model. It is however, through my work in hospitals that I began to have concerns about "Outsider Art" and its field of occupation and criteria for authenticity. If there is a case to be answered by what seems to be a lucrative and flourishing genre for academics and dealers alike then what is it, and where do we place the art of those in emotional or spiritual *crisis, or who are defined as mentally ill or disabled? Trapped, it seems between encumbered medical connotations of the pathologising aspects of art therapy and the vagaries of "outsider art" with its elitist notions of authenticity, it seems that art, the pure creative process needs to be re-claimed by those creative beings **who just want to create** without being challenged to be authentic. A patient-artist in a secure hospital once said to me; "Art gives me a way of recreating spirit, mind and body".[2]*

So perhaps we need to search for a less loaded term than outsider, with its connotations of social marginalisation and neo-primitivism, and simply look at the art itself and our response to it. Speaking the other day to a young trainee art psychotherapist in London he suggested that what was labelled outsider art "spoke to his condition" much more than any other art. He said that he cherished the works that inhabits the pages of books and journals that feature Outsider Art, suggesting that it had always interested and stimulated him. Perhaps this young psychotherapist recognised the true depth of such work when he said "I just feel closer to it - is it the outsider in me? It sears and excites me." So what are we implying here? Perhaps outsider art may be looked at as work that is laden with emotional and spiritual depth? And what can explain the deep interests of audiences, patrons and the art world in general to Outsider Art? I return to what Laurent Danchin describes as one cause for this intense interest in the work:

…bored by the interminable degeneracy of fine art, whose evolution has led to a series of even more vain and intellectualised performances which are hard to follow. A new public is becoming apparent, looking for something else: signs symbols, myths even rituals which can help it survive in this new hyper-sophisticated civilisation which has severed man's links forever from his peasant ancestors.[3]

Perhaps this art of the Outsider has the "breath of life" so deeply and profoundly embedded in it that it touches us on a level that so much contemporary art with its "interminable degeneracy" cannot reach?

One of the peculiar developments in our Western world is that we are losing our sense of the divine side of life, of the power of imagination, myth, dream and vision. The particular structure of modern consciousness, centred in a rationalising, abstracting and controlling ego, determines the world in which we live and how we perceive and understand it; without the magical sense of perception, we do not live in a magical world. We no longer have the ability to shift mind-sets and thus perceive other realities — to move between worlds, as ancient shamans did. Ritual signifies that something more is going on than meets the eye — something sacred.[4]

In a previous piece, I equated the art of so called "visionaries" to the search for meaning and self-realisation in the way that it is not an absolute but one in which the often "fractured and dislocated mind might seek clarity or solace in the creative process itself, in intuitive and spontaneous ways: as Kandinsky once stated, making art from "inner necessity".

There has always been a human concern with the fractured self", right from the beginning of human consciousness. Questions fermented in the psyche: what constituted the fissure within and between minds and bodies, what is its causation and how do we repair the damage? And further, how do we reconcile the boundaries within us all, our environment and within the cosmos, between other beings and the spirits, and when things go wrong how do we rectify the imbalance, the illness? These dilemmas were addressed, until the development of the modern world, as spiritual problems with a divine process for healing. To be disconnected and dislocated from the notion of self in the deepest sense of the word is to be deprived of our potential as human beings and to be deluded into perceiving the world as a distorted and hostile place.

Self-realisation or self-integration can be said to be a tendency, a movement towards a greater understanding and acknowledgement of self in relation to the world. Self-realisation in this context does not imply total understanding, but more an improvement in the awareness of self and a reconstruction of awareness of one's relationship with the environmental, personal milieu and history of the individual which charts the route of one's life journey. This was done using the templates of mythology as a guide. The journey is, in this very process, enhanced by self initiated and archetypal use of images and symbols which acts as a form of mapping in relation to mnemonic and re-collective experiences, and which also includes a future potential.[5]

And so what we have come to call Outsider Art might just be an inclination to heal connections that we have lost. Whatever restraints or difficulties upon cognitive and intellectual capacities there are some people making art for the act of creation alone. They have no audience in mind and are just simply producing objects intuitively and instinctively. The purity of this art sings out in an age of complex and over-intellectualised art. In the absorbing recent exhibition at the Wellcome Trust in London entitled *Souzou: Outsider Art from Japan* it is explained that there is a not a perfect approximation of the term Outsider Art in Japanese. I am not surprised.

Souzou is a word which has no direct equivalent in English but a dual meaning in Japanese: written in one way means creation and in another imagination. Both meanings allude to a force

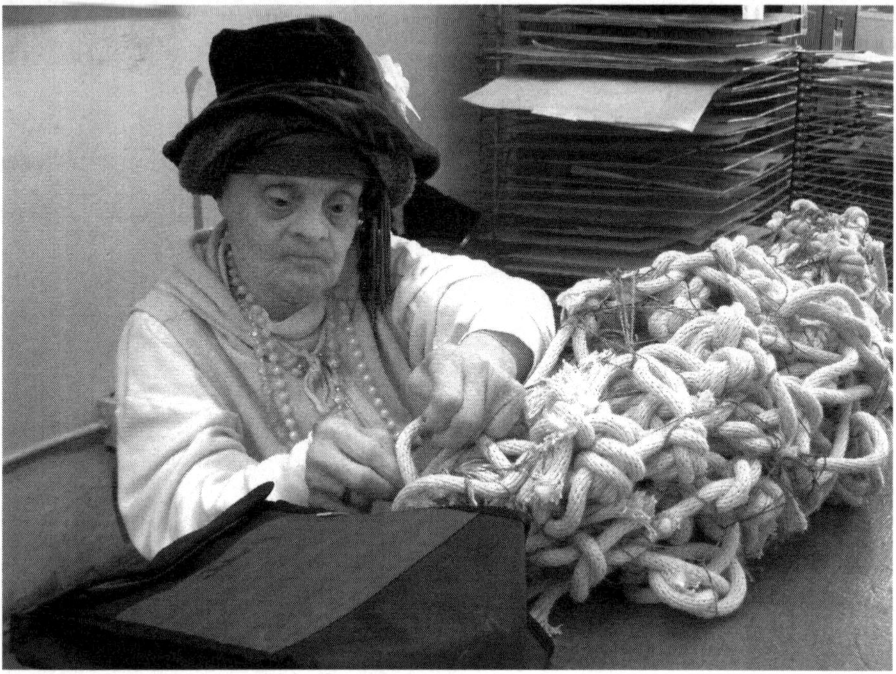

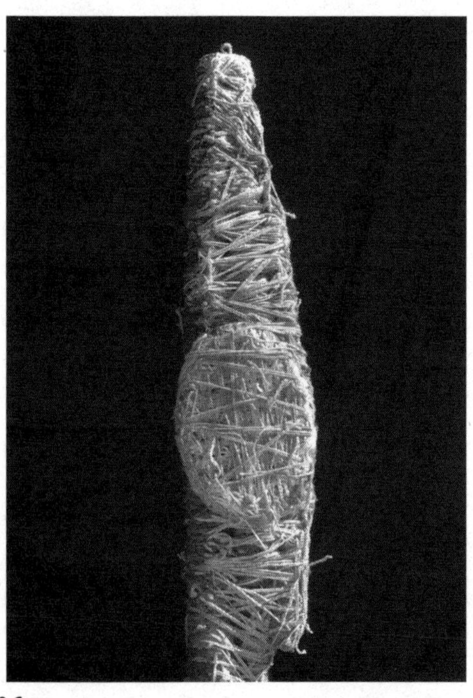

Judith Scott at work (above)
mixed media piece by Judith Scott (left)
images courtesy Joyce Scott
(see www.judithandjoyce.com for more information)

by which new ideas are born and take shape in the world.[6]

One wonders if the title "Outsider Art from Japan" was a title given especially for the Western audience? The work in the show is of the art practice of 46 self-taught artists living and working in social welfare institutions in Japan. It could be said that the artists all had what we define as "learning difficulties" and have produced their remarkable work in the creative sanctuaries of state institutions over a long period of time. Their disabilities may well have meant that they were naturally inhibited from the absorption of cultural influences. Two simple but striking quotes from the exhibition illustrate the point regarding the effects the social marginalisation can have on art making:

"Difference leads to innovation"
Koichiro Miya

"Ideas bubble up from inside"
Masao Obata

Interestingly in the exhibition booklet it states that in Japan, Outsider Art has been more closely aligned with public health and education reform from 1945, when as in Britain, a highly developed social welfare system was established. This echoes my own work in Art Education, work in secure psychiatric units and in the founding of an arts and mental health charity AiM (Artists in Mind[7]) which provides art studio spaces for artist/ser-vice users and works in hospitals and prisons. AiM also holds an archive of work by artists isolated by mental distress. In parallel to the experience of *Souzou* artists, at no time were the artist/patients and service users I worked with, suffering, as they were the whole spectrum of mental illnesses and disabilities, thought or defined as Outsider Artists.

On April 1, 1987, Judith Scott started going to the Creative Growth Art Center. In her first few months at the center, Judith was unexceptional with paint. She scribbled loops and circles, but her work contained no representational imagery, and she was so uninterested in creating it that her sister was considering ending her involvement with the program. Some months later Judith casually observed a class conducted by visiting artist Sylvia Seventy, and using the materials to hand, spontaneously invented her own unique and radically different form of artistic expression. While other students were stitching, she was sculpting with an unprecedented zeal and concentration.

Her special creativity was quickly recognised, and she was given complete freedom to choose her own materials. Taking found objects (often stealing them from other people at the Center) she would wrap them in carefully selected colored yarns to create diverse sculptures in many different shapes. Some resemble cocoons or body parts, while others are *elongated totemic poles. Many of her works also feature pairs; Scott's experience as a twin is essential to her work. Scott's work became immensely popular in the world of outsider art, and her pieces sold for up to $15,000. Her art is held in the permanent collections of the following museums: Art Brut Connaissance & Diffusion Collection (Paris and Prague), Museum of American Folk Art (Manhattan, New York), Intuit: The Center for Intuitive and Outsider Art (Chicago, Illinois), L'Aracine Musee D'Art Brut (Paris, France), Collection de l'art brut (Lausanne, Switzerland), and the American Visionary Art Museum (Baltimore, Maryland).[8]*

The work of Judith Scott, an artist born profoundly deaf, mute, and with Down syndrome is acknowledged as of international significance and worth. Perhaps the degree of Judith's disability places her clearly into the accepted criteria of Outsider Artist yet the more articulate patient whom I worked with at Rampton Hospital is harder to authenticate as an outsider. Although his work is patently from a deep psychological place within his psyche and was made initially secretly and as an exploration of the ambiguities of his sexuality and long periods of incarceration in prisons and secure hospitals, it is not easy for him to be defined as an outsider. There are some artists I know of who proclaim themselves as Outsider Artists thereby opening up a rich potential vein of patronage and a platform for exhibiting. I also know of artists defined and exhibited as outsiders who reject the label and ask not to be defined as such and others who think that Outsider Art should not be separated from the mainstream.

Which brings us to the horrible Rubicon that still separates so-called "outsider," "self-taught," and "visionary" art from institutionally sanctioned official art. Now that even immigration reform can happen, it's time for MoMA — and all museums — to integrate "outsider art" into their permanent collections and erase that distinction for good. They need to allow these artists to take their rightful places in the canon. In addition to the artists mentioned above, visionaries like Hilma af Klint, Emma Kunz, Bill Traylor, Adolf Wolfli, Martin Rameirez, Minnie Evans, John Kane, Clementine Hunter, Hector Hyppolite, and others must be integrated into the canon. At the Fair, there's a 1939–1942 town scene by one of the greatest "outsiders" of them all, Bill Traylor, that would easily compare with any Picasso from the same period. Or, indeed, any artist.

Similarly, MoMA and other museums once drew strict lines between insider and outsider because they were beset by accusations that modern art could be made by disturbed people and untrained artists. Thus "outsider art" had to be left out in the cold, out of fear. Those embattled borders are long gone; the wars were all won. Museums: I say it's time for you to set aside these old chauvinisms. There are no more excuses. You're on the wrong side of history. Your definitions of art are reductive and insular where they need to be inclusive and expansive. You've hit a wall. Change — or wither with your prejudices and die a slow death.[9]

In the preface to Matthew Meadows' book *Insider Art* the artist Grayson Perry says of the art made by prisoners and patients in secure psychiatric hospitals:

Though prison art is traded both inside and outside of gaol, the principal benefit of making art is not financial gain but improved mental health. Making art is perhaps working out who you are, what you want and how you relate to the world... they are expressing heartfelt messages, unselfconsciously to the world, to their fellow prisoners and perhaps more importantly to themselves. In putting something non-verbal on paper we often find out and reflect on what is happening, literally beyond words, in our heads.[10]

There are links here to both process and criteria regarding Outsider Art. The numerous terms used to describe this work bears testimony to its instinct to not be pinned down, not to be called what theorists place upon it. *Raw vision, art brut, naive art, intuitive art, marginalised art* are all aspects of the defining and codifying process. The term I feel most com-fortable with is *visionary art* but that requires its own specific ethos and context.

The visionary realm embraces the entire spectrum of imaginal spaces – from heaven to hell, from the infinitude of forms to formless voids. The psychologist James Hillman calls it the imaginal realm. Poet William Blake called it the divine imagination. The aborigines call it the dreamtime; and Sufis call it alam al-mithal. To Plato, this was the realm of the ideal archetypes. The Tibetans call it thesambhogakaya – the dimension of inner richness. Theosophists refer to the astral, mental, and nirvanic planes of consciousness. Carl Jung knew this realm as the collective symbolic unconscious. Whatever we choose to call it, the visionary realm is the space we visit during dreams and altered or heightened states of consciousness.[11]

When I first visited the Outsiders exhibition at the Hayward Gallery fresh from art school in 1979 it was as if I had seen the art I had always dreamed of, it was as though the scales had been removed from my eyes. It made me laugh, made me cry and it terrified me. Perhaps I had been confronted by the purest psychological seam of art that I had ever encountered before but which I had always suspected, in the deepest recesses of my psyche, did exist. This was an art of truth, an art of the inner world. This encounter is eloquently defined by Roger Cardinal in his preface to the 1979 exhibition catalogue:

The "ferment of individuality" is what I see happening in my work in secure psychiatric hospitals and prisons that I visit and within which I work. They, the "unforgiven", the marginalised, the stigmatised, and those of the fractured experience know what it is to be both on the inside and the outside simultaneously. They make art as a currency of self, as a search for meaning and place, to expurgate anger and internal violence, to come to term with their sexuality and incarceration. The recent institutional use of powerful medication, which often inhibits and in some cases destroys individual creativity for so many people, can be a barbaric solution to psychosis and socially unacceptable behaviours. Patients I have worked with have complained to me about how their cocktails of medication had destroyed the support mechanisms of their creativity. When asked about this, they replied *"They are not interested in my creativity, in my art"*. At the time when art historian and Psychiatrist Hans Prinzhorn was collecting art from the asylums of Europe that explored the borderlines between psychiatry and art there were no powerful anti-psychotic medications to hinder free thought and the expression of patients.

And so Outsider Art seeks new realms of conquest but with an ever-shrinking base it seems. It has to find new territories and regions for its survival and of course it has a grand and illustrious past in collections throughout the world which will be constantly exhibited albeit with the reservations that Jerry Saltz raised that Outsider Art should be integrated as a consequence of institutions *"that still separates so-called outsider, self-taught, and visionary art from institutionally sanctioned official art."*

territorial disputes and exaggerated claims, for example - and to show the contradictory forces that have shaped and continue to propel it. I have argued that what is really at stake is an underlying, and not always fully conscious, set of conceptions about the nature of authentic creativity. Allied to this are numerous concepts such as madness, originality, automatism, privacy and even "authenticity" itself, which need closer examination. Although it is Outsider Art that has brought these into the open and highlighted many of the problems involved, the issues it has dramatised affect the wider world and, because of its subterranean links with that art world, may also question some of its assumptions.[13]

And so as David Maclagan (artist, art therapist and critic) puts it so succinctly what is really at stake is an underlying, and not always fully conscious, set of conceptions about the nature of authentic creativity.[13]

Anthropologists of the mind have their own territories of colonisation and exotic analysis and just as anthropology went through its crisis of identity, so I feel that Outsider Art should re-examine its premise in a more consultative and inclusive way with those upon whom their gaze falls.[2]

And to finish I could not resist this dryly observed short piece of wit from artist Brian Treadwell.

"I used to be an outsider artist, but my intellect got the better of me"[14]

John Holt is an artist at the Sculpture Lounge, Holmfirth. A writer and founder of Arts and Mental Health charity AiM (Artists in Mind) based in Huddersfield. He is also a chaplain (Quaker) at two secure psychiatric hospitals.

Notes

1. Sebastian Wilbur quoted in *Insider Art*. Matthew Meadows A&C Black, 2010.
2. John Holt *Anthropologists of the Mind*. First Published in *Asylum Magazine*, 2003. The article can be found at http://www.escapeintolife.com/essays/anthropologists-of-the-mind/
3. Laurent Danchin *Raw Vision*. Issue 1, 1989.
4. Suzi Gablik *The Re-enchantment of Art*. Thames and Hudson 1992
5. John Holt "Creativity as the Immune System of the Mind and the Source of the Mythic" in *Ways of Knowing Science and Mysticism Today*. Chris Clarke (ed.) Imprint Academic, 2005.
6. *Souzou Outsider Art from Japan*. Wellcome Collection, 2013 [Booklet accompanying the exhibition]
7. More information on AiM can be found at http://www.artists-in-mind.org.uk/
8. http://en.wikipedia.org/wiki/Judith_Scott
9. Jerry Saltz *On the Outsider Art Fair and Why There's No Such Thing As Outsider Art*. Available from: http://www.vulture.com/2013/02/jerry-saltz-on-the-outsider-art-fair.html
10. Matthew Meadows *Outsider Art*. Herbert Press, 2010
11. Available from http://www.alexgrey.com/essay/whatis.html
12. Roger Cardinal *Outsiders*. Arts Council of Great Britain, 1979.
13. David Maclagan *Outsider Art: From the Margins to the Marketplace*. Reaktion Books, 2009.
14. Brian Treadwell's website is http://www.briantreadwell.com

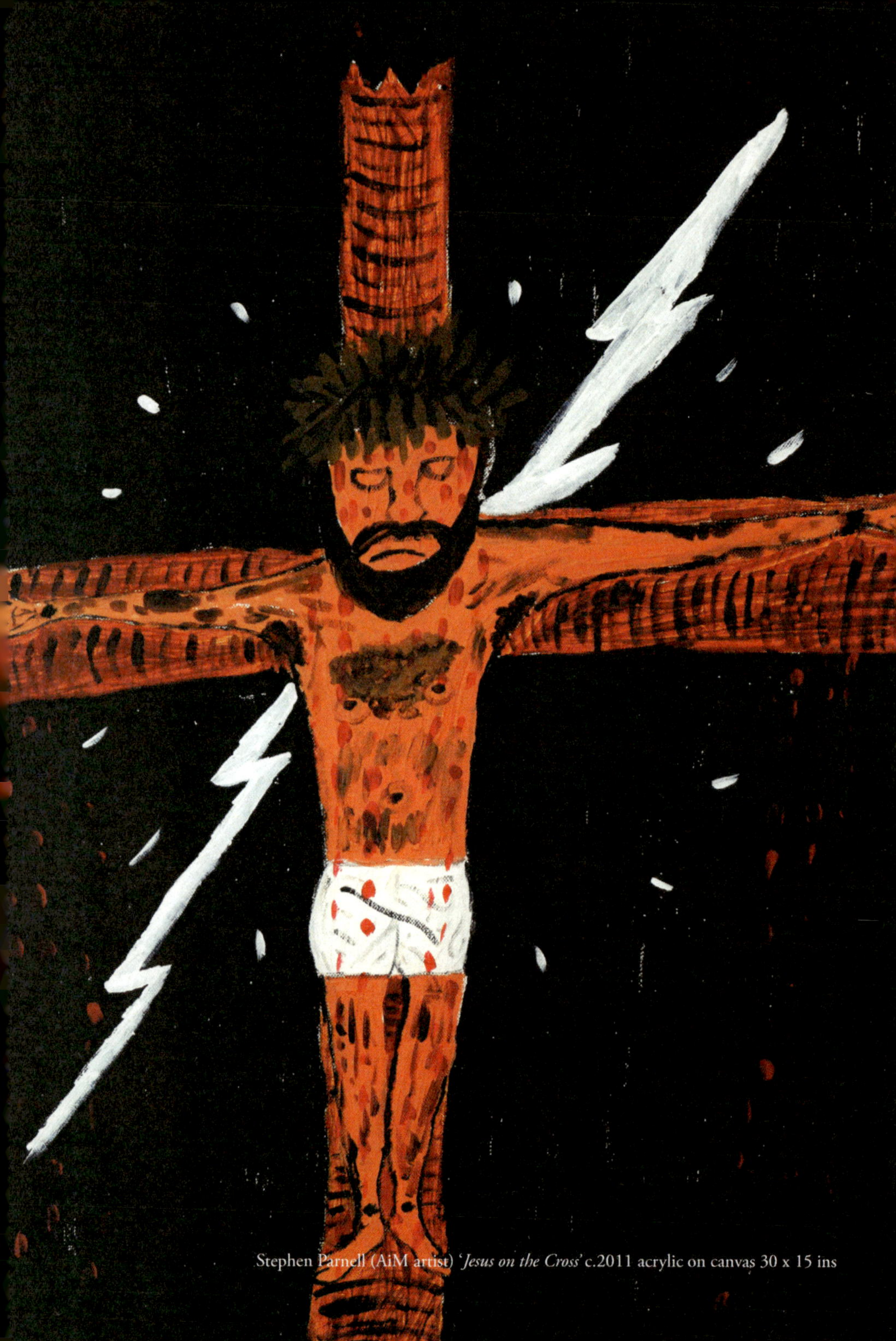

Stephen Parnell (AiM artist) *Jesus on the Cross* c.2011 acrylic on canvas 30 x 15 ins

The work on the next few pages has been produced by a broad range of artists in contexts that might be grouped under the term art therapy. Whether or not this is appropriate - it seems the best current term to describe this work produced as an attempt to develop independence, deal with mental health issues, learning difficulties or to cope with the consequences of addiction. On pages 126-139, artist and psychiatric nurse Stephen Kirin explores the work of three artists that he has encountered. The artworks reproduced on pages 112-125 have been produced in collaboration with the following organisations:

ILS at Coleg Llandrillo. The Funny Phantom and The Flashy Phantom were created by eleven learners who are studying on a course in ILS (Independent Living Skills) for students with significant learning difficulties. The *phantom* images were created in response to Neil Coombs' exhibition *The Phantoms of Surrealism* by the ILS students as part of their studies at Coleg Llandrillo in North Wales.

AiM (Artists in Mind) is a charity started by John Holt and is based in Huddersfield, West Yorkshire. It is a creative sanctuary providing studio spaces for people who are suffering with their mental health. I have worked for the AiM charity for seven years. In that time I have seen many talented people develop their own creative voice through painting, sculpting, film, photography, textiles, ceramics, poetry and writing. AiM enables each person to engage fully with their creativity at their own pace in their own unique way. Mentors provide a creative friendship where artistic ideas are explored and supported alongside regular trips to art exhibitions. Most of the artists exhibit their work in art galleries throughout the country. *Sarah Sheard.*

Tyddyn Môn is an organisation based on a smallholding on the isle of Anglesey in North Wales. Tyddyn Môn provides day care, training and support for adults with learning difficulties, all of whom contribute to the development and running of the farm. The photographs included on the following pages were taken by these adults with learning difficulties as part of a photography project with the artists Tim Williams and Moyrah Gall. The work from Tyddyn Môn is accompanied by a short piece from Roger Cardinal.

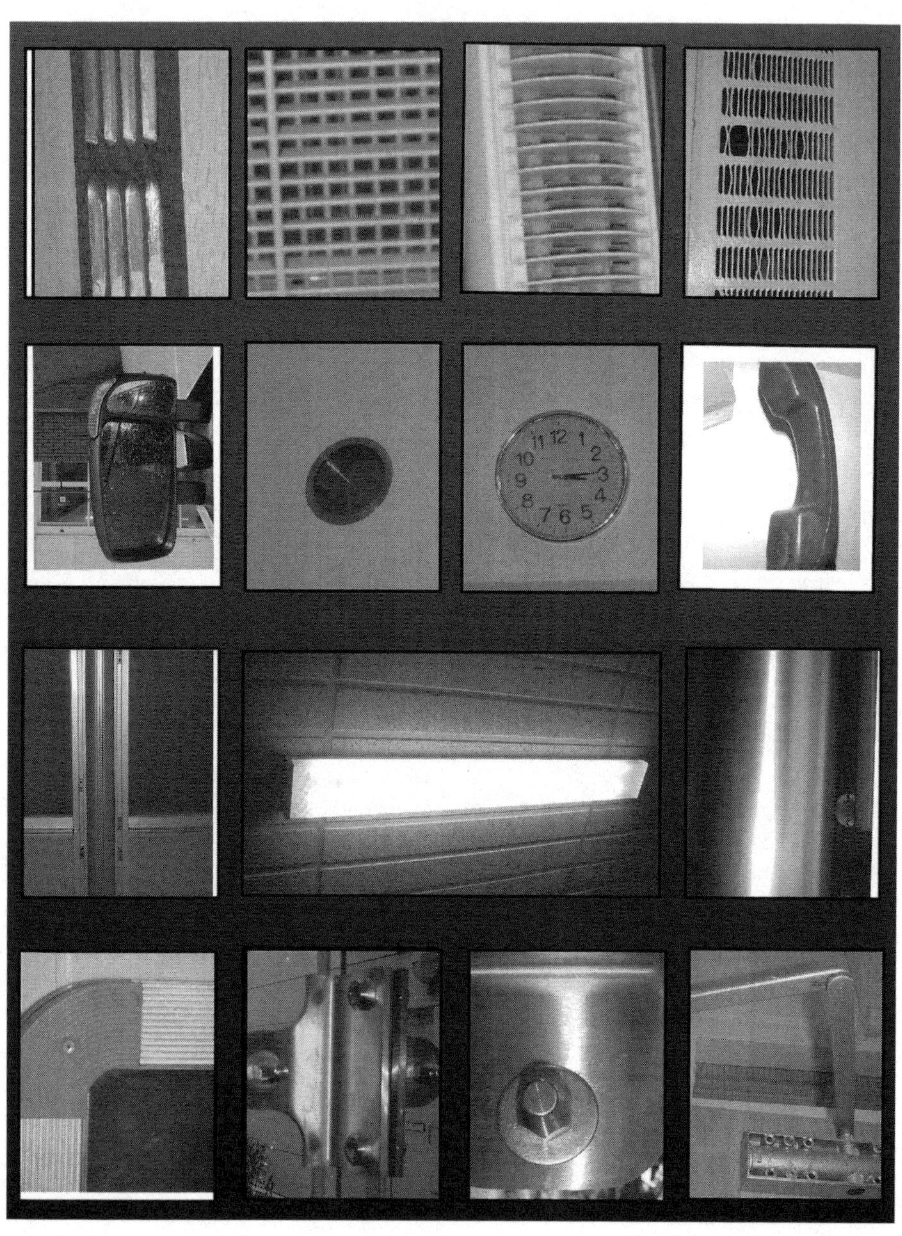

'The Flashy Phantom of Coleg Llandrillo' 2013

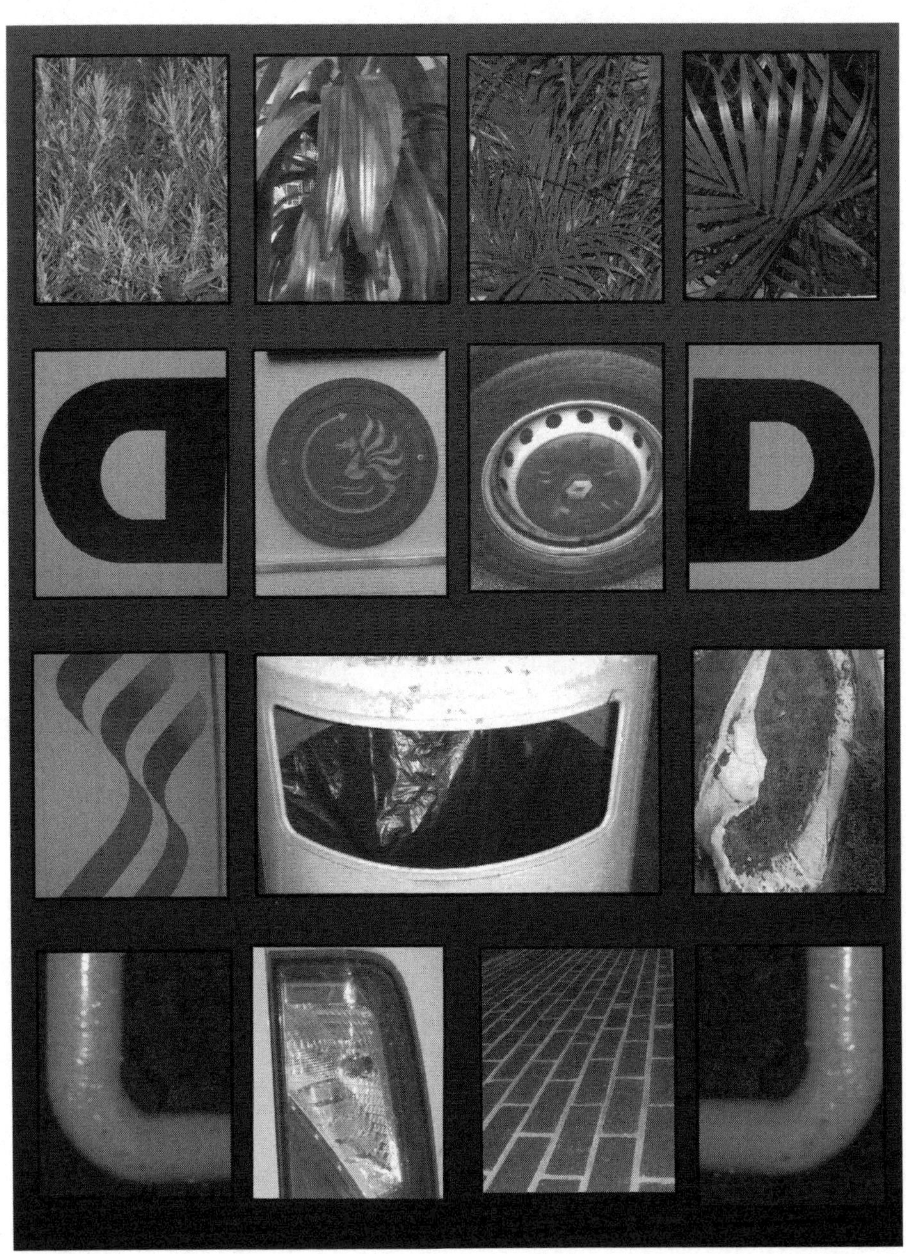

'The Funny Phantom of Coleg Llandrillo' 2013

115

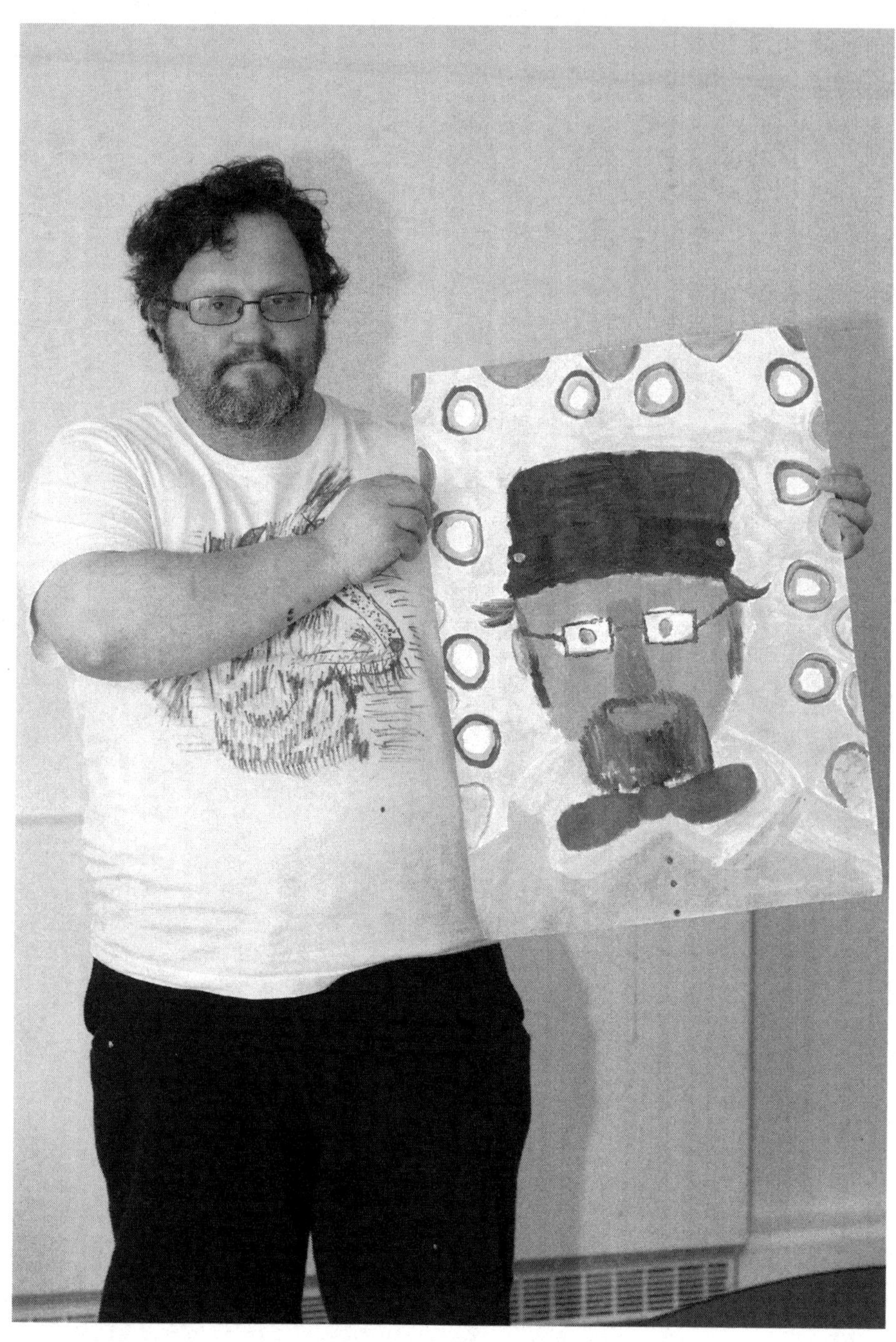

David, artist working with Sarah Sheard at the AiM workshop.

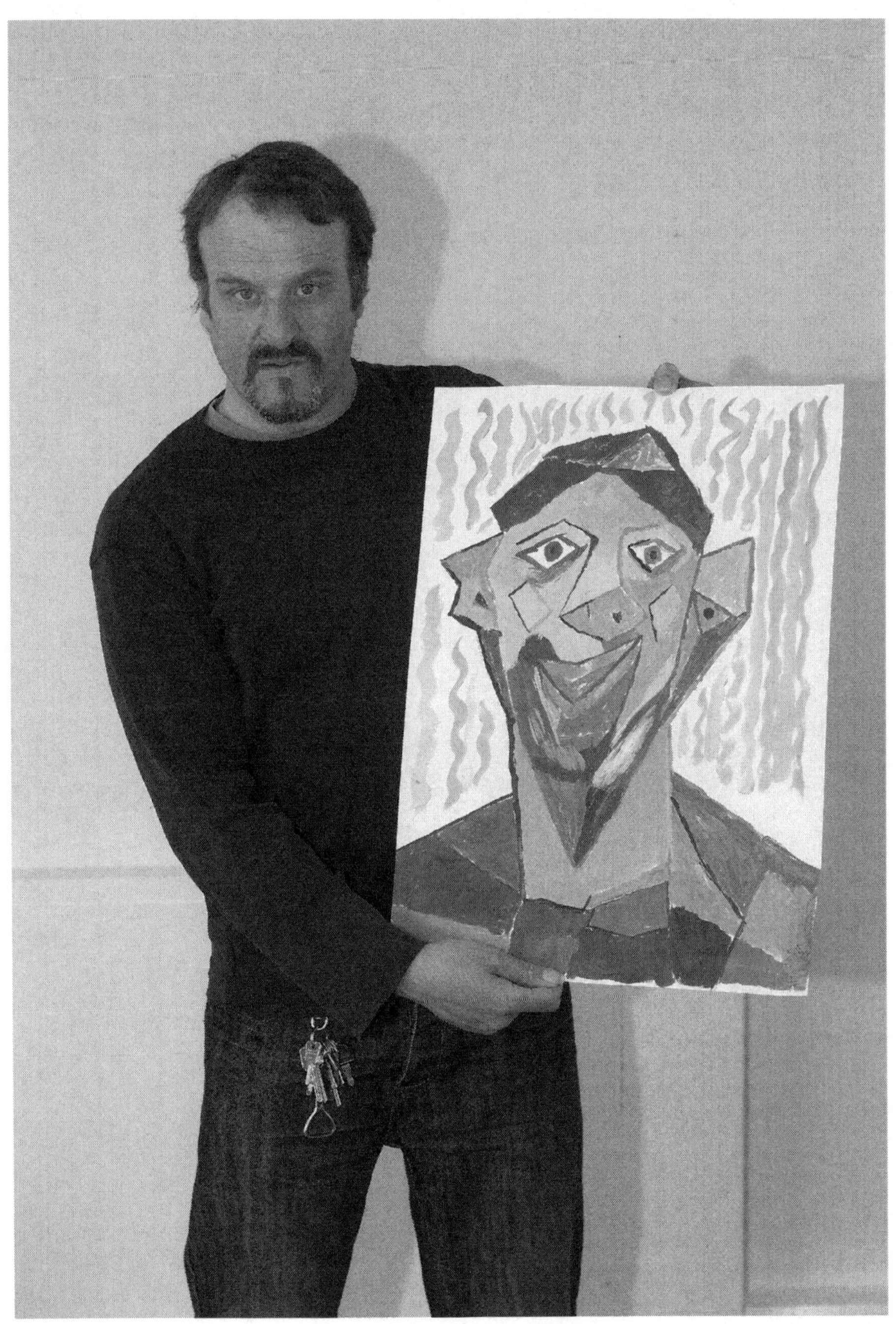

Neil, artist working with Sarah Sheard at the AiM workshop.

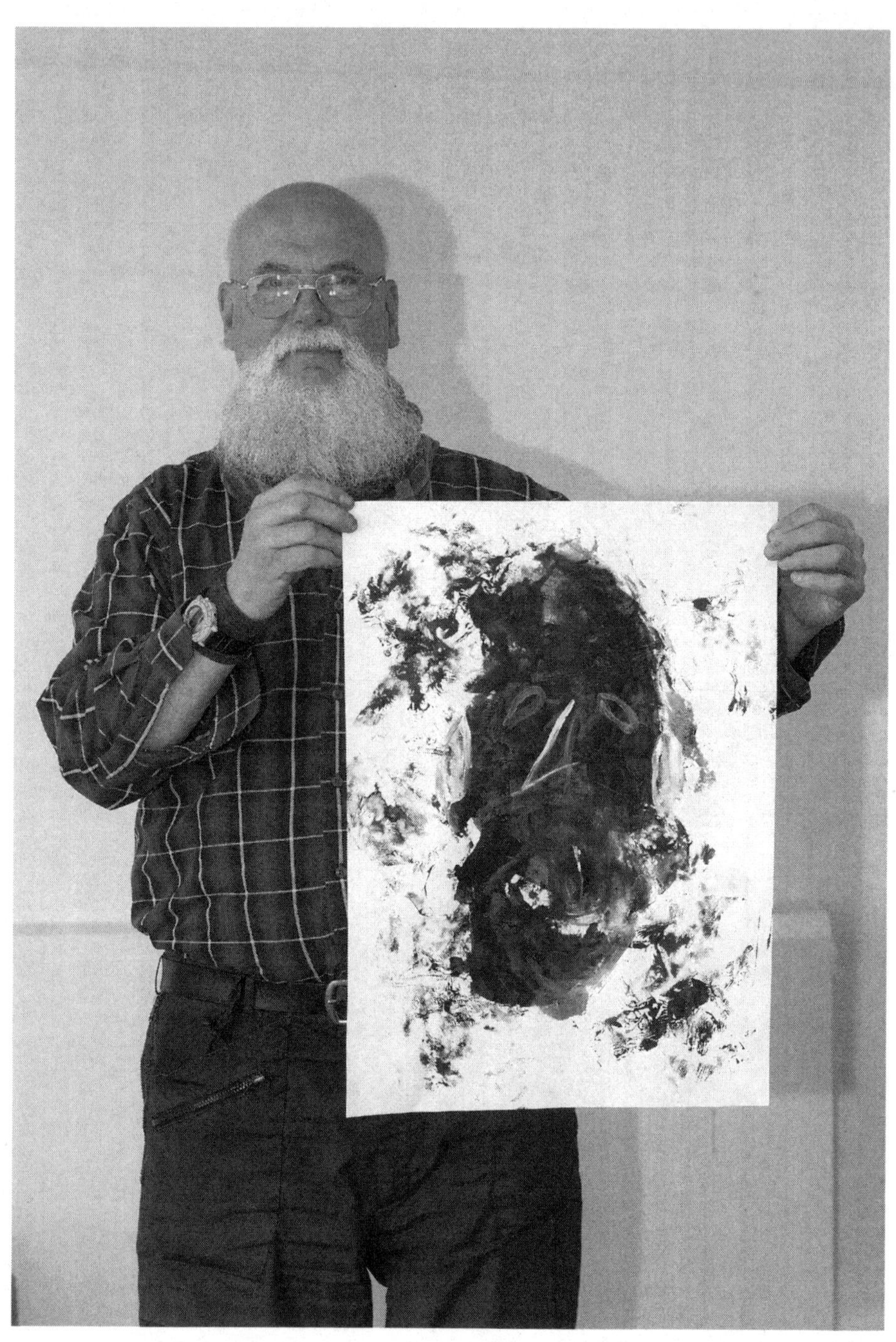

Pete, artist working with Sarah Sheard at the AiM workshop.

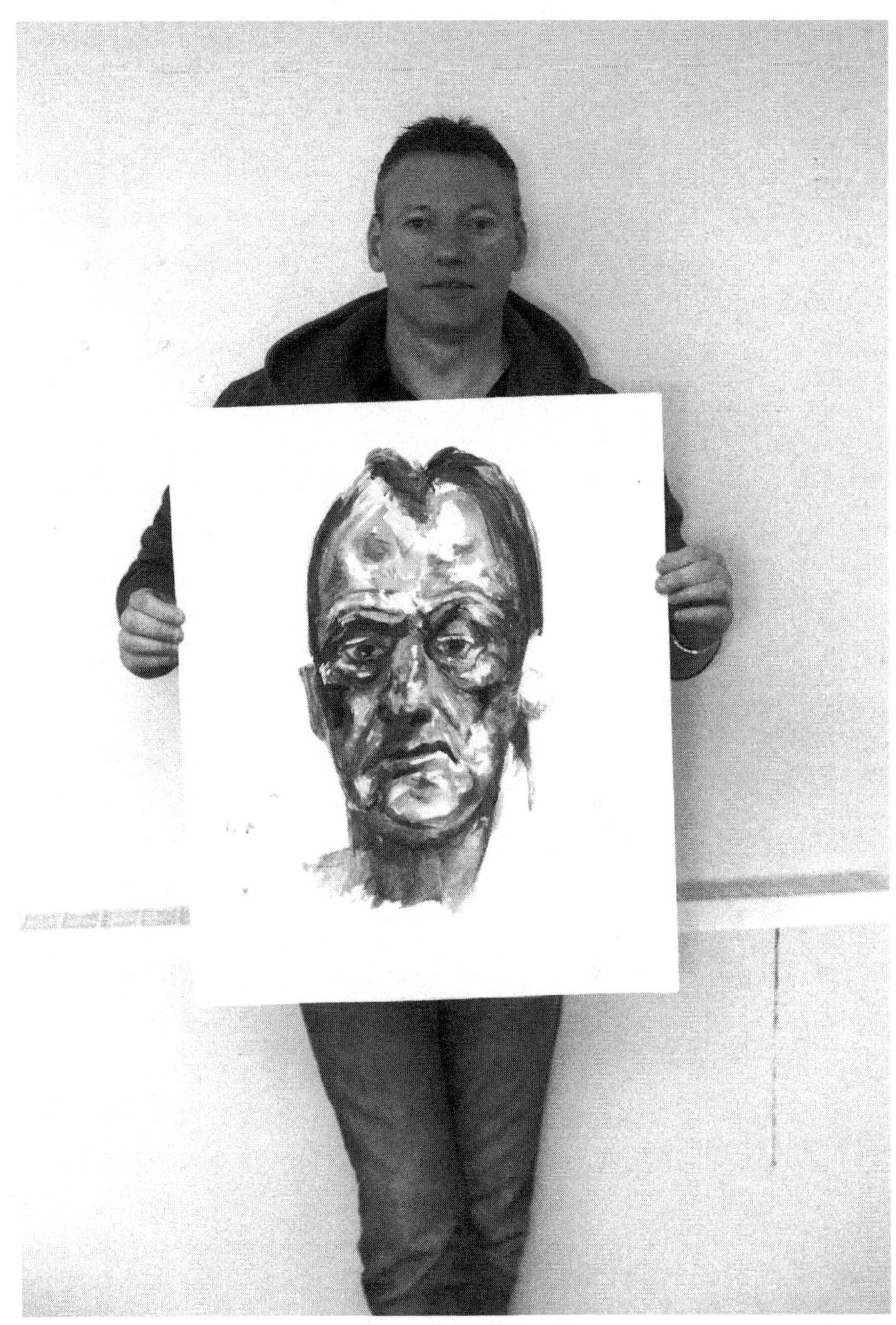

Gary, artist working with Sarah Sheard at the AiM workshop.

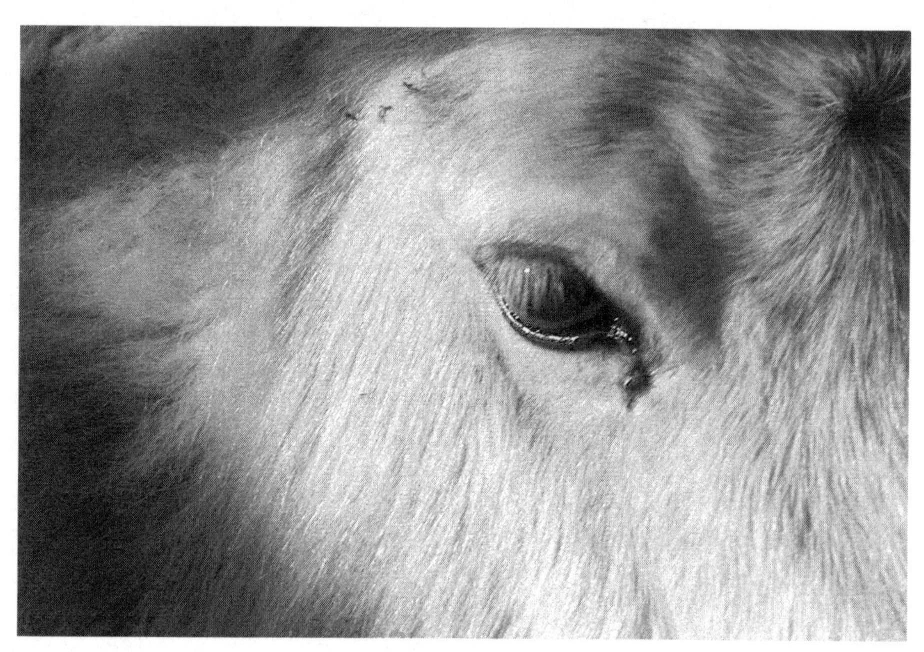

Tyddyn Môn 1

We live in a period strangely attached to signs and especially spontaneous traces. In the context of cinema, the fascination with crime, and above all the reassuring myth of the criminal's fatal mistake, have become a dominant of the crime film, where the resources of forensic science are invoked so as to convince us that the slightest physical contact - a fingerprint left on a glass, a hair on a pillow, a footprint in the mud - will leave an inevitable and unfalsifiable message, nothing less than the unique signature of the individual. We might suppose that we leave irreducible marks of our passing in every place and at all times.

That wilful expressive object commonly called the artwork represents a declaration of presence par excellence. For those who produce artistic compositions - in the form of drawings, paintings, sculptures, graffiti or texts - each scrawl, each arabesque, each loop is the result of a physical impulse transmitting a cerebral or nervous tremor which cannot but confirm the awareness, on the part of the person in question, of his or her own condition of being. We may conceive of this person - bearing witness to himself or herself through the intermediary of a hand that sheds imprints - as an expressive organism entirely transported by the adventure of orchestrating internal affects and ideas.

Although not all those persons deemed to have learning difficulties who attend creative workshops are likely to achieve formal recognition as artists, it remains nevertheless the case that their readiness to undertake the experiment of self-expression deserves our fullest admiration. The entire being of these exceptional individuals seems prepared to set the creative impulse entirely free, with no concern for social or technical convention. They grab hold of the pencil or the brush in order to demonstrate to themselves - long before anyone else - that there is something crucial going on in the gap between the individual and the surface over which he or she is leaning. And once the brush touches the paper, an image is born, the natural child of this fertile contact.

Thus, quite spontaneously, a first step is made towards explaining oneself, a first step which may indeed develop into an autobiographical narrative, sealing the link between author and drawing. Since we usually arrive rather late on the scene

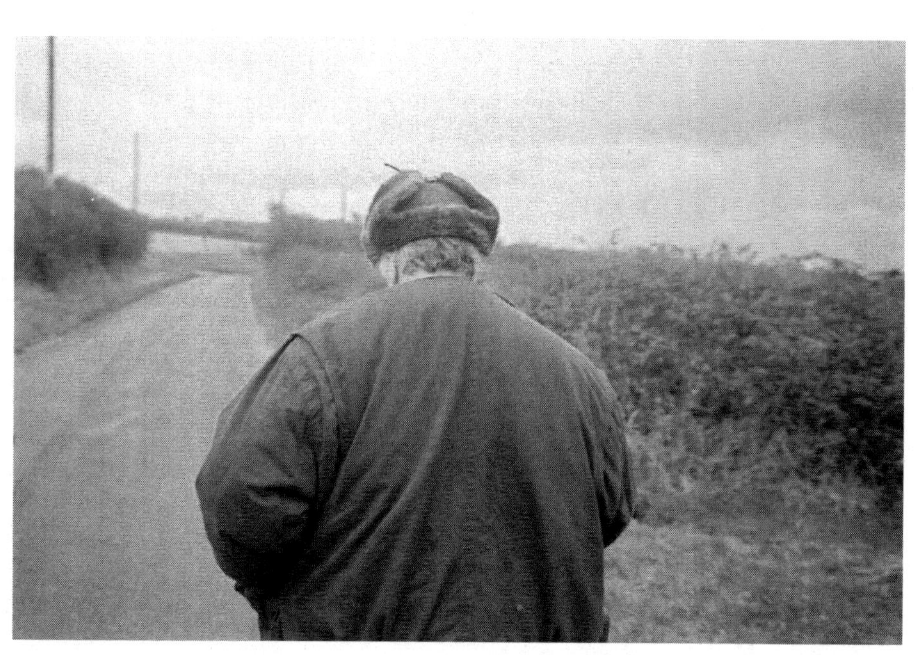

Tyddyn Môn 2

of this sort of self-declaration represented by the work of the handicapped person, we are, insofar as we act as spectators or critics, like a detective who must scrutinize not only the imprints on the paper but also the impressions they leave on his own sensibility. Clearly, what is happening is something more than mechanical objective decoding. A message has begun to be articulated and we are bound to want to construe it. This can only be done through an act of empathy. A valid interpretation can only be a function of reciprocity.

What seems most characteristic of such out-of-the-way art is its urgency, its air of febrile lyricism. These qualities have to do with the artist's continual movement toward self-discovery and self-definition, and thereafter the impulse toward communication with others. From the virtual image to the image realized on a surface, we pass on to the image as received and absorbed by the spectator. It is this last transition which, remarkably, seems to activate the aesthetic emotion

Is this then our cue to speak of beauty? Hardly, or at least not in the ordinary sense. For if there is beauty here, it is a special sort of beauty which goes beyond the simple appreciation of an agreeable texture, a nuance of colour, or an adroit curve. As is the case with authentic Outsider Art, the virtue of such works as these can scarcely be separated from our sense of being caught within a magnetic field: they demand our fullest engagement and undivided attention. Miraculously, what is spontaneous and arbitrary can then take on an absolute authority. We stand before these expressions as before windows which have suddenly been thrust open. Of course, we cannot cross the sill; yet most certainly we feel a subtle breath of wind upon our skin, lulling or darting, soft or sharp, which bears a guarantee of contact and meaning.

Roger Cardinal wrote the first book about Art Brut, Outsider Art (London & New York, 1972).

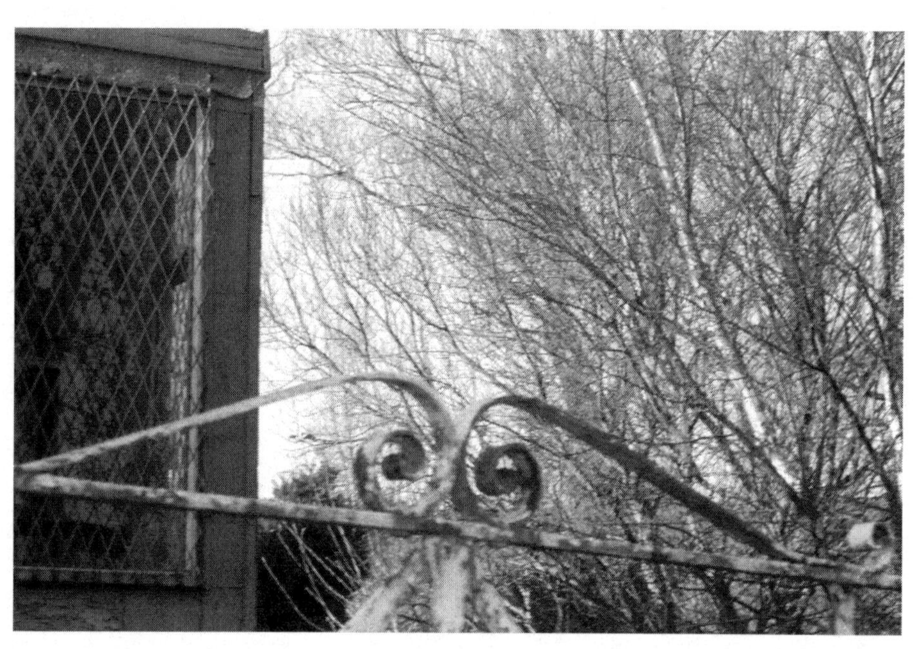

Tyddyn Môn 3

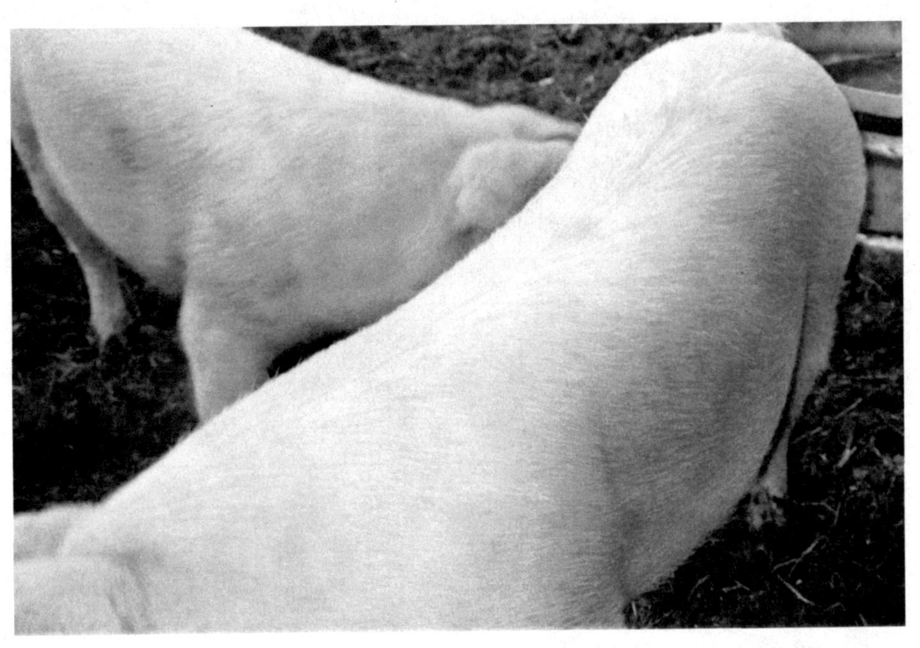

Tyddyn Môn 4

Some thoughts and anecdotes via the 1980,s industrial music scene on the outsider and his/her place in our consciousness,many many thanks to Brian,John and Martin for contributing "the meat"to this dialogue.

"historical detail to set the scene".In 1985 sum of money changed hands to enable private careers advice in an office in Oxford S London,travelling from rural Essex with a concerned mother who saw her sons educatio and future edged in black ,a fickle punk and art obsessed version of myself tolerate stupid expensive questions until a final judgement proclaimed that he should become art student which he already of course knew and subsequently became!During the lunch break ,Virgin megastore across the road(vinyl in those days)had a copy of informati overload unit by SPK(interesting clips on youtube)on the front a bleak image of a lo male in a corridor in a wheelchair,on the vinyl the ugliest squalling feedback and disturbed grunting s that could be imagined (of course I bought it)

Reading deeper into the origins of SPK brings me up to date with this edition of Patricide and the geography of the "outsider".Graham Revell and Neil Hill formed SPK,one a psychiatric nurse the other a schizophrenic inpatient who he had nursed(in strange " SPKesque" echo   which hints at subconscious patterning after that days career advice ,many years later the fickle me became a psychiatric nurse who performed with one of his previously sectioned patients in a performance available o YouTube,"sonic egg Artheads)without realising it the careers adviser that day took t money and led me by the hand to SPK emulation.

SPK took their inspiration from the Socialist Patients Kollective a fascinating detail of radical 1970,s Germany,a maverick Psychiatrist and numerous patients occupied premises and issued manifesto,s proclaiming ill health to be the natural reaction to Capitalism ,and violent revolt the natural conclusion.this was the Germany of Baader Meinhof and the various gun toting groups exchanged members and vitriol,an interesting parallel with the art market of today took hold in so far as the radicalised mental health patients were second class in the pecking order of revolution behind the cooler Krautrock terrorists,inside Art occasionally tolerates Outsider Art in a similar fashion as lon as it gets something from it.Some aforementioned SPK members took part in the Red Arm Faction siege of the West German embassy in Stockholm in 1975 a casual onlooker could be forgiven for believing they were expendable in that "no way out "action.Which brings me back to Neil Hill,he stayed in Australia whilst SPK toured and killed himself in 1984,graham Revell now composes film scores in Hollywood,I,m sure Neil Hil wasn,t expendable but he,s part of a pattern as far as the outsider is concerned whether it be in revolution or Art.Around the same time vinyl by Einsturzende Neubate was purchased ,this time Zeichnungen das patient O T,the reference being to Oskar Tschirtner,a schizophrenic inpatient in klosterneuberg psychiatric hospital in Austri who was encouraged to draw and continued to draw remarkable artworks for the rest of his life .O.T resided in a specially designed inpatient facility at Klosterneuberg ,years before the SPK had been granted a set of offices in Heidelberg university as a academic nod to philosophical experimentation(a series of occupations followed after the university board lost control of the experiment and changed its mind)similarly a building was freed up for patients with artistic ability to express themselves in Austria ,but this time with a continued official sanction in recognition for the revolutionary ability of Art to change people's lives,the house became known as the Haus der Kunstlers ,Oskar Tschirtner continued to live there in the grounds of the psychiatric hospital until his death fairly recently.

The remit of this edition of Patricide leads me ,the fickle Art /Punk of yesteryear to the psychiatric Artist nurse I find myself today scrutinising some seeds sown in the industrial music scene of the late 70's and early 80's ,a revolution of the senses led me to my own occupations and statements and finally my own insider membership of the system,only creativity remains a constant with an earlier me and the pattern of the accepted and the Unaccepted within it,the insider and the outsider and the way the outsider is controlled ,sterilised and made acceptable by the system,the SPK and the Haus der Kunstlers are both examples of this,the first neither accepted by academic or revolutionionary exploded violently,the second was formalised by a hospital into a version of treatment,a liberated response to the artistic impulse in psychosis,but a structure never the less led by an organisation.And today the art markets of the world have continued this pattern by turning the creativity of the outsider ,the mentally And today the art markets of the world

ill,the dispossessed and the junkie into a commodity with financial value and its own identity,but still carefully positioned to one side of the insiders in art,a member of the SPK would have been tempted to read this as capitalist control of the outsider and probably would have occupied the market with grenades in their pockets.

And now

Patricide enters into the dialogue freeing a space for ideas ,but will the ideas be acceptable in the outlets and minds of its readers?Do todays Surrealist sympathisers have an insider or outsider world view?the classicists of French Surrealism so often quoted in these pages also played the inside/outside game.Breton et al identified their foremost admirable sexual outsider from a safe distance whilst safely controlling the realtime Surrealist doctrine,take for example a reference to tolerance of frowned upon homosexuality within the Surrealist pantheon .Andre Breton stated "i accuse the homosexuals of affronting human tolerance with a mental and moral defect that tends to advocate itself as a way of life and to paralyse every enterprise i respect.I make exceptions,one of which i grant to the incomparable marquis de sade"(Surrealist revolution 1928)with one sentence casting the role of sexual insider/outsider within a revolutionary movement ,Whether or not the openly bisexual Surrealist author of "difficult death"Rene Crevel is one of these exceptions is hard to tell,but he was only one of several contributers outside of the mainstream in that particular movement ,and consequently disposable to the insider clique that preferred its queers dead ,ironically in a self fulfilling way Crevel soon would be dead,by his own hand,whichever the system an inside and an outside coexist often with a hinterland inbetween.

in my own hinterland between inside and outside there are 3 friends and acquaintances who sprang to mind immediately when I thought of a discourse about Art

and the outsider they do not necessarily share my world views and they do not necessarily adhere to a surrealist ethic though one contributes to the Surrealist London Action Group (SLAG)it is their words rather than my words that will be the grenades and pills that will provoke the next reactions,i have asked each one 5 questions /requests and hope the images and answers they provide add shape and form to all of our landscapes,and please never give money to a careers adviser ,visit your local music store instead.Request 1.please introduce yourself.Question 2.What meaning does Art have in your life?Question 3.Do you recognise the term "Outsider"?Request 4.Please describe your working practice.Question 5.does the Art market as we know it recognise your working practice?

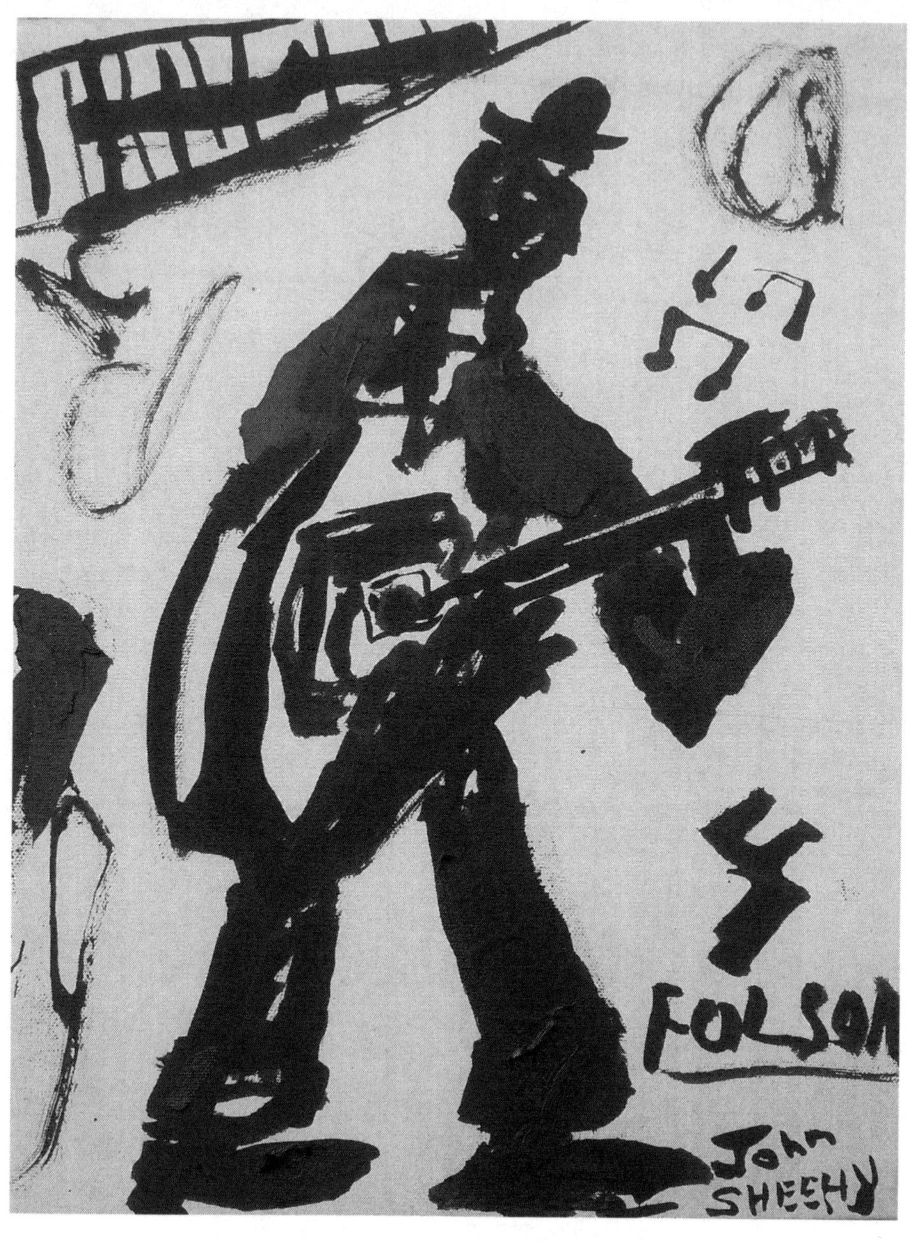

John Joseph Sheehy *'Folson'* 2013 acrylic on canvas 16 x 12 ins
image courtesy the artist

128

Re.
Questions

1st Question

Please introduce yourself

My name is John Joseph Sheehy. I originate from South Western Ireland and have lived in London for near enough fifty years. I worked on building sites for a good part of my life. Covering things like; Hod-carrying, Laying Bricks, Roofing with Welsh - slates, etc.

I've been through homelessness a good few times, living in hostels and night shelters and also slept out, many things have happened along the way and I have been in many scrapes have battled with illness all my life. I came to my art through a day centre and the Big Issue about 13 or 14 years ago these days I make my own art-work and create original images. I don't research or copy. My creativity comes from a divine source, titles appear as each piece develops. I paint, draw, print and work with pottery, sculptures and ceramics as well as art work. I write poems, short stories, small plays and songs, I play the mouth-organ tin whistle and banjo. I sing too but don't play any traditional tunes or

Question1 Continued page 2   John Joseph Sheehy

OR COPY OR ~~try~~ imitate Any other musican or
Sengers. I compose my own sounds and pla
a different tune everyTime
I have To pAINT, SCRIBBle, dRaw, and wRite
dAILy and ~~nightly~~ nightly. I have done
Thousands ~~And~~ And Thousands. I dont kn
How mANy pieces. EVERy poEM And sTORy is f
OF each other and will Be of Any woRk that I
ever do.

Question. 2 : What meaning does ~~it~~ ART have to
    youR life
well it mAy and mighT have a couple of
meanings to my life. Its absolutely cRucial To
me, Its like AIR And wATER. I have To pAINt,
And wRite, dRaw. It can be fuRIOus and
Reckless but it's ALwAys nonstop-, EVen if
JusT scRiBBling. Its not a Techique I follou
it ~~simply~~ simply FOR me., CReating is my life
I suppose Realy you'd have To spend a dAy a
night to get an undeRstanding of This.
    oTHeR ARtist Have foughT my woRk. They Tell
IT INSpIReS and moves Them. I do admiRe
wIALLIAM BLAKE'S WORK ANd TRACEY EMIN'S
dRAwINGs, pRINts and sTITchings, TheiR woRk
is veRy good cReation, it's got a life
    A LIVING lIFE

        John Joseph Sheehy 1sT mARch
                                2013

Page (3)

Question 3

Do you Recognise The Term "outsider"?

I do Recognise the word yes and other
Art Historians and gallery owners have —
Referred To my work as "outsider Art".
I have participated in Exhibitions under the
Titles "Outsider Art" and "Outsider Artists"
and I'm very proud of all the Artists I
have exhibited with. Their work is
Fantastic It does exit and Belong, it's
A species, a strong culture and a daring
presence. A unique Race of Art, which Has
its own Nationality and Belongs in every
Race. It really does come Alive It speaks,
it sings. It attracts. It inspires. It Loves
Its Definitley got IT.

Question 4.

Please describe your working practice

My working practices are Random, often on
The spot. From a day centre workshop - to - working
at my home. It could well Be A Canvas, Board
R on card with Arylic, oils or House paints. Inks
ould Be Crayons, Pastel pencils, Charcoal.
Ino, Felt Tip, Biro, I also use ~~often~~ often Found items
Some Thing out of A skip Even. It might Be
A Box or A window Blind, Any object
There's No End To ~~the~~ The possibilities Really

Idm Joseph Sheehy
1st March 2013

Question 5

Does the art market as we know it recognise your working practice?

I don't think so. As there is not really a definitive way to analyse my work and thereby fitting it into the types of art that is recognised today

There is a big interest also a big interest from Germany France and Norway. But it seems they don't know what to do with it just yet

John Joseph Sheehy

1st March 2013

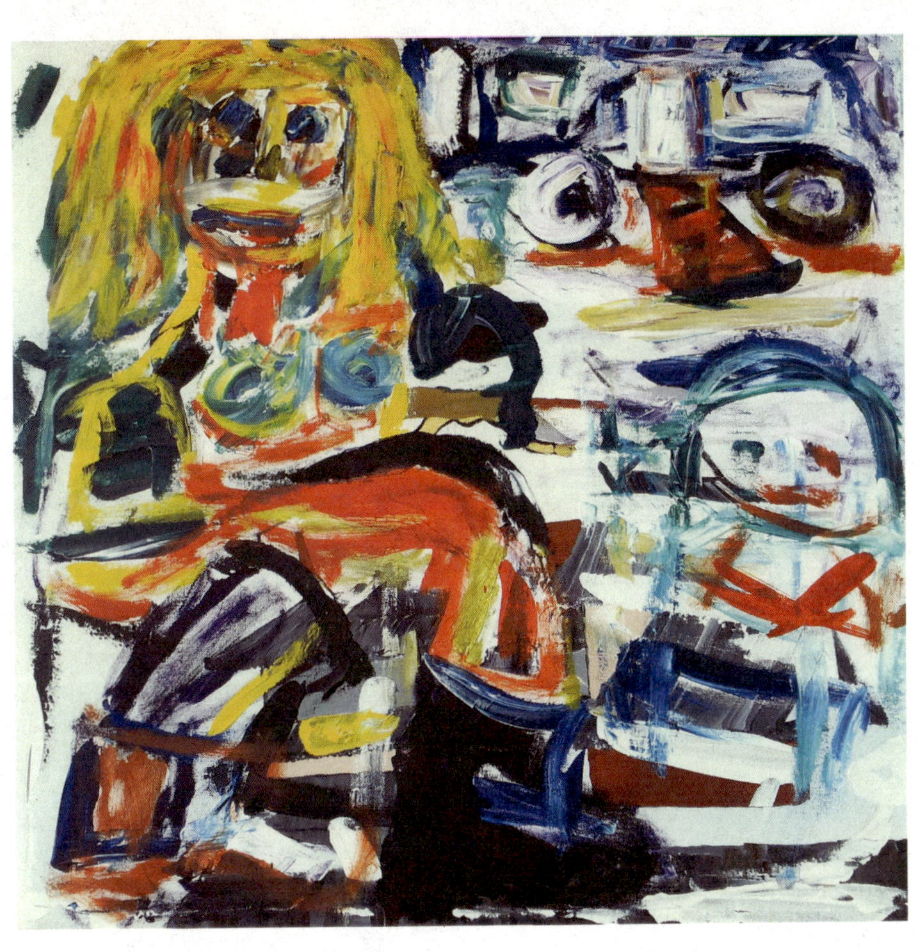

John Joseph Sheehy *'Beside St. James'* 2013 acrylic on canvas 28 x 28 ins
image courtesy the artist

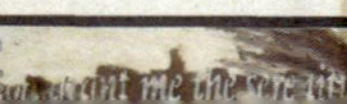

...ally above an off license, on the a...
...as the family ho...   ...ace of
Ap...   ...and ...   ...calling
of ...   ...y live
se...
be...

A self taught painter working predominately in un pretentious figurative/portrait work. Stylistically avent-garde, impressionism with undertones of realism. Born 1968 in the east end of London, an ex R.A.F Regiment Gunner and Alcoholic. Sober now after 27 years of addiction. Art plays a huge part in my Recovery.

My first thought when asked "what is an outsider/do I recognise the term outsider art" Instantly turned to someone weighed down in Gore-Tex and galoshes stood in a muddy field painting yet another pleasant land-scape, but No thats silly. I would like to of thought it was a movement working outside the traditional royal academy pristine perceptions of art, but it turns out I'm wrong!

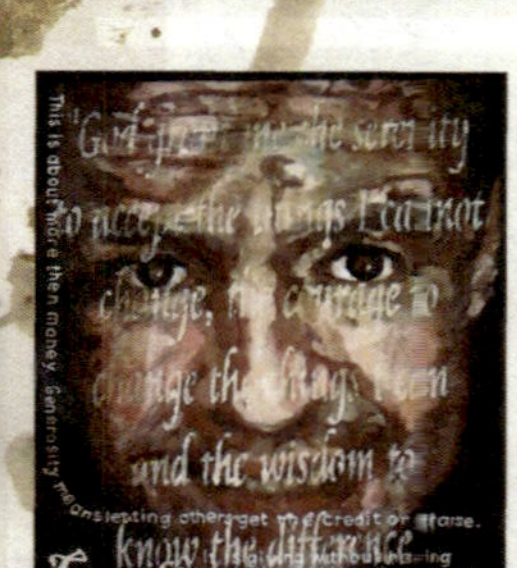

I dont pretend to know or understand exactly what an outsider is but for most my life there has been some-thing within me that had been wide of the mark and Alcohol was never a help, I live an honest program these's days, but still find time to lie to my Self, I am well know I'm an Outsider' whether my pride likes it or not, my art for years was closed and distructive. Only when I had to look at myself, my art became a vessel to Wellbeing I began by registering my exact

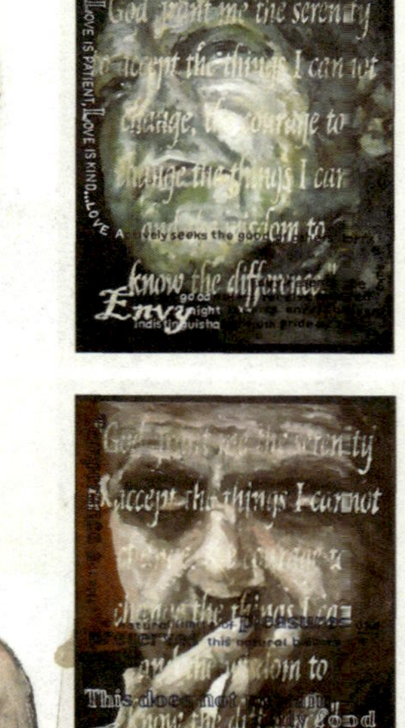

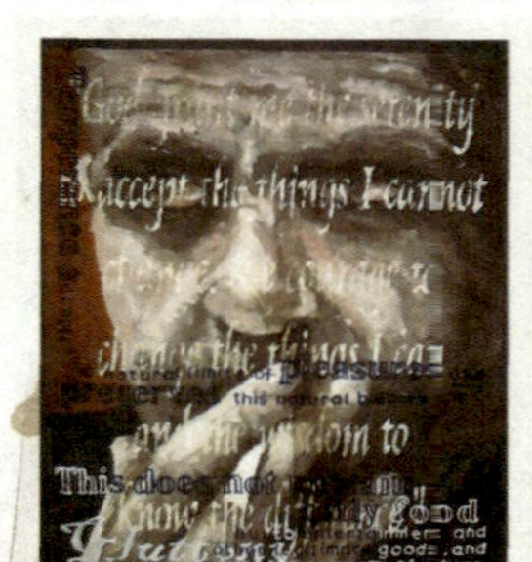

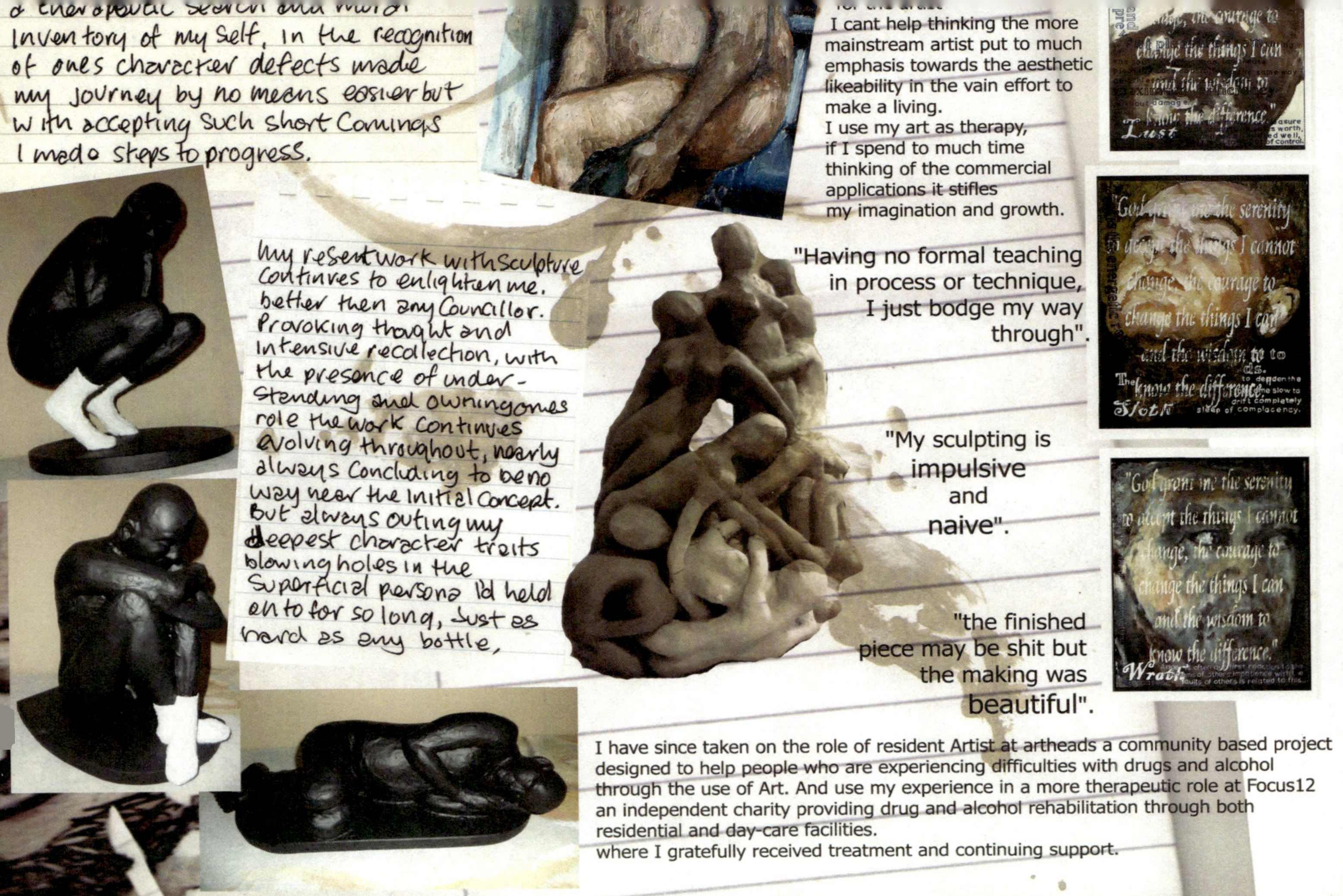

I cant help thinking the more mainstream artist put to much emphasis towards the aesthetic likeability in the vain effort to make a living.

I use my art as therapy, if I spend to much time thinking of the commercial applications it stifles my imagination and growth.

"Having no formal teaching in process or technique, I just bodge my way through".

"My sculpting is impulsive and naïve".

"the finished piece may be shit but the making was beautiful".

I have since taken on the role of resident Artist at artheads a community based project designed to help people who are experiencing difficulties with drugs and alcohol through the use of Art. And use my experience in a more therapeutic role at Focus12 an independent charity providing drug and alcohol rehabilitation through both residential and day-care facilities.

where I gratefully received treatment and continuing support.

inventory of my self, in the recognition of ones character defects made my journey by no means easier but with accepting such short comings I made steps to progress.

my research work with sculpture continues to enlighten me. better then any councillor. Provoking thought and intensive recollection, with the presence of under-standing and owning ones role the work continues evolving throughout, nearly always near the initial concept. but always outing my deepest character traits blowing holes in the superficial persona Id held on to for so long, Just as hard as any bottle,

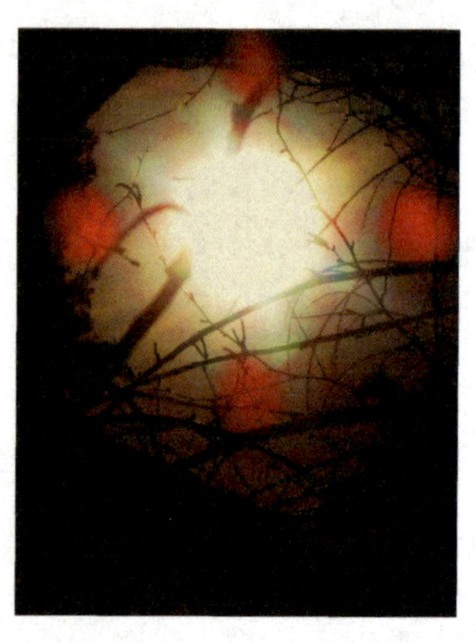

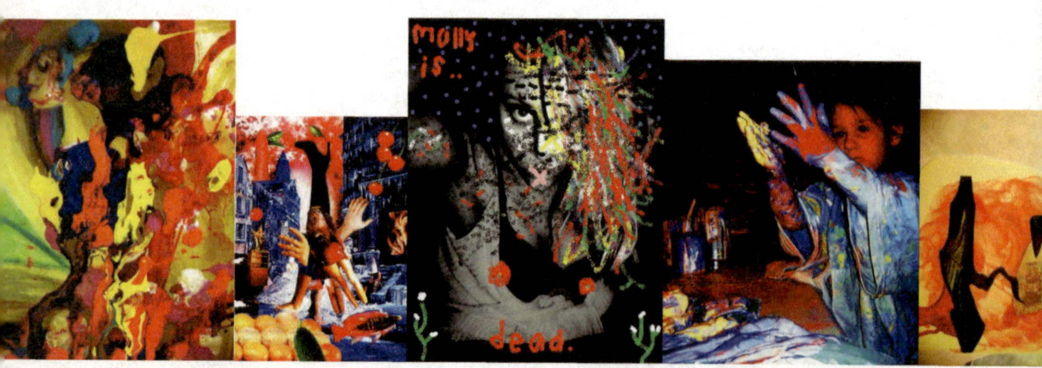
molly
is..
dead.

Please introduce yourself.

My name is Martin Marriott. I've worked all kinds of jobs, from steel-mill to house-painter. I became an artist after my dad's funeral. I reached for a pen and wrote my first-ever poem. More recently, I had a mental breakdown in 2012, which landed me in a psychiatric, ward and then -- in a gross Kafka-esque way -- into Wormwood Scrubs prison. Now I have a flat in London, live on scavenged food heading to the dump, and the now-reduced ESA benefit-pittance-insult, and have committed myself 100% to living the life of an artist. I'm going to start selling my art, to whoever likes it and wants it, so that I can get tube-trains, buy a beer, etc.

What meaning does art have in your life?

The shortest true answer is the one the sublime surrealist poet Benjamin Peret gave: "Fish swim, Man creates." Art is breathing, moving, the reason for waking up, and the reason for dreaming.

Do you recognize the term 'Outsider'?

It might be good to turn things around. There is a tremendous art-party going on, and a whole lot of us are in it, and there's another whole lot at the door and at the windows peering in and smiling. Across the street from our big house are some cars with darkened windows, containing bosses, generals, politicians, and bureaucrats. They know that our party isn't making them a penny, which is all they care about. And our party's noise disturbs them, because they want us to be mechanical work-slaves and passive consumers, (or somehow disappear if we are not currently working for them) -- they don't like us heading for the dance-floor! Yet they have never managed to close this vast house party down, and they never will. For the reason Peret gives. If we see it this way, from inside the party, then those who 'run society', the non-creative ones, are the actual outsiders.

Please describe your working practice.

The practice of art as we usually define it involves materials. In prison, not much available. I found out that toothpaste is a very good sticky glue, used by people inside to pin up pictures of family and girly-pictures. Birds -- such symbols of freedom -- would swoop around the exercise-yard, and I would collect the feathers and make wall-collages in the cell using them and friends' old newspapers. You are also entitled to pen and paper, so I wrote poems.

Right now, I am very lucky to be living in a busy London neighbourhood, with lots of rubbish skips about. There is nothing in rubbish -- literally nothing, that is not a possible art material, from a doll to electronics to old clothes, to twisted metal. I found an old canvas recently -- wow! -- and right now the main materials on it are cigarette ends and beetroot juice. If you find or buy beetroots and boil them, the liquid is an amazingly deep and vivid purple! Curry spices are amazing, used tea and coffee, the colours of broken bottles can be collaged... there really is no end to it, and it can lead to seeing everything that exists as 'wanting to become art.' This seems to connect with tribal art, as well as with how children may turn anything into a game or toy.

So my daily practice involves going out and bringing stuff back, and playing. My flat gets so full I keep purging it. My sister says I am living in an art-gallery. Yes, in the Kurt Schwitters way. It keeps heading out, too, into the common hallways. The neighbours like it, but the landlord called me last week. "Martin -- car tires and old frying pans on the walls -- COME ON!!" So the battle for art continues! Everything has beauty -- his mind is rustier than the pan, so he doesn't yet see that. He's numbed by having his head too far into the money-system. He is losing out on life's pleasures, big-time.

Writing is such a major love for me, and I am currently scribbling every day, and my mind works on them so that I wake each day with new lines and new poem/song ideas. I am writing a collection, which will be called *Vaudeville Kisses For a New London*. It will be, for me, a celebration of being alive.

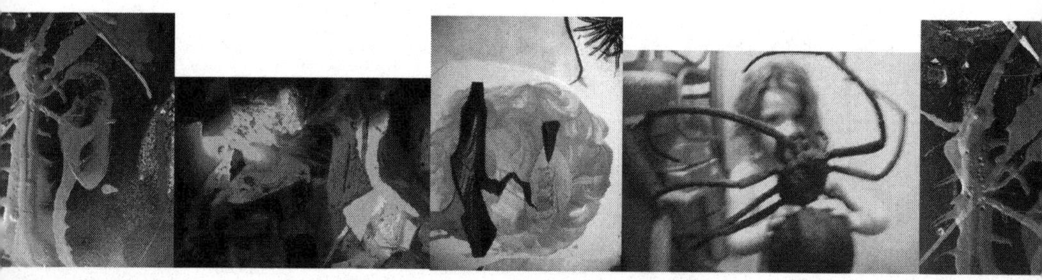

The major turning point for me, towards all I am saying here, was my mental breakdown. More specifically, that I very nearly died. On a rooftop, with a knife, and with razorblades. Various dramas. Very lucky to be alive. So the saying 'you only live once' has immense weight with me these days -- to really do what I want to do and not give my years to a compromise for money. As long as I can physically survive, I'm going to focus fully on what makes me feel most alive, and that for me is creativity, in all its forms.

Does the art market as we know it recognise your working practice?

The art market? I don't yet have any connection with that. A house-painter friend living in Seattle, USA, was painting Bill Gates' house, and he has a Van Gogh in one of his toilets. No one gets to see it.

In a deeper sense, Gates looks at it and he himself isn't capable of seeing it. That's the people of pretensions, investments, etc. But I've seen paper articles recently on 'affordable art', aimed at the rest of us. I like that very much. Art from re-cycled materials is going to become more and more common, if only because of the spreading poverty. And so 'non-artists'- will see they don't need a gold frame and oil paint to express themselves. And most everyone has songs they find very beautiful -- that's art too.

Postscript: 14.04.13
Stephen Kirin

Martin Marriott, John Sheehy and Bryan Thorpe have contributed their own thoughts on the "outsider", I believe their responses are an essential illustration of the human spirit, and thank them immensely for their openness and honesty.

I remain a registered psychiatric nurse working in a system scarred by *One Flew Over the Cuckoo's Nest* and Wally Hope's death. However a system that's evolving in the 21st Century: thoughtful about new recovery-led philosophy, actively challenging stigma and prejudice - not perfect, but changing. Countered against this is an art world that seems to be interested in exacerbating a divide between the inside and the outside. I look for evidence that it's not doing this - suspicious of the old military tactic of divide and conquer. I'm surprised that the people who hold the keys often forget that there are more "outsiders" than "insiders". Critical mass approaches.

Part 2: Responding to the Outsider

EREKTE
ŞiiR! GF
Fr.Loy

Ruhunu
dinle

DA·DA
GÖKTAN
ölmedi

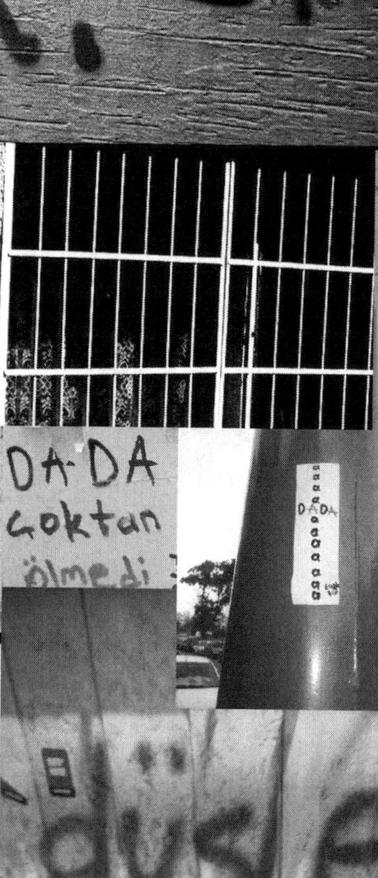
DADA

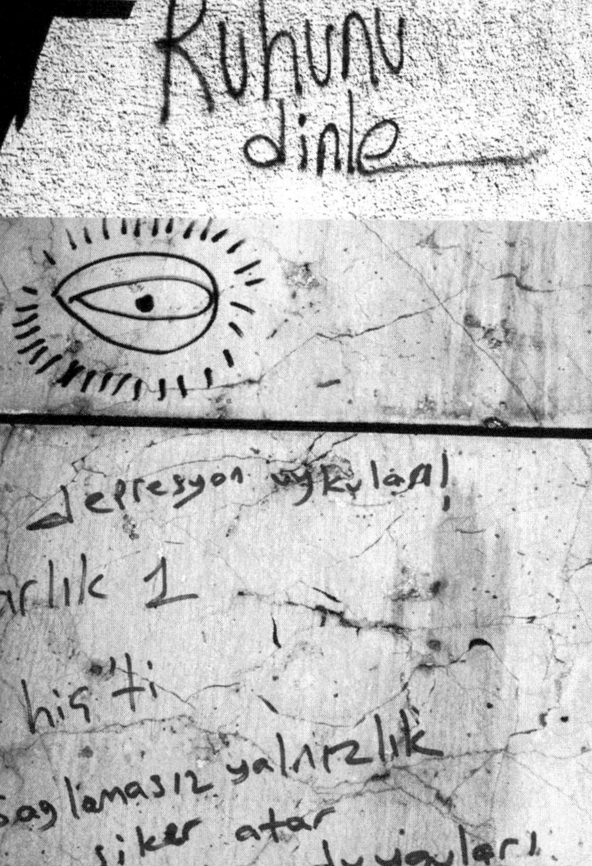
depresyon uykuları
arlik 1
hiç"ti
saglamasız yalnızlık
siker atar
duyguları

düşte
müstehcen

Ghost of The City is my Presentation

Rafet Arslan
translated by Ali Kartal

I don't know why I first took a marker pen and started to write in the street. To express myself, to give a reaction, punkish attacks, automatic scribblings, trying to take the role to save the poem from its published and printed limitations… There were many things motivating me.

I wrote the manifesto *Erect Poetry* and a passionate movement was born from this. From the city where I live, it passed from Izmir to Istanbul and there, especially in Kadikoy it made its residence. *The Erect Poetry Manifesto* became popular within the activities of *Surrealist Action Turkey* and it started to be known on the wider underground scene.

In this period I met people I knew and those I didn't who practiced *Erect Poetry* in the street. The movement developed as an anonymous form of street art. But just after this period, especially in the area around Taksim Square, tens of street poems popped up at the same time written with marker pens in the same hand.

After a while we began to wonder who this ironic and sharp sentence picker poet calling himself AX was? Many people thought that he was a young poet or a fine arts student. But the reality was totally different.

This anonymous street poet was Atilla Çapraz who signed his works AX. He was a total "outsider" and didn't have any artistic concerns or pretensions. The interesting part of this was he had no expectations or validity to the practical, real life. Moreover he was closed to communication, he was speaking with himself via the surface of the city. That is why his words were unique, uncanny and definitely very powerful.

Now by *Patricide*; bringing *Erect Poetry* as a conscious street act, with AX acting as a unconscious ghost together, I would like to introduce you to the "raw" face of Istanbul.

Erect Poetry is Street Poetry

To take part in the experiences of the street, to live new experiences on the street, to reveal the extraordinary hidden by daily reality, to sail to new situations.

The important thing is not only to stay and/or live on the street but to live with the street. Poetry can not only be imprisoned into the printed paper. It should be written onto the walls, onto the electric poles, onto telephone boxes with markers. While we are strolling around the city, poems should be written automatically on the stickers and they should be put on the outer face of the city. They should be thrown from the roofs of the buildings and bus windows. Poems written on the street should go back to their origin, i.e. to the street.

Erect Poetry is against Reality

At the beginning of the 21st century, where daily reality is transformed into an illusion reproduced by the system, Erect Poetry is against reality for the sake of the Real. It swaps reality with dream.

Erect Poetry is Anti-Oligarchic

It doesn't need to take confirmation from those authorities establishing their own institutions under the heavy loads of their ego, and who are giving their fetwa as to whether this is a 'good poem' or this is a 'bad poem'.

Erect Poetry is Independent

It distances itslef from a centralised power. It doesn't depend on an authority. It is independent and free. It advocates the freedom of poetry and its individuality against those seigneurs who decree that poetry should be dependent on rules and traditions.

Erect Poetry is Libertarian

It never comes to terms with lumpen nationalist, conservatist, orthodox approaches which are spreading like cancer through every cell of society.

Erect Poetry Erects!

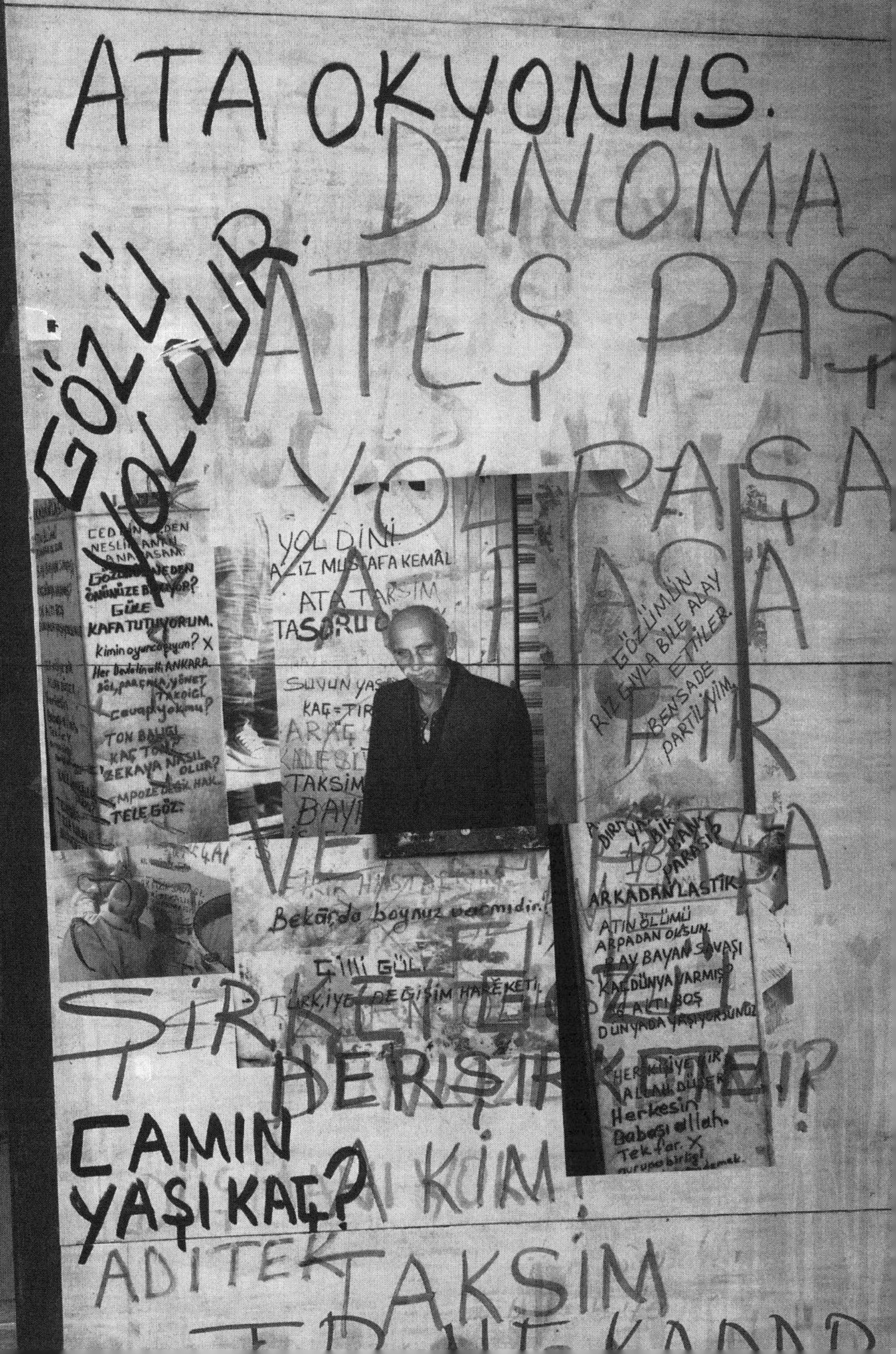

ATA OKYONUS.
DINOMA
GÖZÜR
DÜ ATEŞ PAŞ
YOL
RAŞA
DA

YOL DİNİ.
AZİZ MUSTAFA KEMÂL
ATA TAKSİM
TASORU

SUYUN YAŞ
KAĞ=TIR
ARAÇ
KARDEŞ
TAKSİM
BAYR
VE
Bekârda boynuz varmıdır!

GÖZÜMDEN
RIZ GMYLA BİLE ALAY
ETTİLER.
BEN SADE
PARTİLİYİM.

CED... NEDEN
NESLİ ANA
ANA ASAN
Gözler NEDEN
önünüze B...yor?
GÜLE
KAFA TUTUYORUM.
Kimin oyuncağıyım? X
Her bedelinaki ANKARA
böl. paşanın yönet.
tacaci?
Cevap yokmu?
TON BALIĞI
KAÇ TON
BEKAYA NASIL OLUR?
empoze değil hak.
TELE GÖZ.

Gülü Gül
TÜRKİYE DEĞİŞİM HAREKETİ.

DÜNYADAN BİR
PARASIR
ARKADAN LASTİK.
ATIN ÖLÜMÜ
ARPADAN OLSUN.
AV BAYAN SAVAŞI
KAÇ DÜNYA VARMIŞ?
ALTI BOŞ
DÜNYADA YAŞIYORSUNUZ
HER... BİR
ALLAH DİYER
Herkesin
Babası allah.
Tek for. X
avrupa birliği demek.

ŞİRKETEP?
BERİSİR
ÇAMIN
YAŞI KAÇ? KİM!
ADITEK TAKSİM

Atilla Çapraz (known as AX on the streets) is a man who writes the poem of his life on the walls.

I am an alone and troubled guy. I am alone with my loneliness. I was born in Araç district of Kastamonu in 1961. I am humanitarian. I am a hunter. I lost my left eye when I was three. A blackthorn took my eye. Then, everything became single to me. I started to smoke when I was 12 and have smoked ever since. I played "saz" for a while, but I could not make any sense and gave up. I grew up there until I was 24 years old, then I left.

I left to travel and have worked in several jobs during my life, jobs without insurance and worth. I have never taken a wage for myself and I did not even study after high school. I was accepted at university but I did not find a necessity to go. I was born drunk and became a drunkard. All teachers are cheaters. All professors are cheaters but they all cheat to learn. Books are copies. Being a proletarian is tough. In some ways, I am a teacher too - I see no difference. I ask questions. I write on the walls because I know myself. Look, I have no left eye. It is unfavourable to look with a beautiful eye. This is why death looks with beautiful eyes. I write both when I am drunk and when I am not. A wall is writing. Writing is a wall. Wall writing is an effort of labour.

I am asking: Which one of my eyes is more sinful? The left one or the right one? Why is the first letter of the alphabet A? The basis of my writings, the basis of my brain is single. It is the basic question, the problem. The word is alone. I ask to learn and teach. As long as our kind doesn't grow up, no one can be understood. We give so much effort yet nobody notices us. We write the writings, we receive the punishment. Not them. The basic desire of the human is to write what he cannot answer. I never got married. But I want to get engaged. I never cheated any women. Not even one woman came to me for to get married.

My political view is my tongue. Not on the left nor on the right. I stay at a cheap hotel. I can't stay at some hotels because they are lousy. Lice can't live in the streets. Sometimes I prefer to sleep at hospital yards. It gives a positive way of living to a human. You can't get the voice of injured and dying patients out of your mind. Even if it is just obscenities, humans should write. The effect of books is like the effect of alcohol. They give you a headache first, but, unlike the alchoholic, when it passes away the reader doesn't suffer from the headache anymore.

If there are no minor writings, major writings can't be written. I am beside myself with minor writings.

A verir. Öc alır. Bu anlaşılırsa Tek-Yol'a gelirsin
A gives. Takes revenge. If this is understood, you come to "Only-Way".

Alan-verenle aynı yerde bulunmaz.
The taker is not present in the same place as the giver.

Latincenin adını kim koydu?
Who named the Latin?

Baba yaşımız ne olacak?
What will our father's age be?

Camın yaşı kaç?
How old is glass?

Suyun yaşı kaç?
How old is water?

Korkma bir şey olmaz İstanbul'dan
Don't be afraid, nothing has come up from Istanbul.

Molla Çelebinin öğretmeni kimdir?
Who was the teacher of Molla Celebi?

Araç kozmos. Kozmos makinedir. Makine vekillik. Vekilsin, vekilim. Vekillik inisiyatiftir. İnisiyatiflik de; ya sensin ya benim ya da onlar
The tool is cosmos. Cosmos is a machine. Machinery is regency. I am regent, you are regent. Regency is initiative. And initiative is either me or you or them.

Çizgiyi çizen adamın adı ne? Bunun cevabı toprak kavgasına götürür herkesi.
What is the name of the man who draws the line? The answer of this leads everyone to the fight for land.

Lines Exploring the Meaning of Life
John 'Jazzman' Clarke

I have this shiny electric banana the world is beginning to talk
I have this arch-backed pink rabbit it keeps falling off the bedroom shelf
I have this marmalade cat called 'Cream'
He's evil & doesn't realise what's good for his health
I have this unforetold destiny and keep losing my precious house-door key
I have a fetish for talkability
My first cousins' surname is Corr they live in a posh pile just south of Dublin
On the picturesque coast road to Dalkey
My near-neighbour who I quite fancy
owns a beast of a dog named 'Caesar'
He's definitely not a believer
Naturally I keep 'em both very much at arm's length
I have a weary life right now with aches & pains showing up
in places I didn't know even existed
But don't O don't Lord let me become all bitter & twisted
calmly resignedly listening to Michael Buble

Everyone wants me to write them a song
It's true I've been dragging my feet for far too long
in that specific illustrious department
Why only yesterday I suddenly discovered what that strange
feeling in my heart meant
Is love the answer I don't know
it all depends upon the nature of the question
WHAT IS THE MEANING OF LIFE again I don't know
it so much depends upon what war-zone you happen to be in
If this world is but temporary then what are we doing here
& what should be our lasting approach or impact
& who on earth should we share them with
I just happen to have this whole heap of mangled material
that might help solve such searching pressing questions
Then again they absolutely might not
It's all a matter of dynamics & emphasis or pseudo-philsophical
analysis I suppose

The alchemy of essence is a burning cauldron of desire
"I'm terrible at identifying singularities"
I still dream of the deafening explosion of possibilities
You simply can't progress without progression
Sometimes the eyes gush waterfalls
Coolness is a sanctuary to which I often flee
Lizards are so cool
They strongly identify with imaginative force & purity of spirit
The colour of sensibility is a rectangular funnel of aching simplicity
Blessed be the uncanny rapport between extremes
where the margins of restlessness coexist representing curious
furious fractured features of permanent unbridled annoyance
Everything Japanese suits me apart from the proliferation
of steaming crustacea you can smell a mile off
My next book will be an in-depth treatise in the form of a Manga Original
spanning themes of revenge solace & ultimate searing capitulation

I've since developed a peculiar mode of silence
that will remain a mystery to you all
as if you were really & truly bothered that is
THE MEANING OF LIFE is being where you are
taking a left turn when you meant to go right
When everything else fades from view you need to be able
to touch someone - intimately - if you need to
The years are a trick life plays on us
As the pink of the tongue welcomes you in
like a sprawling sequence of music you conquer
because the contest no longer exists
It's the leverage that exposes the substance
An air of collective pressurised euphoria swiftly assumes control
Polystyrene semaphores rule ok
Somewhere off the beaten track an evident dynamic reveals itself
unknowingly
The unwritten rules of engagement change with each passing day
beaming a shamanic token
of arbitrary disinterest & indifference.

17th April 2013

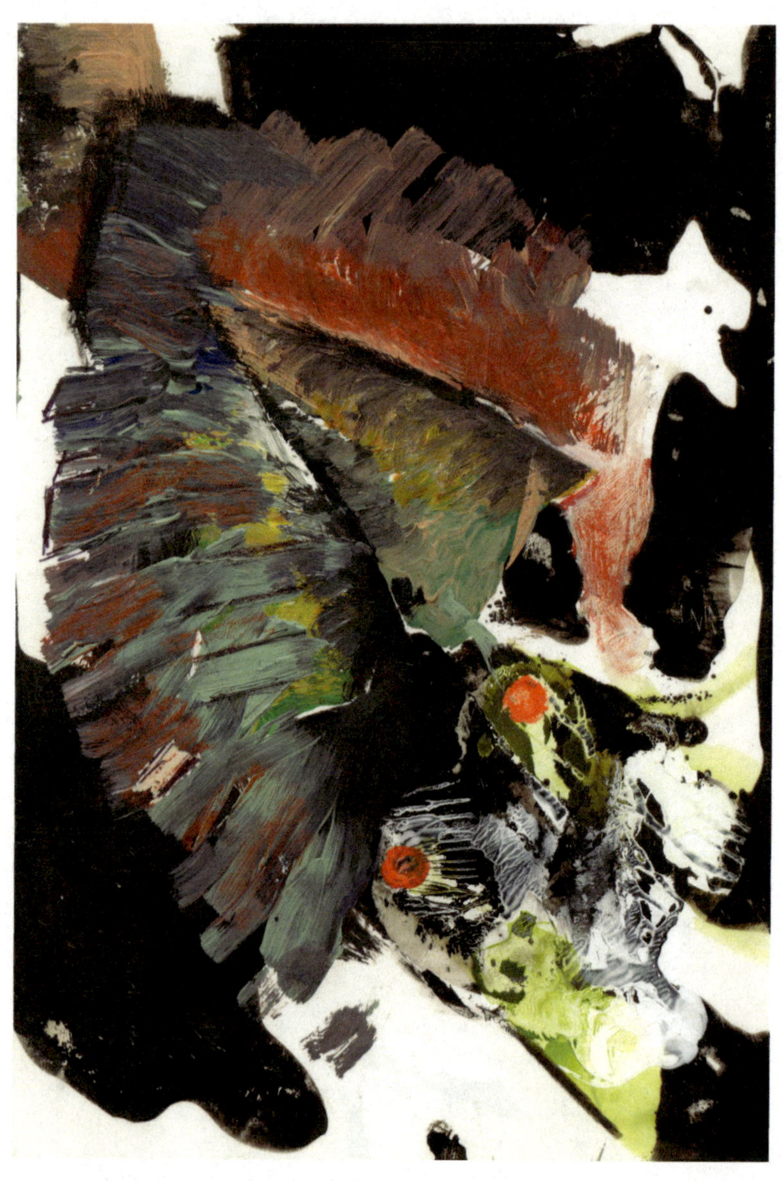

John Welson, Gregg Simpson & Rik Lina *'Outside'* 2012 mixed media on card 6 x 4 ins
image courtesy the artists

It could be reasoned that urban exploration is a form of evolving and non-codified outsider arts. While our ability to move through space becomes ever more restricted by the dramatic wings of terrorism and surveillance, many possibilities for urban adventure remain open to us. From the more passive aimless stroll of the Flaneur to the more engaged Surrealist drift and then into the Situationist's 'Derive' and 'Unitary Urbanism,' modern explorers, city spelunkers or 'vadding' enthusiasts and Parkour players have a lot to draw from.

'Vadding' and 'Infiltration' from which a collective and a magazine were named, often involve trespassing and potential exposure to hazardous circumstances. Groups of friends have been known to don protective clothing, gas masks, flashlights and climbing gear in order to navigate steam tunnels, storm drains, abandoned silos, ruins, bridges and similar locales. These activities are extensively documented.

One can see from early works of Breton and Aragon and the later writings of Franklin Rosemont how investigations of chance, drifting and things considered 'psychogeographical' were, and remain, a part of surrealism. The Surrealist Group in Stockholm coined the term 'Atopos' to describe a 'useless area' which

has slipped outside the capitalist-police grid and which might offer strategic or playful options to the discerning space-poacher. Surrealists from Paris, Madrid, Leeds, London, Chicago and elsewhere were already engaged with or began to develop similar pursuits. The 'Game of Slight Disturbances' from Leeds involved objects being placed around urban spaces which group members then searched for, while Madrid actions included anonymous public alterations and chalking poetic phrases. The London Surrealist Group's simple guidelines for experimental walking and the SLAG group's playing in streets, alleys and fields as part of their festivals are other examples. Some have sought to navigate certain cities using maps from entirely different cities, or to construct new maps based on subjective feelings and exceptional geographical features encountered.

The Situationist International despite their extensive borrowing or 'detourning' of certain surrealist ideas and practices since the late 1950's, considered themselves superior because of their analytical focus and critique of the Spectacle. Though one cannot rely on their descriptions of what surrealism is and their denunciations of the movement as being recuperated, they left a lot of the vocabulary that people use today. *Psychogeography* was a 'study of the specific effects of the geographical environment, consciously organized or not, on the emotions and behaviors of individuals' while *Derive* was called 'a mode of experimental behavior linked to the conditions of urban society: a technique of transient passage through varied ambiences.'[1] Both of these are relevant to 'draining' or entry into drains and tunnels, or to abandoned buildings and public facilities. It brings suddenly to mind an abandoned Oakland train station where persons unknown had built a wild swing from chains and a tire inside the darkened interior, or the time I found myself playing musical toys with a friend inside a huge two-storey Seattle construction site; entering university steam tunnels, climbing high towers on a windy night, and taking part in nocturnal chaos magick rituals in enclosed concrete squash courts also come to mind. A friend used to walk to different towns along train tracks and although I never got as far, it was always fun. I fondly remember a date who showed me a series of fire escapes which allowed roof access to one of Portland's tallest buildings. A defunct creosote factory by the Willamette River was renamed 'Pirate Town' and became a place for colorful artwork, bike jousting and even a punk show. The ruined ship extending into the water from the shore was another slightly eerie attraction.

Although urban exploration and creative interventions based around it are often undertaken for their own sake, without any overt critique or contestation of what the *Seattle Council for Urban Space Poaching* (CUSP) call 'carceral space' and time, this doesn't lessen the sense of wonder and discovery that people feel when entering lost and unauthorized territories outside the comfort zone.

I'm rather critical of the 'apps' that are allegedly designed to encourage urban adventure. We must re-learn how to move through spaces without constant reference to tiny glow-screens; nor should such exploration ever be reduced to a hip form of tourism. One can play urban games and discover minute details of interest almost anywhere; don't underestimate the simple joys of wandering with chalk or making random sculptures from found objects.

Those who seek the gold of space with more fervent ambition may need to prepare themselves to enter certain places in order to make of them playgrounds, as unexpected risks can arise which means that some forms of urban exploration are literally undertaken at the risk of one's life. Of course I don't want anyone to be swept away in a storm-drain so a little common sense is called for. One needn't risk injury or trespassing charges to become engaged with their own wanderings and creations off the beaten path.

1. Definitions from Preliminary Problems in Constructing a Situation. Internationale Situationiste #1, June 1958.

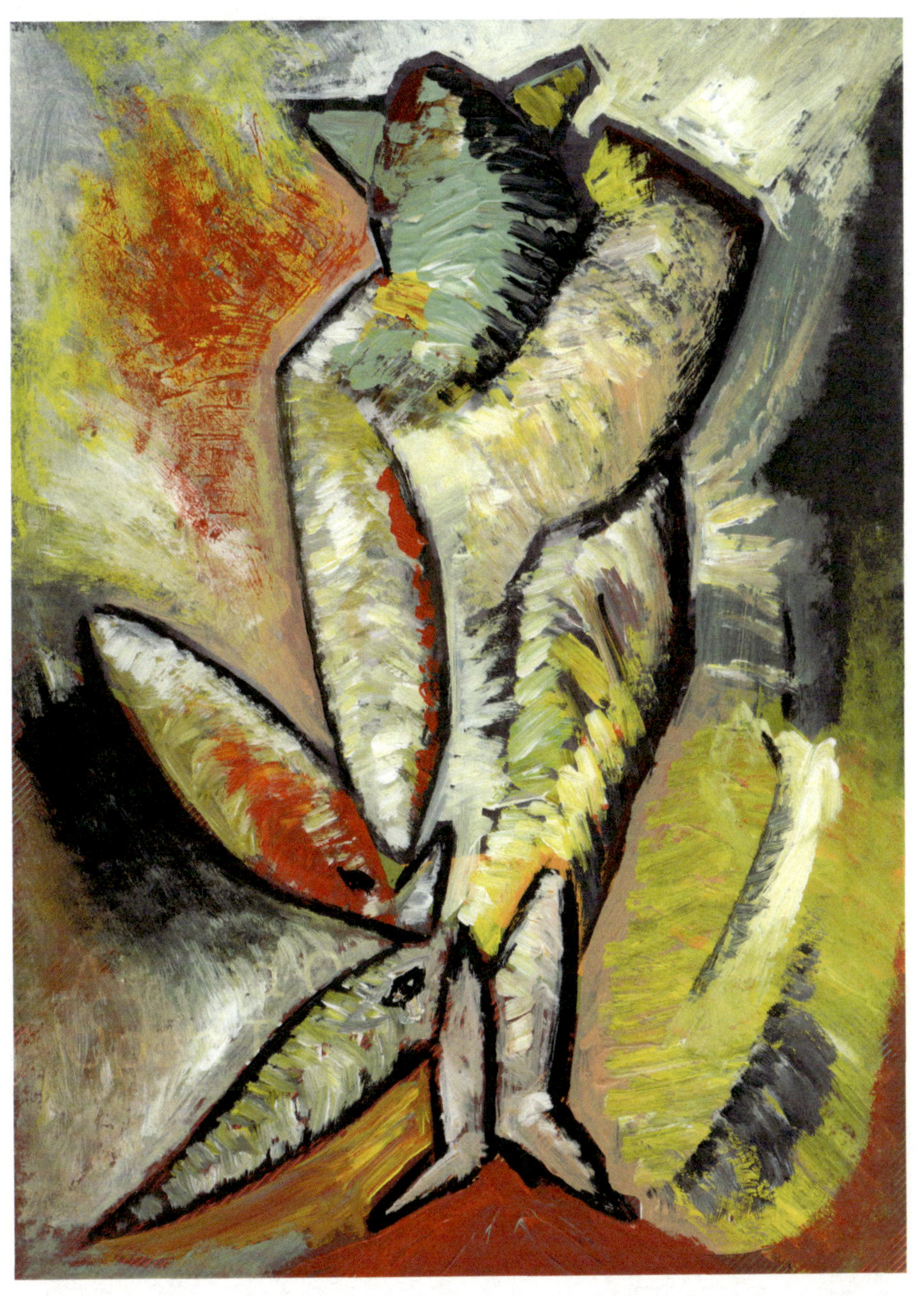

John Welson *'Untitled'* 2013 acrylic on card 8 x 5 ins
(after Sava Sekulic *'Untitled'* 1981 housepaint on cardboard)
image courtesy the artist

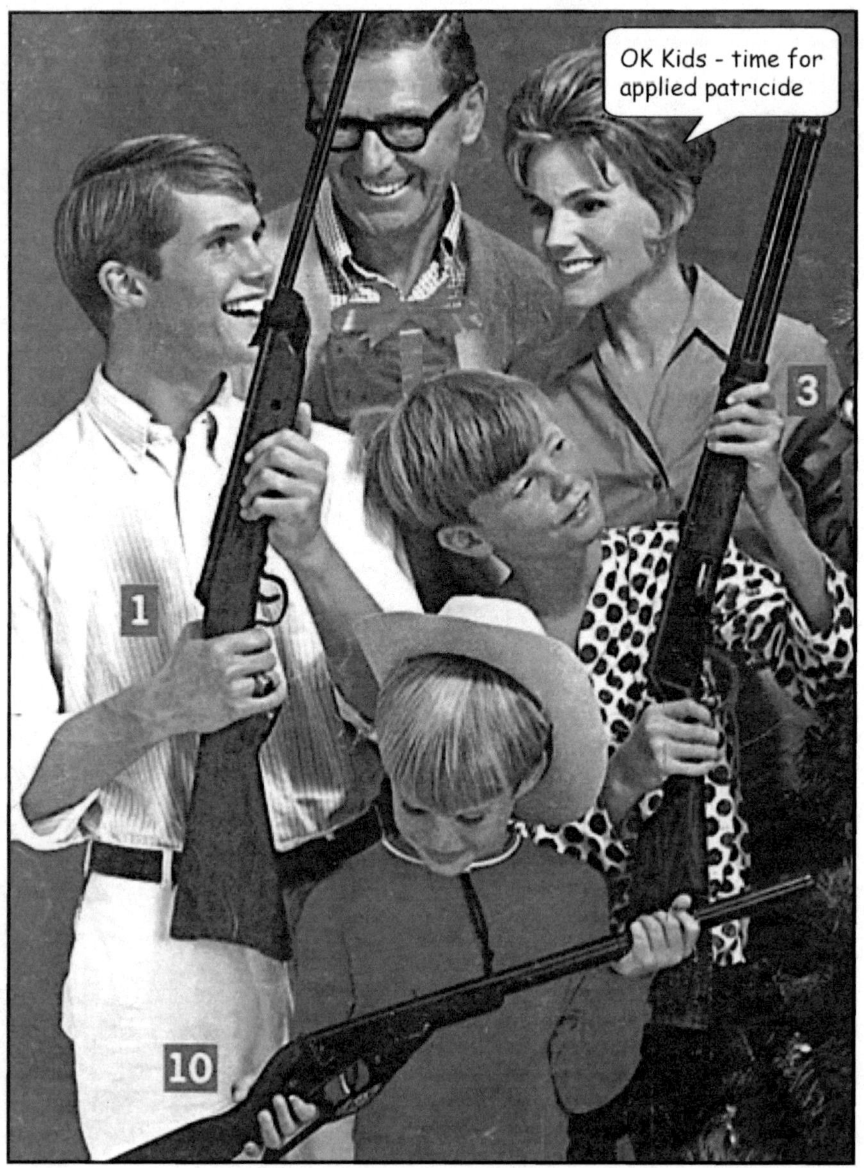
OK Kids - time for applied patricide

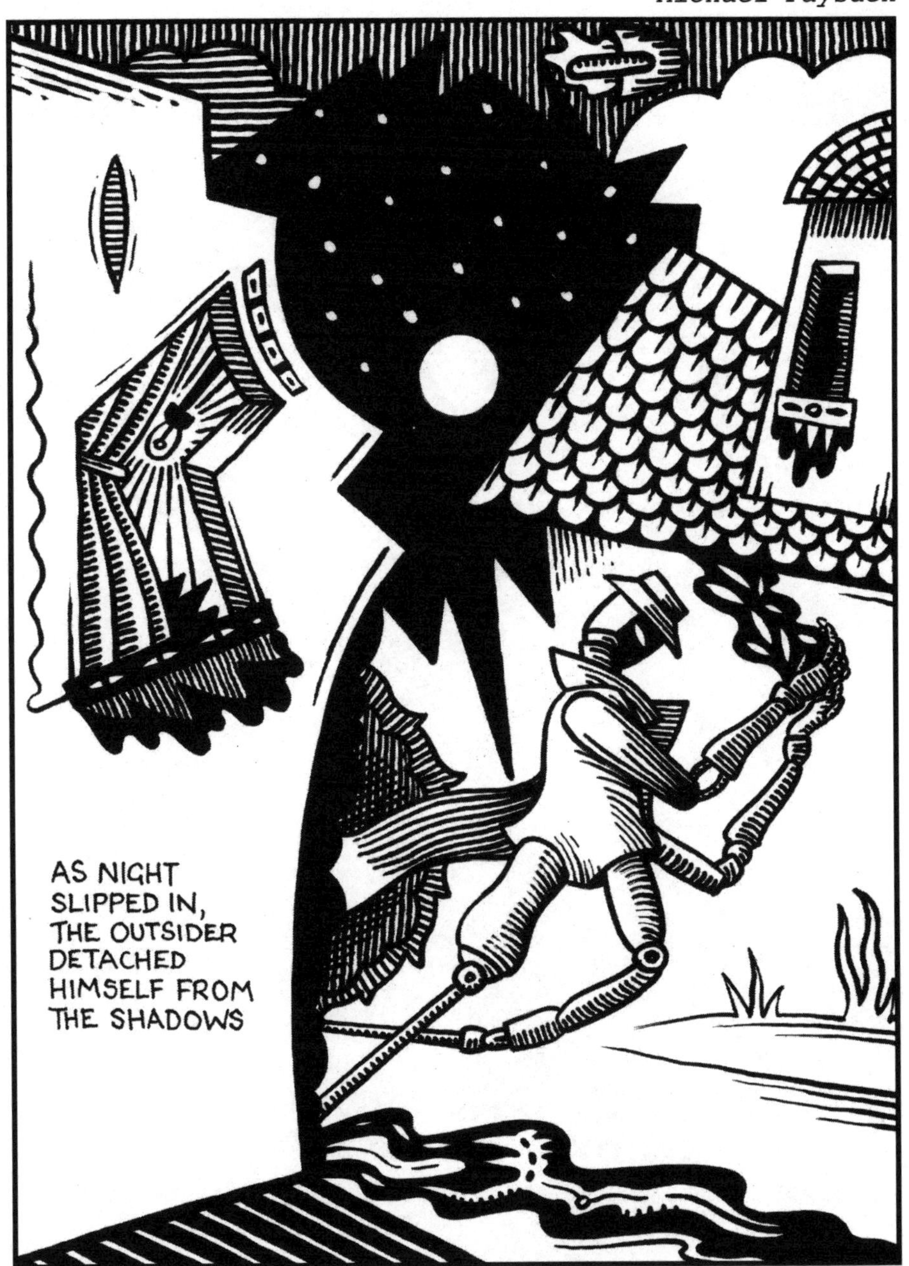

AS NIGHT
SLIPPED IN,
THE OUTSIDER
DETACHED
HIMSELF FROM
THE SHADOWS

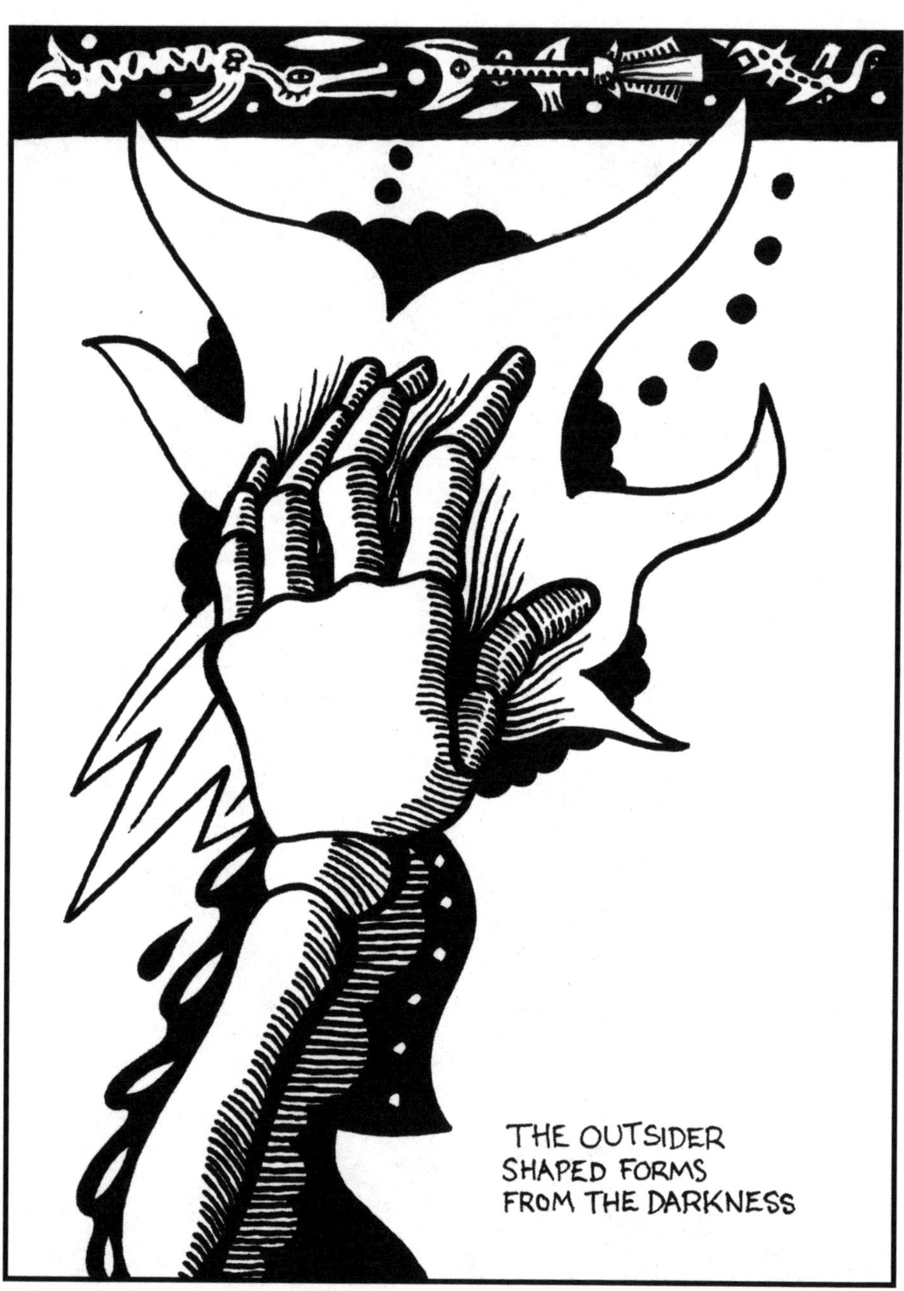

THE OUTSIDER
SHAPED FORMS
FROM THE DARKNESS

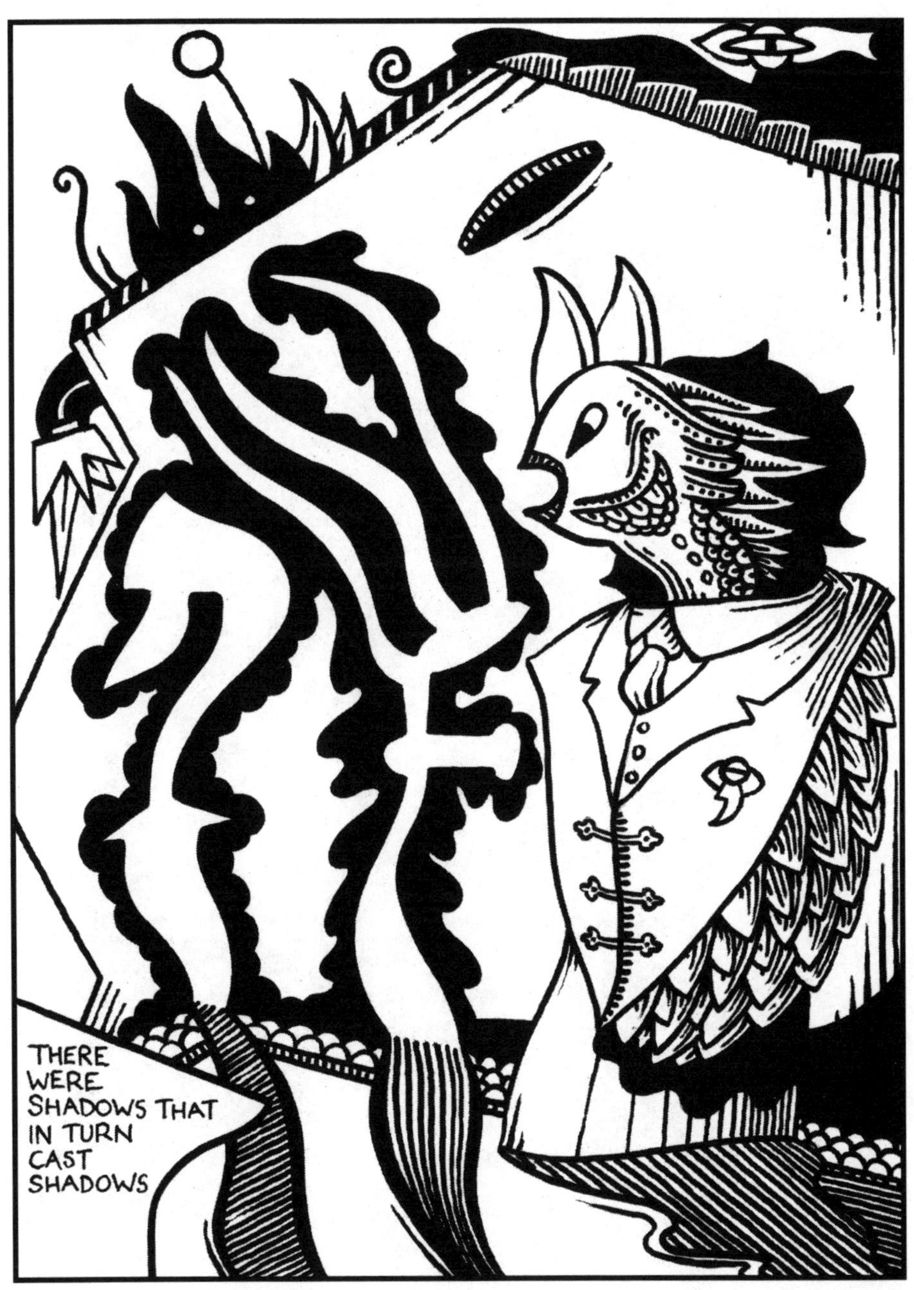
THERE
WERE
SHADOWS THAT
IN TURN
CAST
SHADOWS

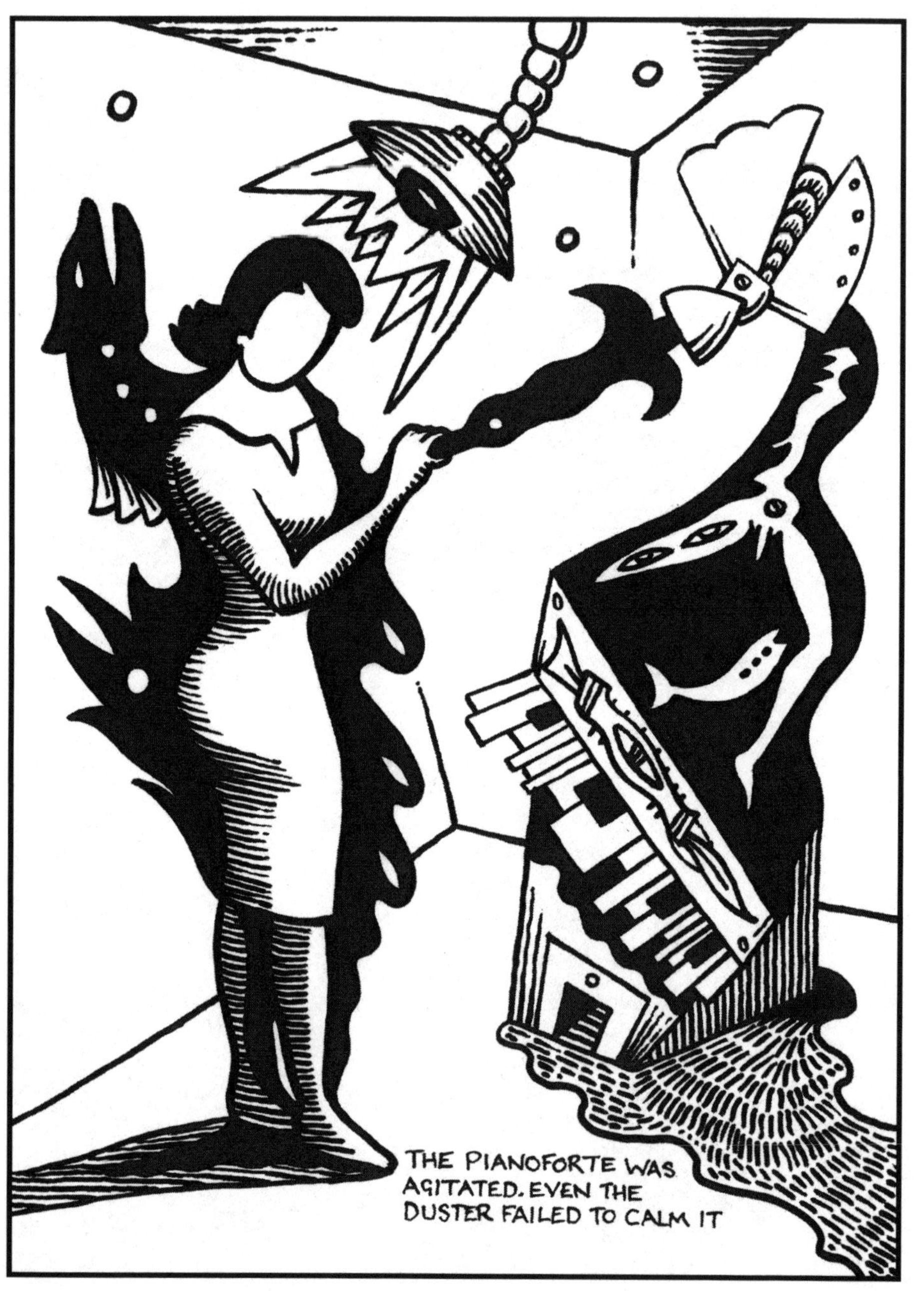

THE PIANOFORTE WAS
AGITATED. EVEN THE
DUSTER FAILED TO CALM IT

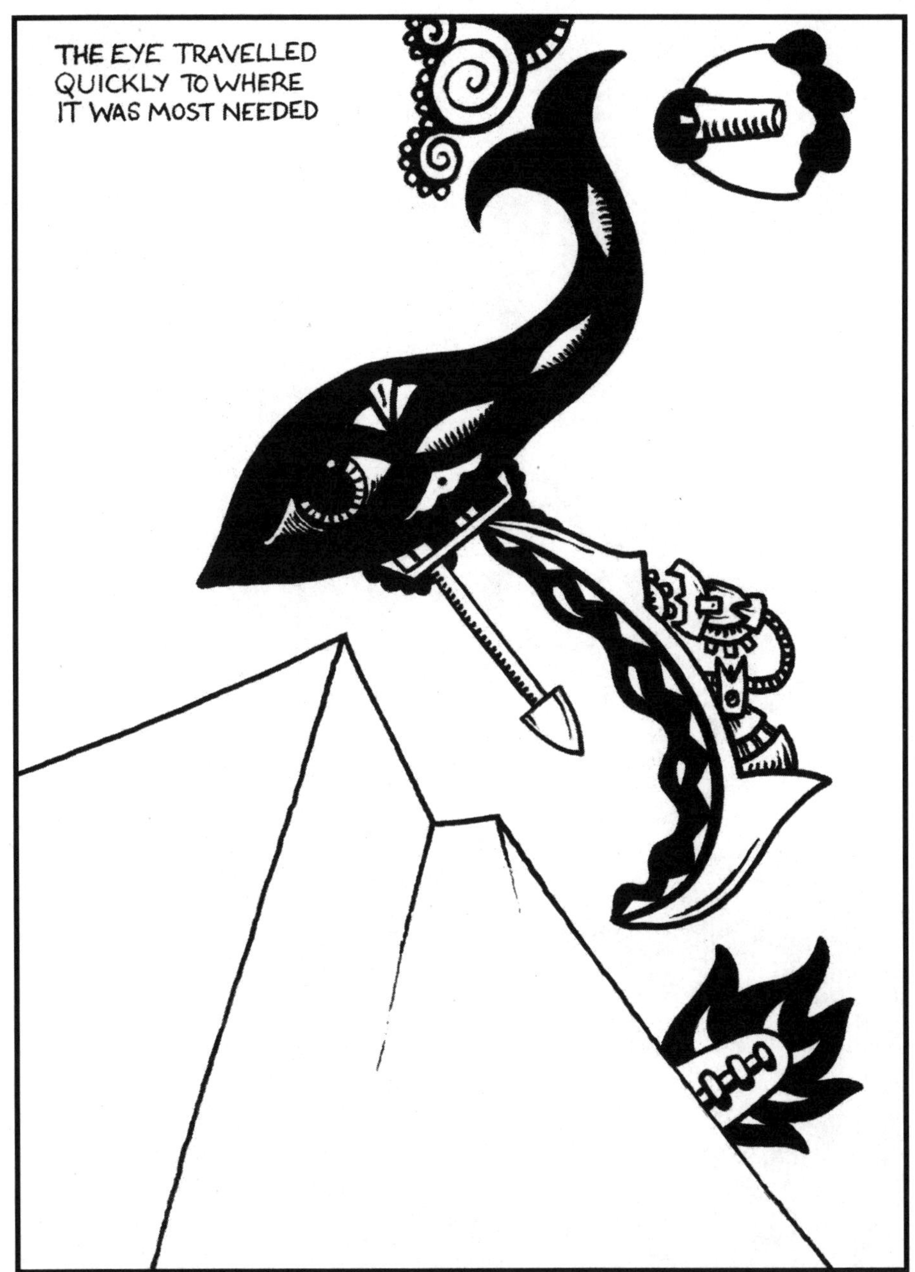

THE EYE TRAVELLED
QUICKLY TO WHERE
IT WAS MOST NEEDED

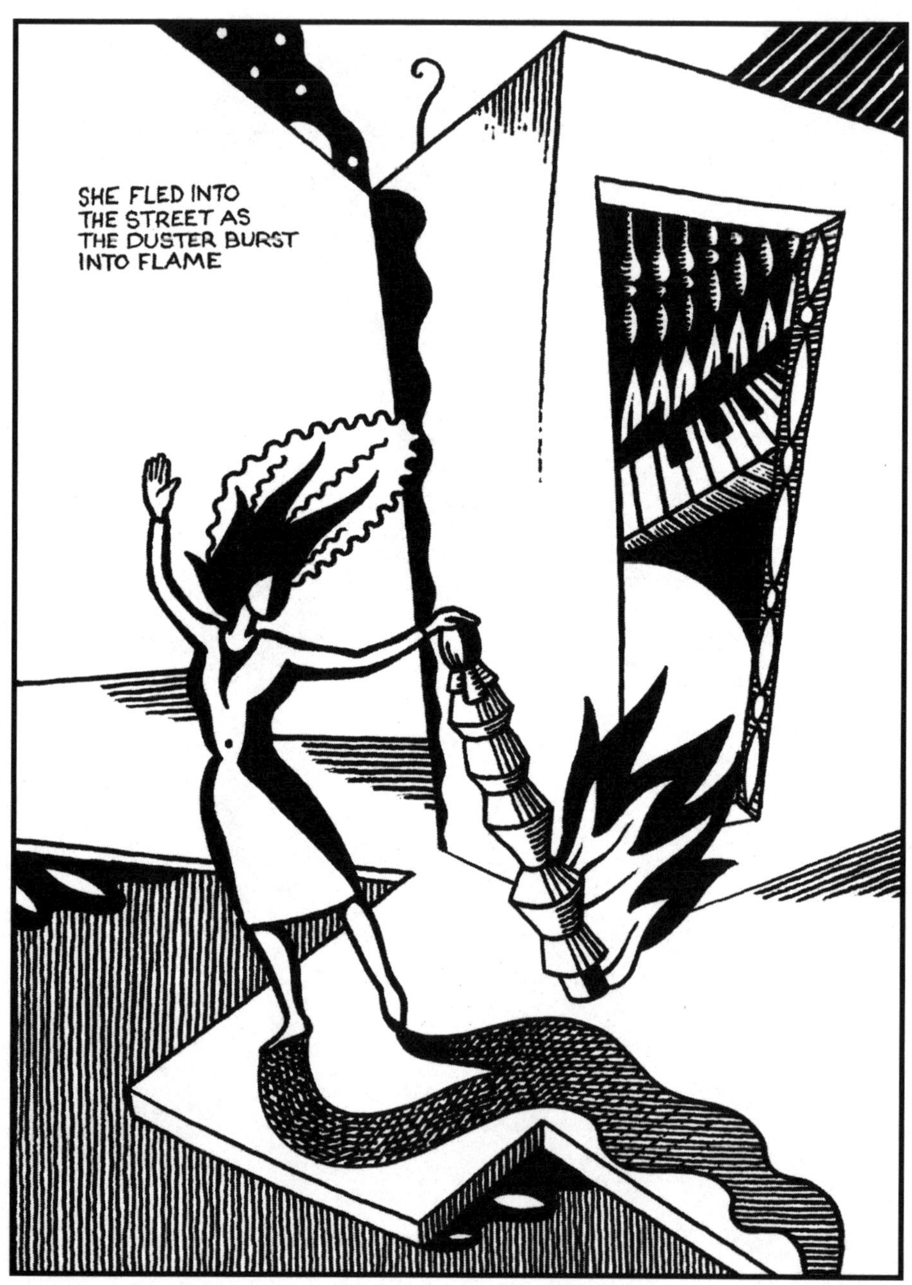

SHE FLED INTO
THE STREET AS
THE DUSTER BURST
INTO FLAME

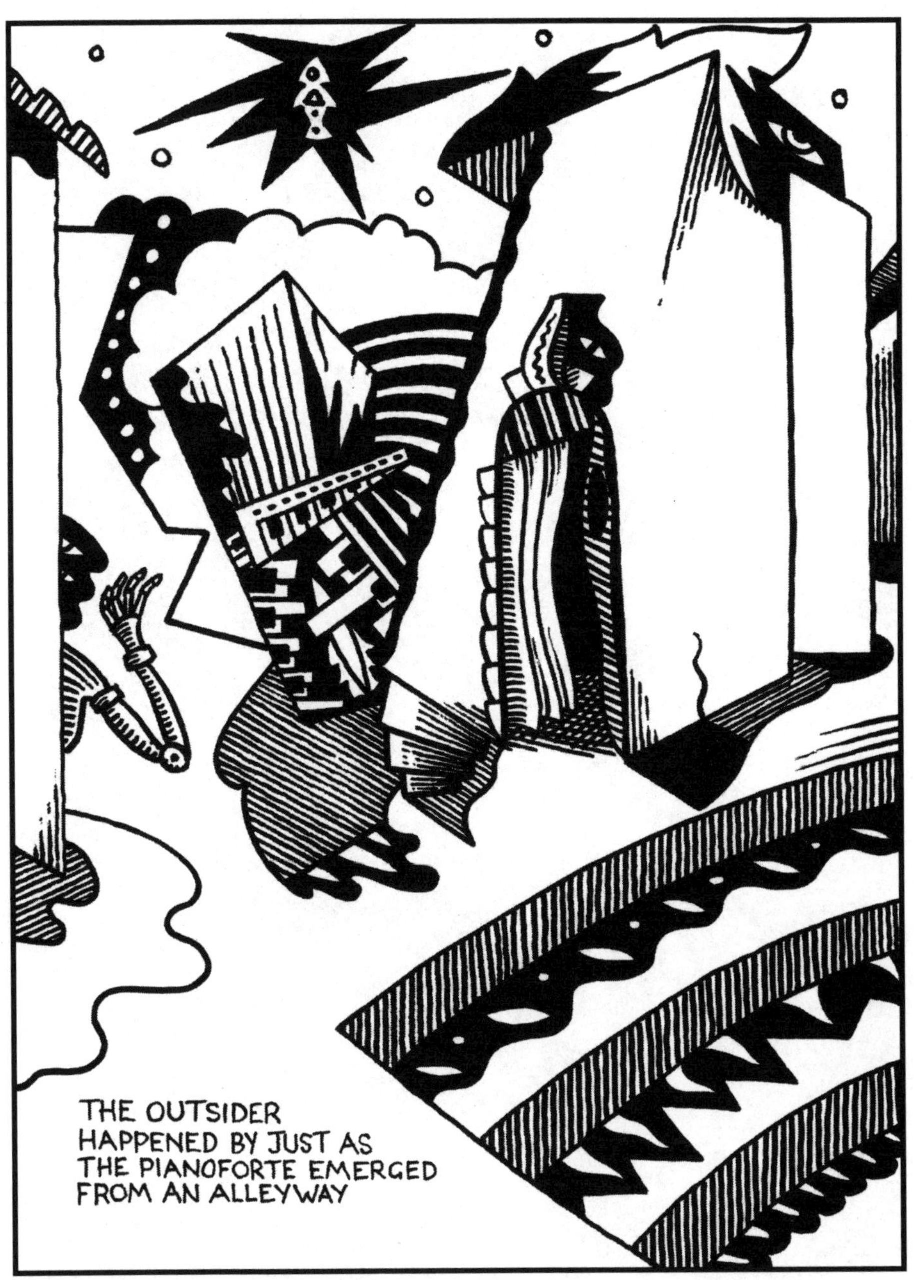

THE OUTSIDER
HAPPENED BY JUST AS
THE PIANOFORTE EMERGED
FROM AN ALLEYWAY

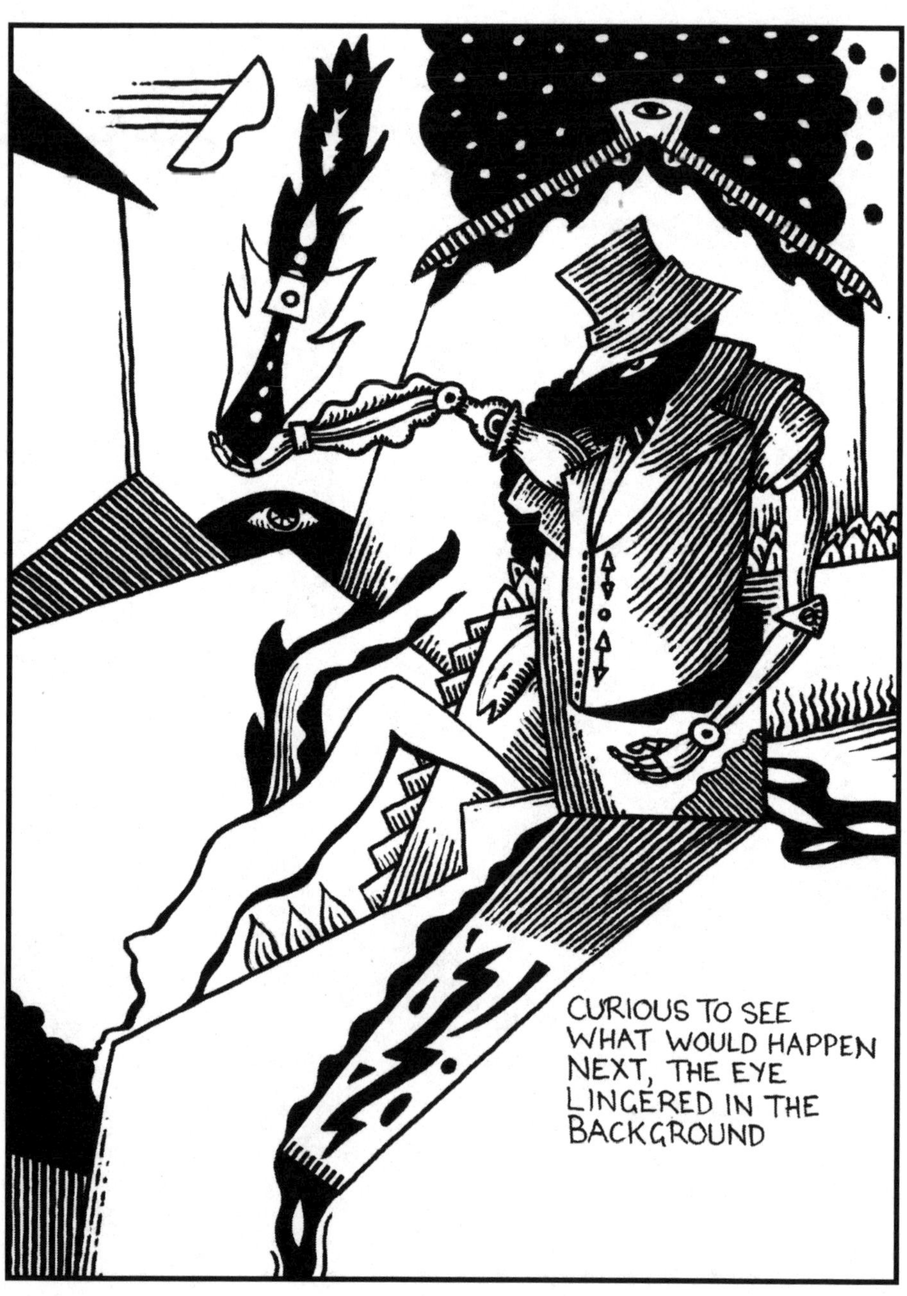

CURIOUS TO SEE
WHAT WOULD HAPPEN
NEXT, THE EYE
LINGERED IN THE
BACKGROUND

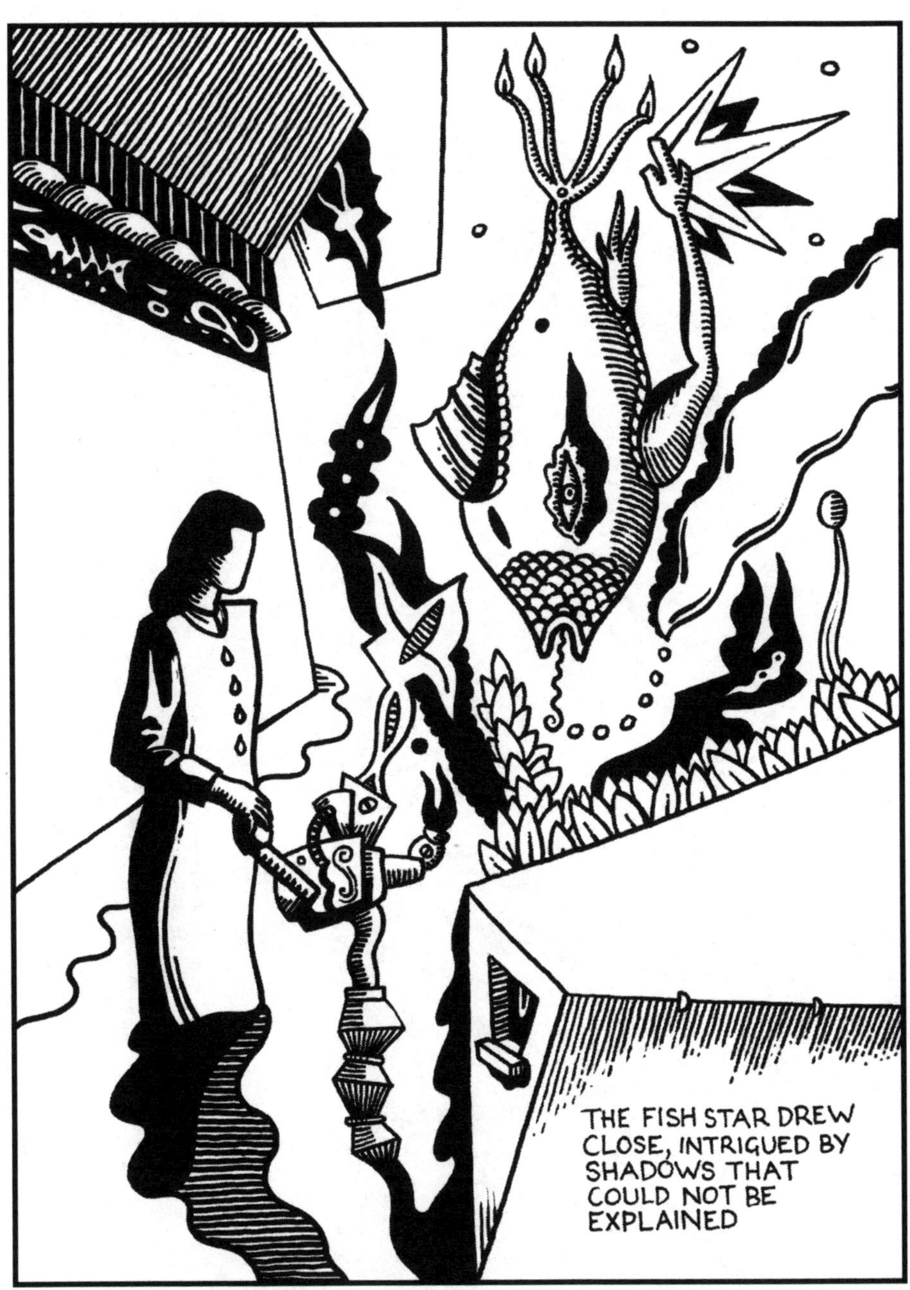

THE FISH STAR DREW
CLOSE, INTRIGUED BY
SHADOWS THAT
COULD NOT BE
EXPLAINED

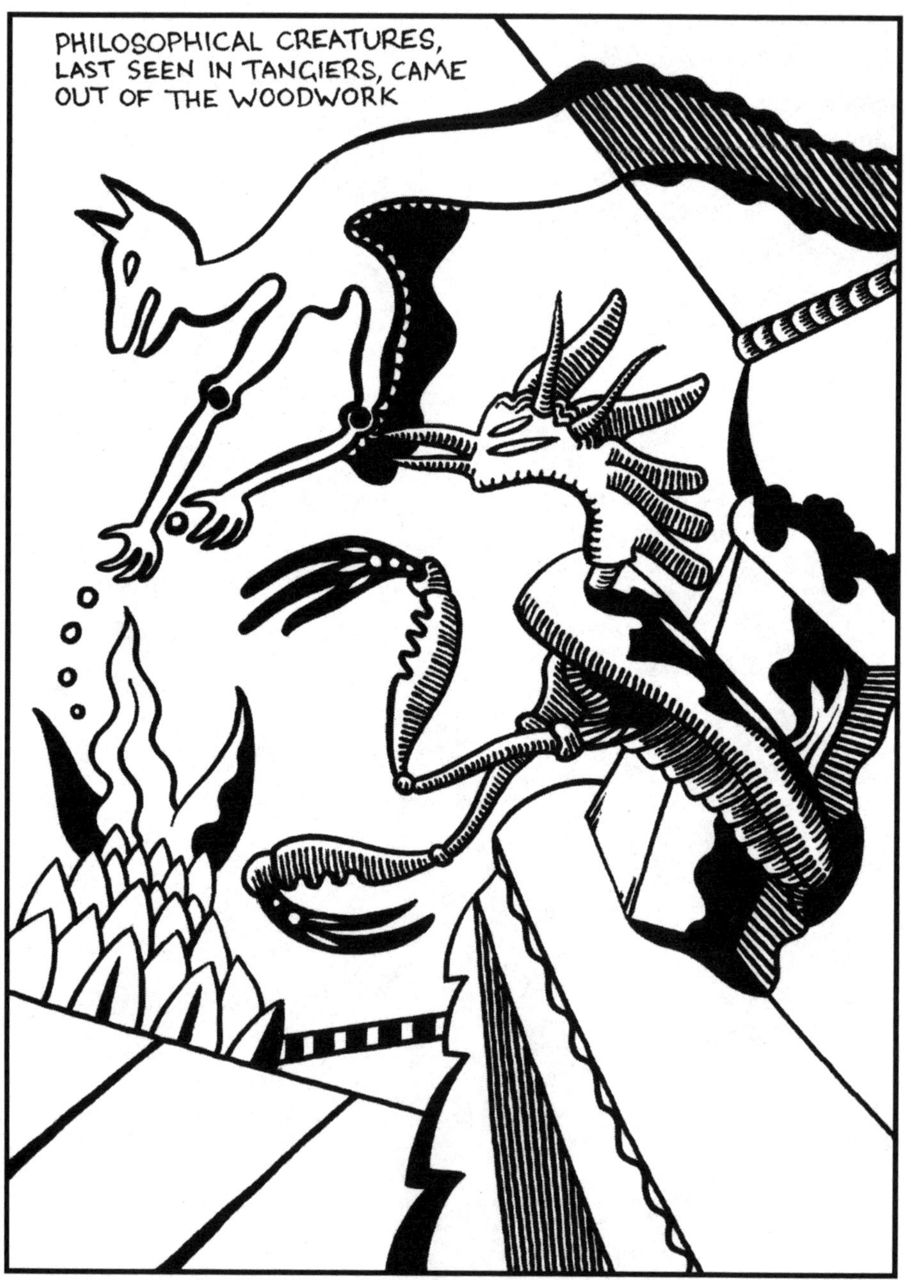

PHILOSOPHICAL CREATURES,
LAST SEEN IN TANGIERS, CAME
OUT OF THE WOODWORK

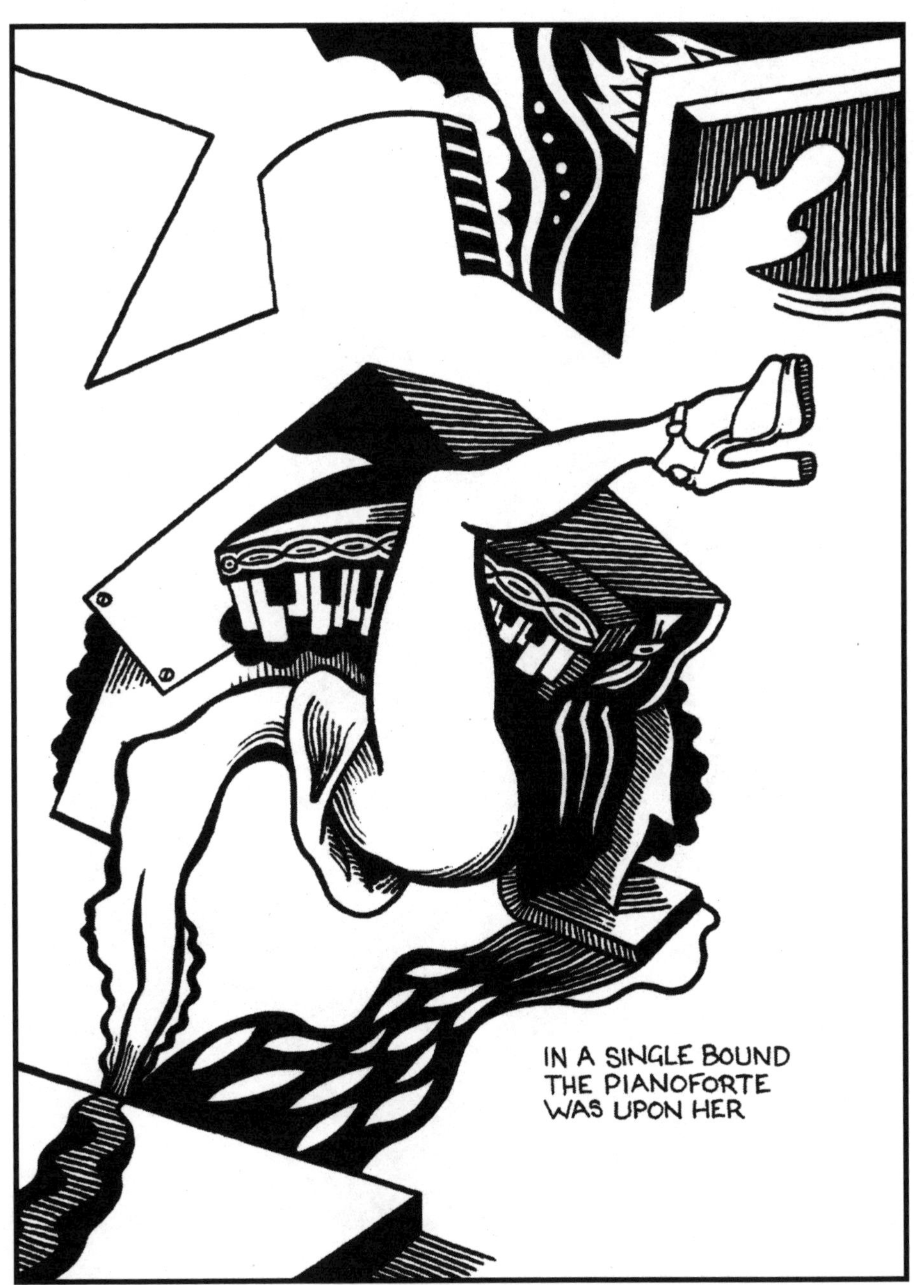

IN A SINGLE BOUND
THE PIANOFORTE
WAS UPON HER

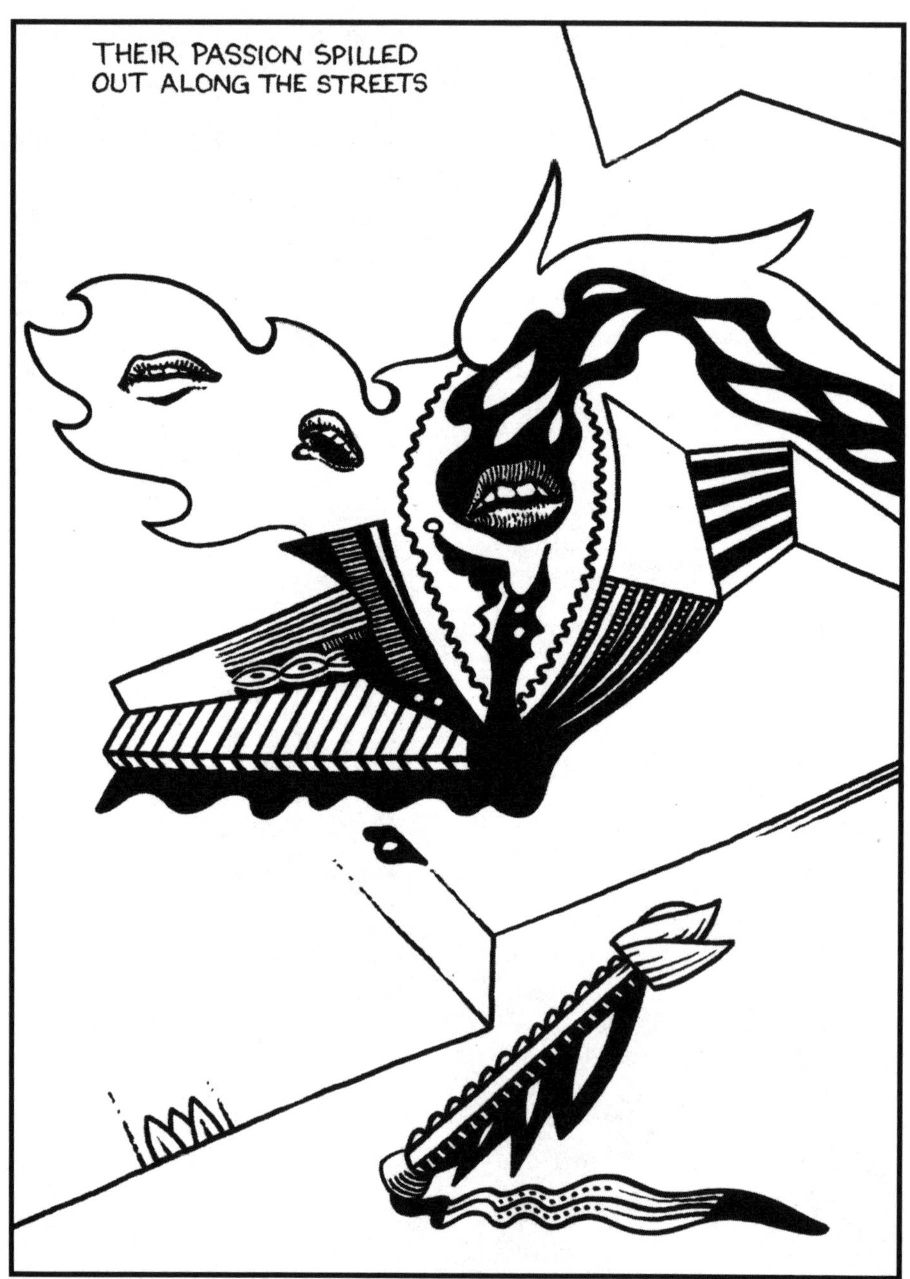

THEIR PASSION SPILLED
OUT ALONG THE STREETS

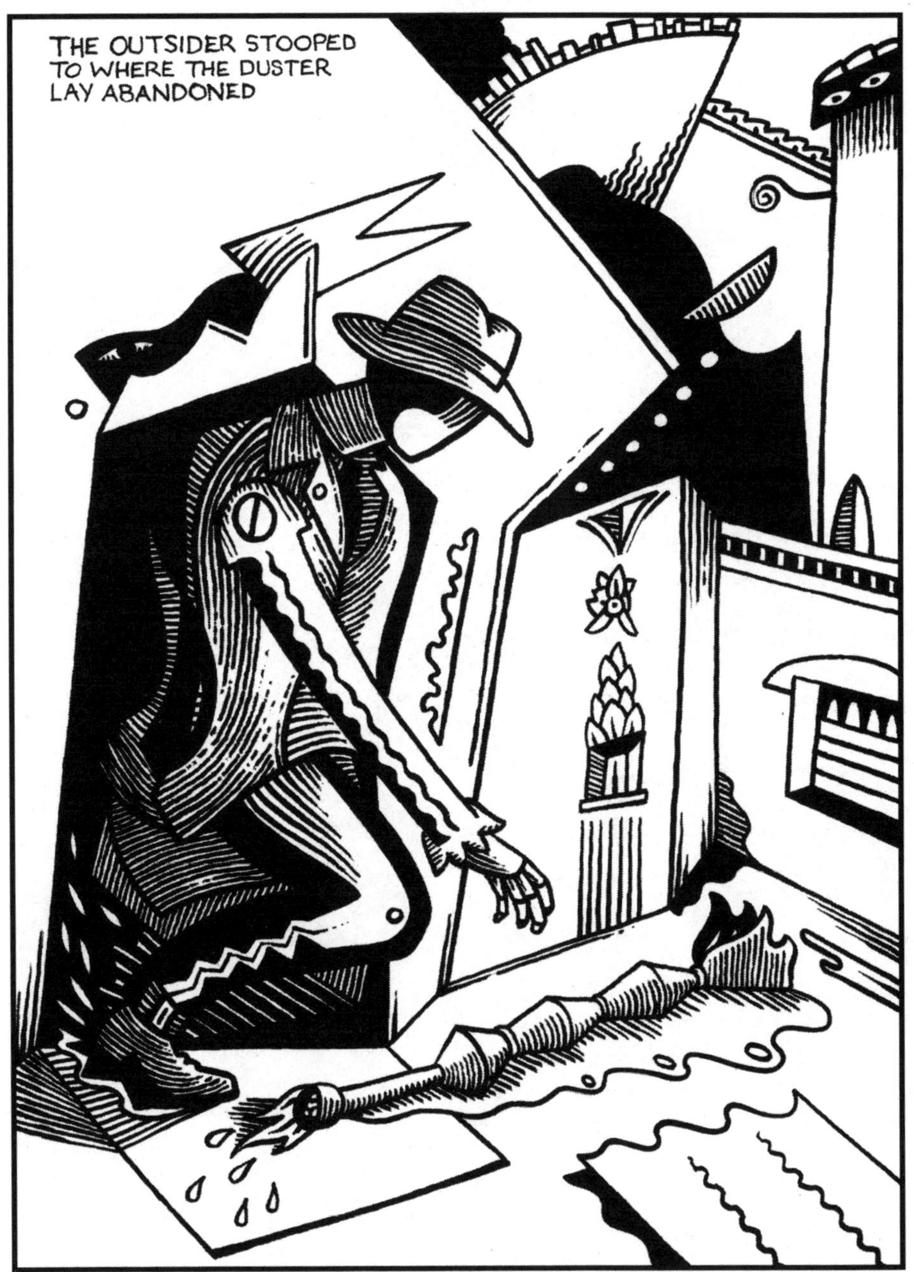

THE OUTSIDER STOOPED
TO WHERE THE DUSTER
LAY ABANDONED

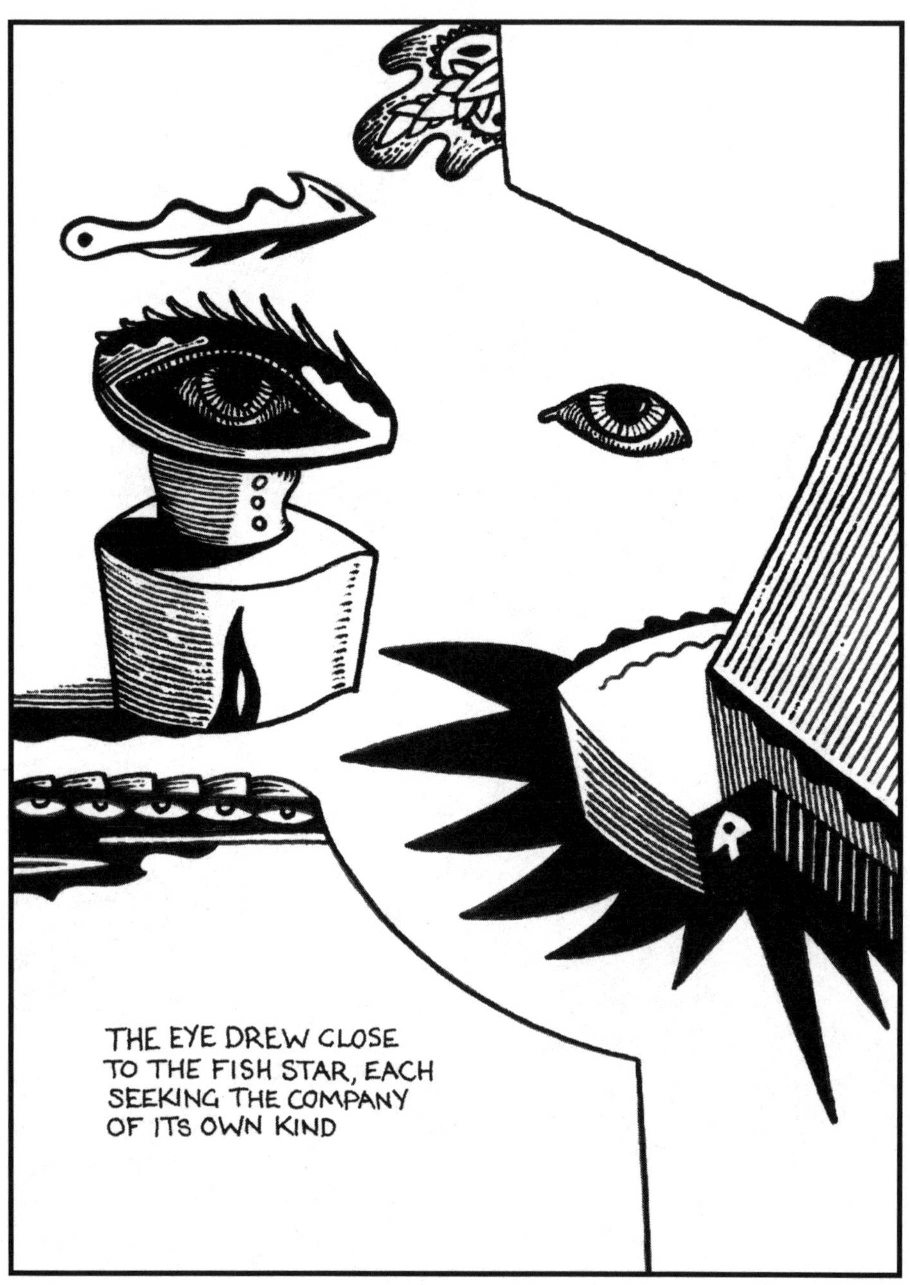

THE EYE DREW CLOSE
TO THE FISH STAR, EACH
SEEKING THE COMPANY
OF ITS OWN KIND

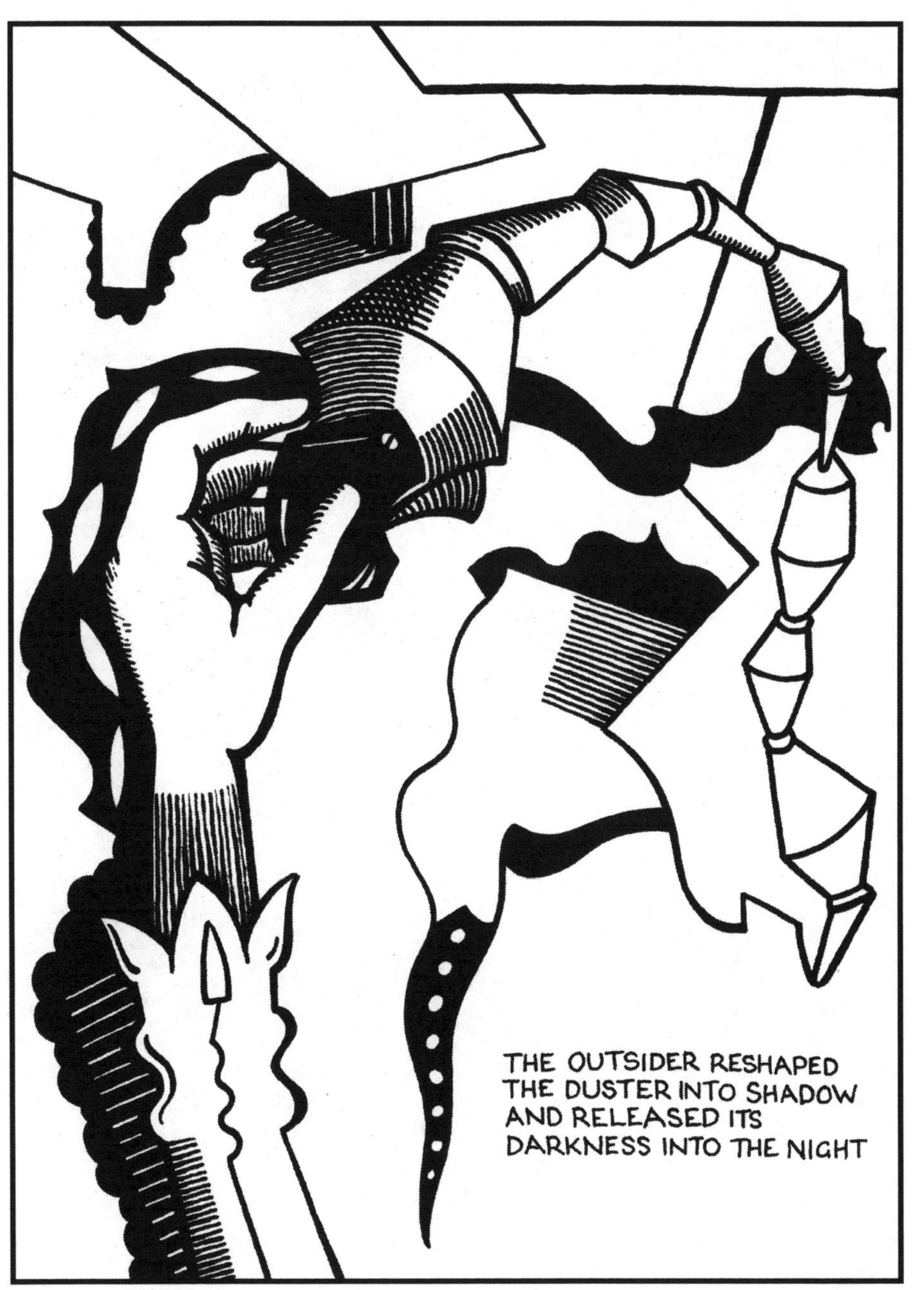
THE OUTSIDER RESHAPED
THE DUSTER INTO SHADOW
AND RELEASED ITS
DARKNESS INTO THE NIGHT

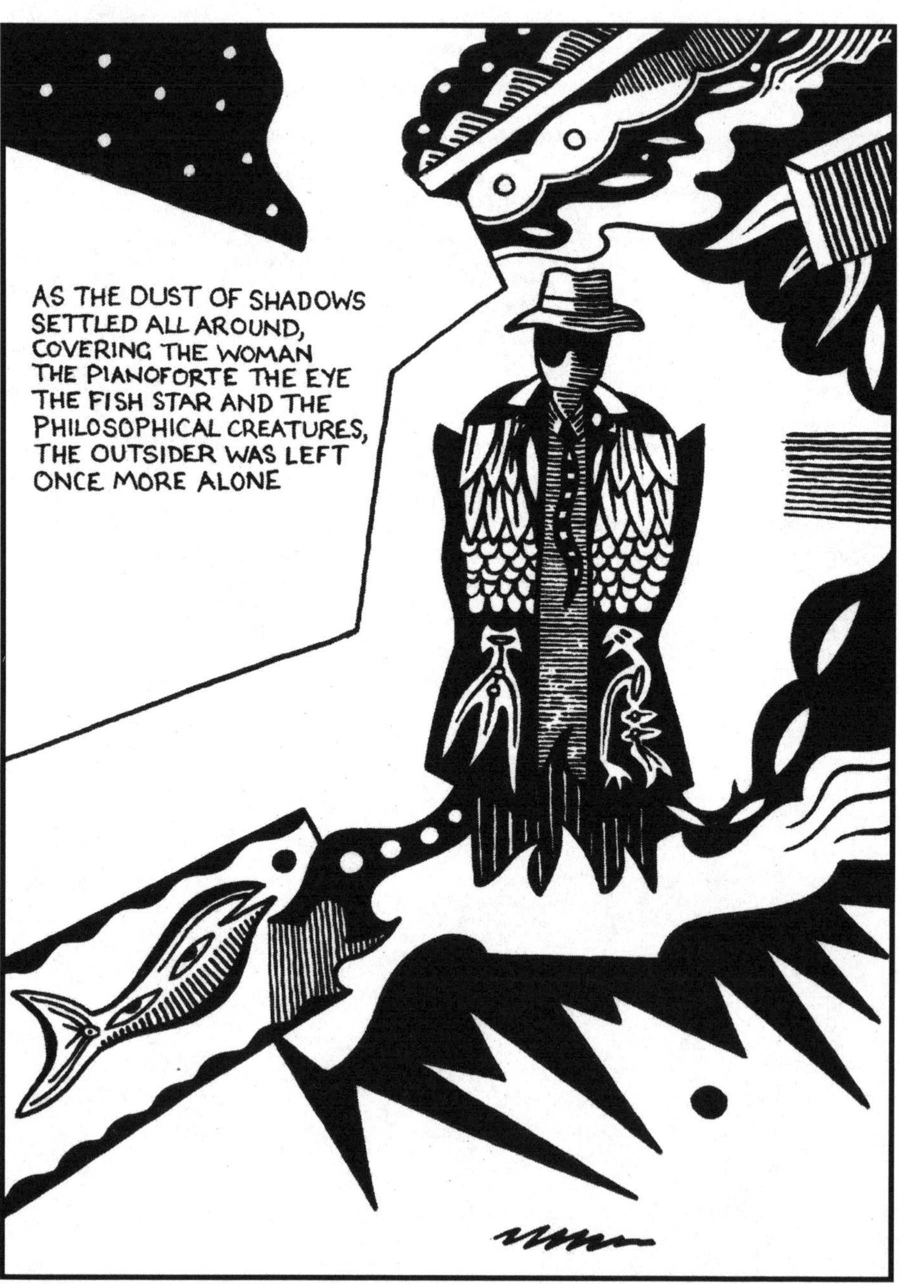
AS THE DUST OF SHADOWS
SETTLED ALL AROUND,
COVERING THE WOMAN
THE PIANOFORTE THE EYE
THE FISH STAR AND THE
PHILOSOPHICAL CREATURES,
THE OUTSIDER WAS LEFT
ONCE MORE ALONE

The Outsider
Mark A. Murphy

What is seen is not always recognised;
it is always this way in dreams,
we take the strangers there for granted,
their anonymous heads stuffed

with mortal man's illusions.
Who really sees the flesh for what it is –
the sick and the insane, paralysed
with the fear of what they will become?

And what of the man, half-crazed,
so long alone in his bathroom at night,
grinding his teeth and biting his fists
as if it would ward off the inevitable?

No one will speak for him, nor call to him,
nor bring him back from the brink
of his ordinary oblivion. Some men
are born to this deadly longing.

For others, the calling remains
only a shadow at the edge of the looking glass.
A prayer, if you will, for the bold men
and the fools, a moments meditation

before you close your eyes and weep.
What is seen, then, will be washed away
by sleep, and it will be just as it was
before you woke with a stranger in your bed.

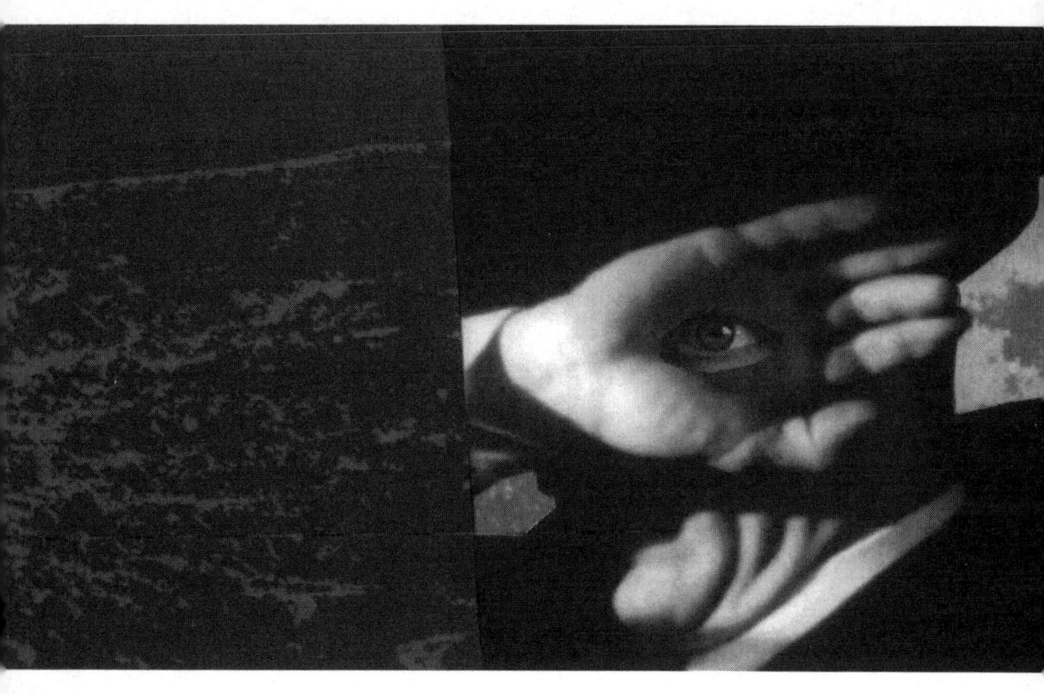

Lise Holm *'No Comment'* 2013

There are those who would have us believe that the world is composed of insides and outsides. One can be on the inside of a classroom, they say, or on the outside learning nothing. One can be on the inside of a society made of people who walk around making families, going to work, bound with the invisible threads of their and peers' faiths and parents' fears, or one can be outside of this, out beyond the boundary fence and in one of the secure psychiatric wards which scatter the wilderness beyond. It is here you will find, they tell you, the 'outsiders' of outsider art.

The case of Ida Lane is known well enough within scholarly circles. Certainly she ticks the requisite boxes of an outsider artist: no known tuition in arts of any form; no observed interest in having her work seen by others; an opaque tangle of cognitive and behavioural disorders. The last of these aspects is by no means a necessity to the definition, if we are talking technicalities, but the truth is that even experts in the field are as powerless as the next person to the witching-hour romance of psychosis. Lane is 'Lady Aporia, the aphotic mirror to our exegesis,' says influential outsider art scholar Mary Kazowitz in a (perhaps rare) moment of self-awareness; she is, in Jackson McCauley's typically pun-fondling prose, 'the darkened lane of our collective childhood, where we long to play but dare not even look'.

Beyond these circles, however, her case never attained the fame bestowed upon others. Arguably the closest she got to popular consciousness was as an episode of the 1976 documentary series *Perspectives*[1]. 'There are a few roads in life we're told not to venture down,' the narrator leaves us with (in an earlier abuse of our subject's name), 'and Ida Lane is one of them', this accompanied by a shot of an actual country lane, enclosing twilight, a bassy synth-note of impending doom. Here we find the level at which the initial discovery of Lane's work, in a room in the east wing of Bromswood Asylum in that same year, was pitched: a half-hour ghost story shown after the ten o'clock news as harmless escapism from transport union strikes, a nail bomb in County Armagh — matters of *the inside*.

Perhaps it was this unserious reception which hobbled her story's getting much proper attention across the following decade; perhaps it was that she did not appear to present anything sufficiently new from Austria's Weismann, Hungary's Balász[2]; perhaps, as Elizabeth Aitkin suggests, even in the 1980s society could not countenance the idea of psychiatric illness in women being as complex and legitimate as in men; perhaps, as Gabriel

Enkoute suggests, Ida's was the crime, even in the 1980s, of being not just non-white but worse: half white.

In any case, after the 1976 finding of Lane's work in Bromswood[3], Lane's case survived the next thirteen years in the form of yellowing newspaper clippings and magnetic tape wound on forgotten newsreels, until, quite suddenly, serious attention emerged from art theory quarters in the form of Kazowitz and McCauley[4], among others. This quickly drew the more firebrand elements of psychology and the first major paper on Lane, Professor Gareth Clarke-Wills's *The impact of trans-cultural schizoaffective disorder and chlorpromazine on therapeutic art practice*, was published in 1990 to a reasonable circulation[5]. Ida had arrived.

And by Ida, of course, we mean her figures and wraiths which are now creeping shadow-men, now jungle beasts crouched on the wardrobe or coiling under the bedframe, now altogether formless swathes of midnight chaos. Indeed most of the time they are this. In the photographs we find every square millimetre of Bromswood's Room 18 crusted with charcoal. On the slats of the blinds, on the insides of drawers, on the glass of the lightbulb hanging from the three-and-a-half-meter ceiling which she must have worked at like some netherworld Andelucci in his basilica, all these demon-shapes dressed in her howling palette, the shades of which seem to exceed in range the hues of our entire spectrum while being of just one colour, that which we, in our hopeless *insider* language, can only call black.

But why are we so drawn to this morbidity, to outsider art in general? For one thing we are compelled by its indifference to our viewing it[6], and so we are disarmed by its complete lack of pretension. It is here, while so disarmed, that Ida's snakes pull us beneath the bed. At the risk of an unwelcome prescriptiveness from myself as to how the work should be absorbed, I will tell you that Lane's art is not something to be enjoyed. When you peer at it, it is enjoying you. Do not pretend otherwise.

Amokamokamokamokamok, reads one of the many text-fragments found in Room 18, scrawled in tiny letters along the top of the skirting boards which run around the walls. The 1976 *Perspectives* documentary used this as a counterpoint to all the morbidity, an example of Lane's 'good' side doing battle with her 'bad': *am ok am ok am ok am ok am ok*, this mantra ringing her little world as protection from the monsters of the psyche. Clarke-Wills, who had made a far deeper study of the recovered files, knew better. Lane, half Malay, had a relentless taste for a certain Malay word which is found in English. The text on the skirting board is *amok amok amok amok amok*.

To 'run amok[7]' is something Anglophones are familiar with in its general sense of havoc-causing, be it a child scattering its toys about or a man attempting to kill a number of people. The recovered observations and progress reports on Lane indicate a constant and spasmodic use of the word which was likened by one of her doctor's[8] to a psychosocially developed Tourette's syndrome, although this was never officially diagnosed and taken to be more a subsidiary tic to her central psychoses. Early 1990s scholarship, however, placed great emphasis on this predilection of Lane's.

As with Clarke-Wills, Arnold, etc, we only have the files, artworks[9] and some scattered hearsay with which to establish a picture of Lane, and consequently it emerges to be as shifting and amorphous as one of her lurking charcoal figures – if indeed figures is what they are. What we know biographically derives from the sessions spent with her during treatment. Lane[10] arrived in Britain at some time in the late 1940s from Malaya, having left during the aftermath of the Japanese occupation. Her date of birth was unknown but the year1935 was a recurrence during discussions of this, so she is noted as possibly 17 at the time of committal to Bromswood in 1952. She was understood to be the daughter of a British Army officer who had been stationed in Malaya and spent the Second World War as a POW to the Japanese. Lane was with her father during his internment[11] and returned with him to Britain a number of years after Japan's surrender, possibly in 1949.

Her committal to Bromswood occurred following a breach of the peace offence in London. Her father was uncontactable at the time and never subsequently found; it was presumed that her mother had never travelled from Malaya, if she survived the occupation, and that she may never have had any relationship with Lane.

From the files we see that in her first few years in the asylum Lane was merely despondent, although she evidently had a comprehension of English. Following no change in her disposition she was in 1955 put on the new antipsychotic drug chlorpromazine, which many psychiatrists believed would revolutionise psychiatric care and even abolish insanity altogether. Around this time Lane began to produce drawings on paper. She started speaking more, and this word, 'amok', became a common theme in her speech and art, although the drawings were not recognised as such and always destroyed, despite Lane's elaborate attempts to hide them. There are indications of several instances of 'ducking', or holding a patient's head underwater, during all of which she said nothing. This silence was taken to be a sign of her worsening condition and over the next few years she became subject to the menu of 'physical interventions' favoured by psychiatrists of the time, including ECT[12] and insulin therapy[13], and she was even mooted for a pre-frontal leucotomy (a lobotomy), but this was being phased out as a practice towards the end of the 1950s.

With 1959 came the Mental Health Act and a decisive move away from the asylum system by seeking to replace it with increased reliance on the new antipsychotic medications, and so it was proclaimed 'As we cracked the enigma code, so too have we cracked madness' by Conservative politician Michael Answell[14]. Lane's art came to instead be identified as 'occupational therapy' and she was for the first time permitted to keep her drawings, which she amassed prodigiously. Her behaviour had come to oscillate between periods of depression and heightened mania but proceeded nonetheless in predictable cycles[15].

In 1962, however, she attacked a nurse and was put on a new form of chlorpromazine called Heragactil[16]. The motive for this attack was either unknown or simply unrecorded[17], but either way her violent episodes became more frequent, as did her recourse to the mantra '*amok, amok, amok*', and it was agreed to increase her dosages. She started covering her bedroom walls in charcoal, redrawing it as fast as the orderlies could wash it away. Large dark patches began to appear in different parts of the asylum[18]. She would make marks across her face and body to effect what looked like tiger stripes, this provoking more ducking, and by 1965 she would answer only to the name 'Hantu'.

Kazowitz was the first to identify this name as a reference to the spirits or folk-demons of Malaysian and Indonesian myth, traditionally believed to possess people to varying ends, depending on the hantu. The one associated with amok is Hantu Belia, the tiger spirit. This was called upon more as a literary device in Kazowitz's essay, but Clarke-Wills made this one of the core aspects of his analysis in *The impact of trans-cultural schizoaffective disorder and chlorpromazine on therapeutic art practice*. He notes, drawing from Eugene Baharom's earlier work on the phenomenon, that amok has in fact been a clinically diagnosable condition since 1849, being initially identified as a 'culture-bound syndrome' which arose in the specific milieu of the Malay Archipelago's ancient island-tribes, their animist beliefs combining with isolated, claustrophobic societies and a sense of honour which was acute to the point of being completely alien to the outside world. This pathogenesis, or the belief in it from traditional theorists of amok, was enough to permit learned people to see Malays as inherently murderous while with deft academic's feet sidestepping the label 'racist', and so it was extremely popular. Later came the counter-claim (made foremost by Baharom herself) that this was nonsense and the only thing culture-bound was the *method*[20], while the *desire* to kill blindly was a response to any number psychotic conditions which emerge (in varying forms and to varying degrees) all over the world[21]. Amok is the simple effect of complex but common causes, and is manifest across all humanity.

Or really only half of humanity. How of many of history's mass killings, attempted or successful, were conducted by women? It happens, yes, but so rarely that Clarke-Wills suggests of Lane's case that her infatuation with the idea was just that, something she had at some point come to understand as part of her original culture and then become fixated on as a means of clawing onto her home while marooned in a foreign environment[22] and then portraying this imagined notion of madness through an artistic bent fuelled by medications. 'Madness', says Clarke-Wills, 'was a way for Lane to comprehend her loss of self, and so she became mad… This brand of madness[23] was culturally masculine, or perceived as such by her, and thereby she could cling to the paternal figure she had lost by revealing him through her behaviour.'

Behaviour which was in the late 1960s becoming severe. While much of the asylum population were making increased use of new 'open door' policies, Lane was under increased security, put under constant observation[24] on two occasions in 1967. This saddening decline in Lane's case was enough, if we are truthful, to keep her in the imaginations of theorists into the mid 1990s and eventually to propel her across the Atlantic where she gained a degree of popularity in American scholarship[25], prompting what is now known as the Second Wave of ideas on Lane.

One notable figure of this time, again floating somewhat hazily on the art/psychology fault-line (Lane draws such people), was Linda Pearlman. She claimed with all the fanfare which her illustrious university gifted that Lane had entered Bromswood completely sane and developed what could be described as mental disorders through isolation, medication and aggressive physical intervention. In fact this is little different from what Clarke-Wills suggested six years earlier, but Pearlman was able to build it on several analyses of the asylum system which had emerged in the intervening period, all suggesting this experience of 'entering sane and leaving crazy', in her words, to have been fairly common.

Still in 1996, a stranger notion came from Ron Baedeker, architect of a theory named – with the subtlety of a billy club – the 'Commie Hypothesis', which pertains to the motif growing in the art of Lane's worsening years: marauding rifle butts; military boots tapering at their tops like the viewer is cowering at their toes; helmets blocking out the sun. She is recorded as addressing the asylum staff as soldiers, transposing their positions into military ranks, and, crucially to Baedeker, doing so in terms which explicitly addressed their being British, expressing the racial contempt she felt they held for her. With this in mind Baedeker suggests that she did not arrive in Europe with her core trauma being the Japanese occupation of Malaya; he says it was rather at the hands of the British having suffered the first years of the Malayan Emergency[26] as, he says, part of some probably familial connection to members of the Malayan National Liberation Army. A pitying British army officer brought her home and subsequently abandoned her. Kazowitz later said this theory had 'too much romance to be true', although her use of the word 'romance' in this grizzly tableau perhaps says more of her than of Baedeker's hypothesis[27].

One place the Marxism connection went down very well was in a Montréal, where radical thinker Adrian Gourac was becoming a vociferous champion of Lane's work. His book, *La Femme dans les Murs*[28], proclaimed Lane to be 'the lurking tigress in the tall grass of Subconscious; the true agent of art brut'. Her cultural displacement and alienation, says Gourac, provided her with an expressive space almost completely free of the inherited and tired tropes with which other art is constructed. This means that her art is not simply raw in its lack of education; it is also raw in a far more primordial sense – it is *before* the shapes and figures which are imprinted on us through enculturation. This is why, Gourac argues, it seems to always shift as it is viewed, never quite a wholly comprehensible object or scene. The standard vocabulary which restricts other art to being no more than different configurations of the same ideas is not present. He likens it to a sentence which has been made without words. The book

gained a cult following in artistic circles of Canada and then Europe, and its ideas were solidified (and bombasticised) into his next publication, *Le Manifeste du Tigressisme*[29].

The manifesto is strongly reminiscent of the mid twentieth-century examples from Jean-Baptiste Proveaux and Alain Lavazza[30]. The degree to which it is either parodic and satirical or utterly serious is difficult to know with Gourac, but certainly there is a lineage to be traced from Proveaux's conscious building of his movement around the discovery of László Balász. Gourac equally declares outsider art (claiming, as everyone does, to possess the true definition of the phrase) to be the unequivocal future of art and indeed all human consciousness[31]. Through this eccentric soapboaxing he succeeded in popularising Lane to the point that there were even a number of devoted 'tigressists' in Quebec and surprising locales of the world[32], and this coalesced with a peak of academic chatter in the year 2000 – as Lane was thirty years before at the peak, or nadir, of her recorded psychoses, producing work now no longer of any discernible form or subject.

In March 1970 it was announced that Bromswood was due to close that summer. Lane was informed. In her records we find the final note under the 1st of April: 'Room 18. Dead. Morning. Do not clean.'

It is as if Lane had become so inured to the institution that she had become a projection of it, or it a manifestation of her, and with its death came hers, her body hunched in the charcoal-deep of Room 18.

But, as we all know now, the east wing of Bromswood housed private sleeping quarters for just 17 patients and due to safety regulations this arrangement was not deviated from at any time. We know now that the facility's heating system was converted from coal to gas in 1926 and there were no fossil fuels stored on site after that date. We know now that the photographs of Lane's bedroom walls were printed on a specific type of resin-coated paper which was not on sale until 1971, years after many of them were purportedly inserted into Lane's records.

At this point you must pose yourself a question: If you have been presented with something which, through your understanding of the context given, comes to appear in a certain way and in turn conjures certain ideas and even feelings within you, as would, say, a piece of art which you have been informed was produced by someone with no artistic education, then would the emerging falsehood of that thing, its context, the entire world built up around it, make the ideas and feelings arisen from it equally false? When all perceptions of art and indeed life are suspended by such threads of context, prejudice, ideology, the fact that your

mother played it to you when you were six, then what is the true meaning of the emotions we draw from it? What, then, of our beliefs when the nature of simply being alive and *perceiving* is to be lied to, again and again, by ourselves and others?

The details which undo Lane's case emerged through the work of a research-er[33] for another TV documentary, this one to have been broadcast in 2001 and set to coincide with the opening of her estate to the public in a purpose-built gallery and a nation-wide publicity campaign. It became clear, right at the moment at which her story was to bubble over into wider public knowledge and even a place in the canon of great twentieth-century artists, that Ida Lane was a phantom.

In the ensuing furore Kazowitz, Pearlman and Baedeker fell from circulation, their academic stock never quite what it was, while McCauley and Gourac merely used the revelations to generate further theories and book sales[34]. No one, however, has broached the fact that the drawings are materially the same as they ever were, and what this means.

The person who produced them is still unnamed and currently understood to have been a nurse at Bromswood, returning there in the early 1970s to cover the walls of 'Room 18'[35], take and develop photographs of them then plant these along with fabricated records and drawings in the Charge Nurse's office. We must now put to ourselves: When the drawings are without doubt the work of a talented and unnervingly original artist, in what sense were they 'fabricated'?

Lane shows us with phantom hands just as she did with real ones that authenticity is not a requisite of truth. We cannot pretend that we have not had an education or been subject to all the moulding forces of the world so that we might create art which is free from the conservatism of inheritance. Outsider art, for all of the miraculous rawness it gives us, cannot be the future of expression because any conscious moving towards it could only manifest in the form of philistinism. Slashing paintings and burning books, as Gourac suggests in his more terrifying moments, would just turn us into children.

We can instead know the art of the past, know when it does not apply to lived experience today, kill it, and then keep at all times in the corner of our eye what Françoise Melchiot calls 'the nearby corpse of education'. The outsider artist[36] can make enormous and underivative worlds in this way – and so what is it that he or she is really on the outside of? We are on the outside of this as we are on the inside of that, all of us dangling from our threads of prejudice while snipping others, retying old ones, lost in education, ignorance, reality and make-believe. This is the very essence of what we try to negotiate through art, and so perhaps that which is itself true but voiced by ghosts, our own ghosts or others', is that ineffable thing: the lie that speaks the truth[37].

1. Now obtainable on the internet.

2. The central European bias of the famed early twentieth-century examples is no coincidence. Even in post-war Britain psychiatrists were extremely conservative in there diagnoses (if not their treatments) of the mentally ill (see the TV documentary *The Madness of Europe* – Paul Carr dir.). Kazowitz suggest this to be principal reason that Lane was not 'discovered' while secured at Bromswood: she never had a doctor who could see her work for what it was.

3. The asylum had been abandoned since its closure six years previously and was being surveyed for redevelopment as a hotel. A large cache of 'bloody awful-looking' (McCauley notes a surveyor as saying) drawings were found in the charge Nurse's office and passed to the local NHS trust which still owned the site.

4. Lane features (along with the usual suspects from Germany and Japan) in Kazowitz's essay in the seminal outsider art anthology *The Outsiders*, and has a whole chapter in McCauley's more populist book *Art Brutus: the knife in the back of commercial art,* published within a month of each other in 1989.

5. Much of the present piece's background on Lane comes from both this paper and Clarke-Wills's 1992 follow-up (with J Arnold) *A return to therapeutic art practice: Heragactil and its variants' affect on left anterior temporal lobe function,* both carried in the psychology (now neuropsychology) journal *Autodidact.*

6. This appealing more to the original meaning of the term, stemming as it did from mental institutions across Europe and the world, before today's 'outsider art fairs', before the hokey handicrafts of Richard Tamerlain, Hannah Kristen, Kaito Yamashita and the ubiquitous (and actually rather wealthy) 'Foz'.

7. A common etymology is that *amok* arrived in English via the Portuguese *amuco or amouco*[a], in turn from the Malay *amuk*, derived from *mengamuk* ('rampage'), with this originating from one or a combination of India-based forms: (1) the Amuco (or Amouchi), a group of professional assassins from Malabar; (2) the Malayalam word *amarkhan* ('warrior'); (3), the Sanskrit words *amokshya* ('they who cannot be loosed' – as from a vow, etc) or *moksha*, a word used in the samsara aspect of Hinduism, Buddhism and Jainism (among other Indian religions) to mean, curiously, 'eternal freedom from social programming'. An interesting, if somewhat flighty, parallel in English is the word *monster* sharing the same etymological route as *demonstrate* (Katsoros, 1986).

   a: Amok's transition to the Western palate came through Portuguese explorer João Bustos Calçarão, who noted while passing through Sarawak, 'It has become known to me that any of the native population are able, upon no provocation, to assault and kill all those around. Those who do so are labelled *Amucos*, and their behaviour is a window to the savagery beneath all the Yellow Peoples', to which postcolonial theorist Émile Vasquez (contemporary of Enkoute at Neesdon College) remarked, 'the true savagery is Calçarão's violence to the meta-ambivalence congenital to the praxis of the jungle-island life-paradigm', and that Malaysian peoples 'are not even yellow'.

8. Doctor 'OP'. Staff are referred to only by their initials in the files, parts of which are sadly illegible.

9. Numbering 65 drawings and 25 photographs of Lane's room and possessions.

10. 'Ida Lane' was the name of a music hall singer active from the mid 1930s and known to have sung in wartime ENSA shows. Much of the staff at Bromswood would have been ex-Forces and so likely familiar with Ida Lane[a]. It was common practice at Bromswood for un-named committals to be given the monikers of popular entertainers[b].

    a: Note that even this was merely a stage name.

    b: Separate records list cabaret singer Gloria Suchet and comedian Rodney Walts as residents at the time. Walts's biographer recently stated that this was actually him.

11. This was proposed in the notes due to the common presence of soldiers or soldier-like entities in the drawings, generally portrayed in a very negative light (see drawings #51, #58 and #61, and the photograph of the back of the bedroom door). There are very few accounts of the Bromswood staff using her work as a means of analysis; this is one of them.

12. Electroconvulsive therapy. Known to many of us through Daniel Leifey's visceral performance in the 1978 film The Year of the Troubles (Kristoff Aaronson dir.) – we can imagine Lane's experience to have been similar. ECT's benefits are still a matter of debate. Due to the use of anaesthetic it is today at least visually a different practice and still used on occasion in Britain, while its use elsewhere, such as in India, is reportedly seeing a year-on-year increase [although statistics on this vary – ed.].

13. Or insulin coma treatment, as it was then known, in which large injections of insulin were used to induce the body's burning up its sugar and so reducing blood-sugar levels to the point of coma. The belief was that comas were beneficial to the troubled mind and it was used predominantly to treat schizophrenics. The nature of the benefit was never properly substantiated and the practice came to be responsible for at least 44 deaths across the asylum system (Jameson, 1993).

14. One of the earliest public references to the enigma code. Information on much of the code-breaking work of the Second World War was not officially released until 1974, so Lord Answell's statement was fittingly enigmatic and lost on many. Incidentally, or perhaps not, Bromswood Asylum lay in his constituency.

15. Clarke-Wills's diagnosis of schizoaffective disorder is drawn largely from the episodic alternations between mania, hypomania and depression in Lane's reports. The designation 'schizoaffective' is an attempt to reconcile a combination of different conditions manifested in the same patient, predominantly a mixture of schizophrenic behaviour and mood disorders.

16. Chlorpromazine was sold as Thorazine in the US and Largactil in the UK. Smithson & Brown obtained the license to develop derivatives of Largactil in 1961 and among their products was Heragactil[a]. Unlike other antipsychotics, which are merely a type of sedative [to put it crudely – ed.], Heragactil did not so much inhibit motor function as 'quieten' (or so the promotional literature put it) certain parts of the brain. Clarke-Wills and Arnold suggested in their collaborative article that this permitted other parts of the brain to become 'louder'.

> a: Staff nicknames for the drug included 'terrorgactil' and 'pterodactyl' due to the swooping visions it would sometimes induce. Smithson & Brown never accepted this side-effect publically. Kazowitz makes a perhaps flowery comparison between Heragactil-drugged Lane and the Greek goddess Hera, wife (and sister) of Zeus who is often engaged in acts of maddened vengeance.

17. The difference between the unknown and the unrecorded is something with which we must constantly contend while forming analyses from Lane's notes, and a difference probably ignored by many of the more bombastic commentaries, be they psychological, sociohistorical, art theoretical, or popular. It was, if we are honest, the death of many of our understandings regarding Lane.

18. Ron Baedeker used the photographs of Room 18 and computer imaging techniques to produce a pioneering 360-degree collage which stimulated much analysis. It revealed the walls on both side of Lane's bed, when viewed in their entirety, to show through the other drawings and shapes the emerging outline of feline paws, anatomically relatable to a big cat's, which if rendered to scale would produce a sixty-meter-tall tiger.

19. The practice of ducking was not officially sanctioned and references to it in Lane's notes are either sly, 'Took Room 18 for bath this

PM', or dressed in slang-terms such as 'cucking[a]' and 'the Deluge treatment[b]'.

> a: A more direct reference to the 'cucking-stools' or 'ducking-stools' of Middle-Age witch trials of which ducking is disturbingly reminiscent. In fact the practice was used only in small part for 'witches' – it was deemed proper for troublesome women of all varieties.

> b: Probably referring to the Biblical flood and the 'wicked and corrupt'(Genesis 3:4-5) who were to be washed away.

20. The long, curved parang blade was always near to hand in enclosed island life, as were victims.

21. As Hitam Abdullah killed nine fellow government officials with a parang[a] in Kuala Lumpur in 1903, so Bernie Kopelman killed nine fellow postal workers with a hunting rifle in Denver in 1984. Baharom draws upon hundreds of examples and shows ably how the same behaviour is refracted through different cultural lenses, with these 'lenses' sometimes happening to stifle the behaviour altogether and so creating the impression (falsely) that some societies are free from amok. For example, depression and alienation are no higher in the US than in the UK [insofar as these things can be measured – ed.] yet the incidence of mass shooting against indiscriminate targets, often ending in the death or suicide of the attacker, is significantly higher in the US. Baharom says it is very simply because firearms are always nearer to hand in the US, particularly in the family setting, and so the amok which is latent everywhere can here be realised in this localised form.

> a: Notice the Victorian discourse as to the amoking Malay's love of the parang and the particular kind of violence it wrought. In the Algerian War of Independence the Front de Libération Nationale's use of the 'douk-douk' pocket knife was seen in strikingly similar terms by French colonists. What outsiders cannot help but see as an inherent love of certain method of violence is often merely the use of what is to hand.

22. While ironically seeming to have a conception of amok that has been accentuated through European eyes – probably her father's. Clarke-Wills highlights this as a pertinent example of how Lane is not simply of one culture and displaced into another; she rather sits entirely between them, subject to the distortions that each has of the other while truly knowing neither of them, nor indeed anywhere.

23. Clarke-Wills (a psychologist, remember) uses this word advisedly. 'Madness' here is the notion of the thing, with all of its vagueness, romanticisation and inadequacies. His diagnosis of schizoaffective disorder is separate from his claim that Lane was merely using the idea of amok, at least initially, rather than actually suffering it.

24. This is to be within eyesight and arm's length at all times. It is actually very rare within psychiatric care.

25. Kazowitz is American, of course, but teaching in Edinburgh she had remained largely separate from the US academy.

26. The Japanese occupation of Malaya lasted from 1941 to 1945, while the Malayan Emergency[a] is considered to have spanned 1948 to 1960. There is overlap here which allows room for Baedeker's hypothesis.

> a: The rise of communist groups in Malaya who sought to expel British colonial forces due to economic unrest following the occupation.

27. It must be noted, however, that despite the greater amount of supposition required in realising its story of Lane in 1949 (at this time the MNLA was scattered and disorganised; direct conflict with the British was rare), it does make for a more plausible abandonment-scene than in previous theories.

28. 'The Woman in the Walls', published in 1998[a] with its title taken from of an earlier poem by Gourac.

> a: English translation made by Stephanie Auclat, 1999.

29. Originally co-written with Anatole Djebar, though his name has been expunged from it by popular awareness and probably by Gourac as well. The manifesto was cannily released simultaneously with an English translation produced (somewhat idiosyncratically) by

Gourac. The aims laid out on the first page are as follows:

1. Tigressism rejects the correlation of the uneducated with notions of 'the past' or of 'stupidity' and instead holds the future of art and humanity to be illumined through the steady deconstruction of learned forms to the ends of superior animalistic intelligence.

2. Tigressism rejects any and all separation of the masculine and feminine whereby amok is supposed to be merely carried by the surrogate Lane when she is in fact demonstrating amok merely through her own behavioural mode as a man would his.

3. Tigressism rejects the relegation of magic to the canvas or story-book and instead rejoices its quiddity in the eyeball, the blister[a], the bedpan, the scream, the walls.

a: Auclat later rendered this herself as 'blister pack'.

30. Whose movements, örültégisme and blanchisme respectively, did not last even into the 1940s, although there is a case for the political dimension of Lavazza's blanchism diffusing into far-right elements of his native Switzerland in the 1950s.

31. This notion is clad in a Marxist revolutionary framework of dialectical materialism which has since been much criticised, especially by Marxists. They also did not appreciate Gourac's recourse to the near deification of Lanc (he at one point calls her 'the Jungle Madonna'), and nor did the psychologists.

32. Martinique; New Caledonia; São Tomé (to name a few). The impact of the internet on such artistic movements is an interesting and under-researched field. It is on the one hand hugely enabling, making face-to-face contact obsolete in the expansion of an idea, but equally it provokes very immediate and concerted cynicism which the more insular artistic communities of the last century did not have to contend with. The quasi-religious aspect of the older -isms' growth is now quickly dissembled into a 'like' on social networking sites and taste-targeted advertising. I have heard that 'liking' tigressism will induce sidebar advertisements for Tiger Power energy drink.

33. Whose identity was withheld for a number of years in a perhaps overly cautious bid to avoid reprisal from militant tigressist factions. We now know it to have been Jack Althorpe, recently appointed Director of Factual Programming at TVN.

34. McCauley published a book in 2003 detailing the complex conspiracy by which the British Secret Service had hoodwinked his peers into accepting the idea of the Ida Lane hoax, in his belief because Lane's work held hidden clues as to the depth of British atrocities committed during the Malayan Emergency. Gourac published a pamphlet in 2005 which hailed the hoax to be the greatest 'mass-deceptive art piece' in history and espousing the messianic qualities of its conductor who he believed to be alive and living in the Kalahari Desert. Gourac was last seen boarding a plane to Windhoek in 2006.

35. Possibly this was even that nurse's bedroom while the asylum was running. Either way it cannot have been part of the plan for the walls of the room to be washed clean during initial work on the hotel conversion in 1976, which was subsequently abandoned. Bromswood still lies derelict and we cannot know for certain which room was 'Room 18'. Periodically new pieces are found in forgotten rooms by those with a macabre curiosity for the place. They emerge clutching drawings, reporting walls blackened with pictures which were not there on previous visits, always looking for that holy grail of Room 18. Whether the new work (some of it uncannily similar to the originals, it must be said) is faked by the explorers or planted by others is irrelevant. Bromswood is a building haunted by falsehood.

36. Or simply just an artist[a].

    a: Or simply just a person.

37. This phrase is commonly accredited to cubist Juan Arroyo, but the truth is that he purloined it from surrealist Pepillo Barnetta who in turn had taken it from a poster for the 1931 American film 'Lying with Truth', a pulp noir about a callgirl named Mandy Truth. The tagline of this film was 'We're only on the inside of a joke when we start laughing'.

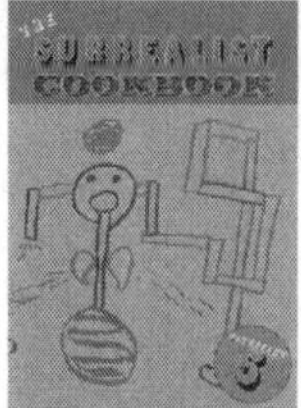
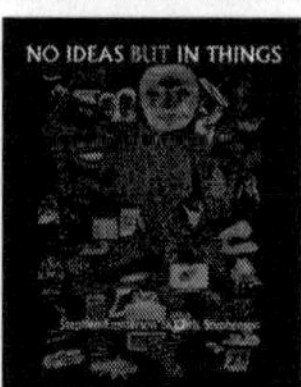
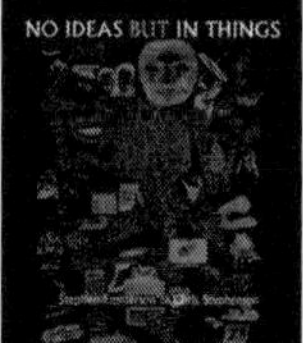
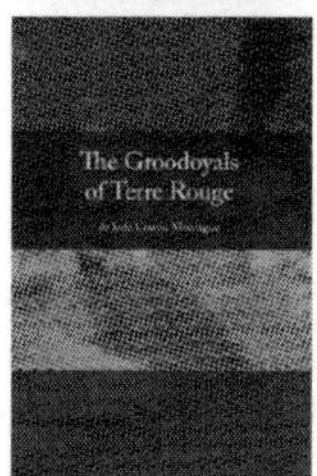
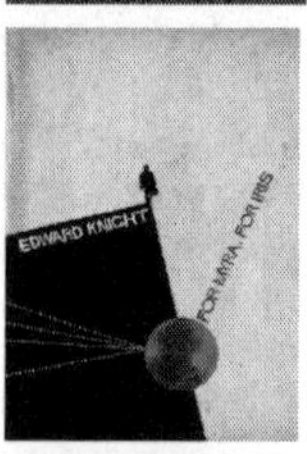
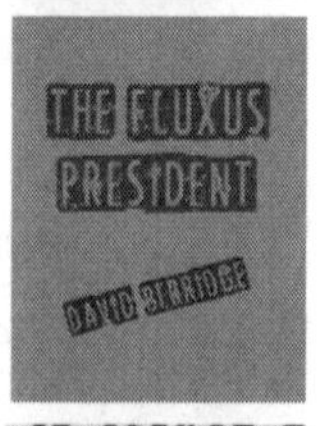
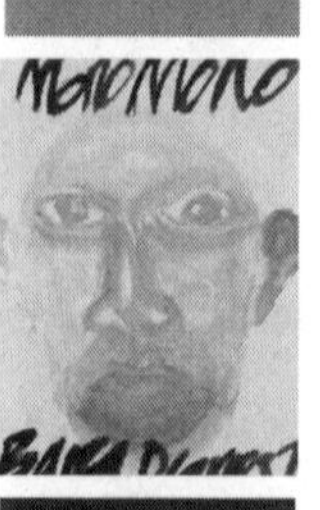
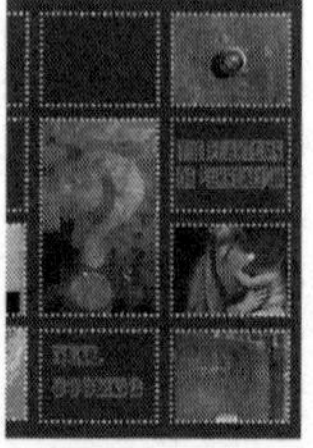

Also available from Dark Windows Press...

Dark Windows Press publish a range of interesting books in short print runs and limited editions, below is a selection...

The Surrealist Cookbook edited by Neil Coombs

"This is rather a strange book, which is probably a good thing" *Yum.fi*
ISBN 978-0-9571644-6-8

No Ideas But In Things by Stephen Emmerson & Chris Stephenson

"a non-connotational word tennis match... they get all the wrong words right" *James Davies*
ISBN 978-0-9571644-9-9

The Groodoyals of Terre Rouge by Jude Cowan-Montague

"An exquisite collection – I found the poems very moving, and the pictures are a delight." *Sarah Rayner*
"a beautiful memoir, full of sunshine" Sabotage Reviews
ISBN 978-0-9571644-8-2

For Myra, For Iris by Edward Knight

A first novel by the young British writer Edward Knight.
ISBN 978-0-9571644-3-7

The Fluxus President by David Berridge

"For anyone remotely interested in art writing, this book is most definitely for you." Sabotage Reviews
ISBN 978-0-9571644-2-0

Monomono-Banza Diaries vol. 1 by Eze Chimalio

A graphic novel that deals with sex, death and politics in a disturbing and restless world.
ISBN 978-0-9571644-0-6

The Phantoms of Surrealism by Neil Coombs

With essays by Krzysztof Fijalkowski & Catriona McAra.
ISBN 978-0-9571644-4-4

You can buy the above & others from **www.darkwindows.co.uk** or alternatively order them from your local independent bookshop or multinational on-line retailer (distribution by Central Books).

DECEMBER 23, 2022
JUNE 1, 2035
MARCH 5, 2021
DECEMBER -, 2024
MARCH 5, 2021
OCTOBER 4, 2058
APRIL 20, 2035
DECEMBER 8, 2023
FEBRUARY 1, 2021
NOVEMBER 8, 2069
MAY 1, 2020
JUNE - 2010
MARCH - 2058
JULY 5, 2021
APRIL 5, 2069
JUNE 11, 2021
APRIL 2, 2010
FEBRUARY 15, 2058
NOVEMBER 6, 2020
JULY 16, 2021
JUNE 7, 206-
OCTOBER 16, 20-
SEPTEMBER 3, 210-
DECEMBER 13, 20-
MAY 13, 207-
DECEMBER 13, 20-
FEBRUARY 5, 20-
MARCH 2, 20-
JULY 10, 202-
APRIL 5, 20-
OCTOBER 6, 2034
MAY -, 2010
OCTOBER 3, 20-
JULY 4, 20-
NOVEMBER 10, 2034
DECEMBER 13, 2024
JULY 7, -
MAY 3, 2080
FEBRUARY 10, 2070
MAY 6, 2024
DECEMBER 5, 2010
MARCH 4, 2034
NOVEMBER 7, 2070
DECEMBER 13, 2080
FEBRUARY 1, 2069
JULY 6, 2035
OCTOBER 13, 2034
MARCH 15, 2069
OCTOBER 1, 2010
MARCH 22, 2080
JULY 5, 2069
FEBRUARY 3, 2034

NOVEMBER -, 2026
APRIL 1, 2007
JUNE 23, 2006
SEPTEMBER 25, 2026
OCTOBER 2, 2015
FEBRUARY 7, 2036
MARCH 8, 2005
NOVEMBER 1, 2015
APRIL -, 2005
OCTOBER 6, 2036
MARCH 14, 2006
JUNE - 2005
SEPTEMBER 7, 2026
APRIL 3, 2015
NOVEMBER 1-, 2015
MARCH 20, 2015
JUNE 5, 2026
OCTOBER - 2035
JUNE 10, 2005
NOVEMBER 13, 2015
OCTOBER 3, 2036
MARCH 14, 2006
JUNE 7, 2006
NOVEMBER - 2035
SEPTEMBER 10, 2035
OCTOBER 11, 2007
JUNE 5, 2026
MAY 3, 2026
DECEMBER 6, 2005
JULY 11, 2007
JUNE 6, 2026
NOVEMBER 11, 2036
OCTOBER 5, 2036
MARCH - 2015
SEPTEMBER 7, 2035
MARCH 14, 2006
NOVEMBER 13, 2015
MAY 11, 2007
JULY 4, 2036
DECEMBER 12, 2005
MAY - 2009
FEBRUARY 2, 2007
JULY 3, 2099
APRIL 18, 2009
MARCH 8, 2007
DECEMBER 5, 2008
JULY 12, 2099
OCTOBER 4, 2089
FEBRUARY - 2099
MAY - 2009
JULY - 209-
FEBRUARY 15, 2008
DECEMBER 7, 200-
MAY 11, 2089

APRIL 23, 2077
AUGUST 5, 2078
JANUARY - 2088
MAY - 2057
MARCH 2, 2057
APRIL 8, 2078
JANUARY 2, 2068
AUGUST 13, 2077
MAY 31, 208-
MARCH 11, 2067
NOVEMBER 2, 2067
APRIL - 2077
JULY 2, 2088
JANUARY 7, 2078
MAY 31, 2080
MARCH 9, 2057
APRIL 1, 2067
AUGUST 6, 2077
JUNE 4, 2088
JULY - 2080
FEBRUARY 4, 2078
AUGUST 13, 2088
JUNE 1, 2087
SEPTEMBER 13, 2088
JULY 8, 2062
JUNE 17, -
JULY 5, 2078
MARCH 12, -
JUNE 7, -
MAY 8, 2087
APRIL 4, -
OCTOBER 11, 2037
DECEMBER 5, 2037
JULY 6, 20-
NOVEMBER 13, 20-
JUNE 9, 20-
APRIL 5, 204-
OCTOBER 5, 20-
MARCH 10, 2017
OCTOBER 4, 205-
JUNE, 2027
APRIL - 205-
NOVEMBER 3, 20-
MAY 5, 201-
JUNE 7, 2028
MARCH 6, 2038
MAY 4, 202-
JUNE 11, 2017

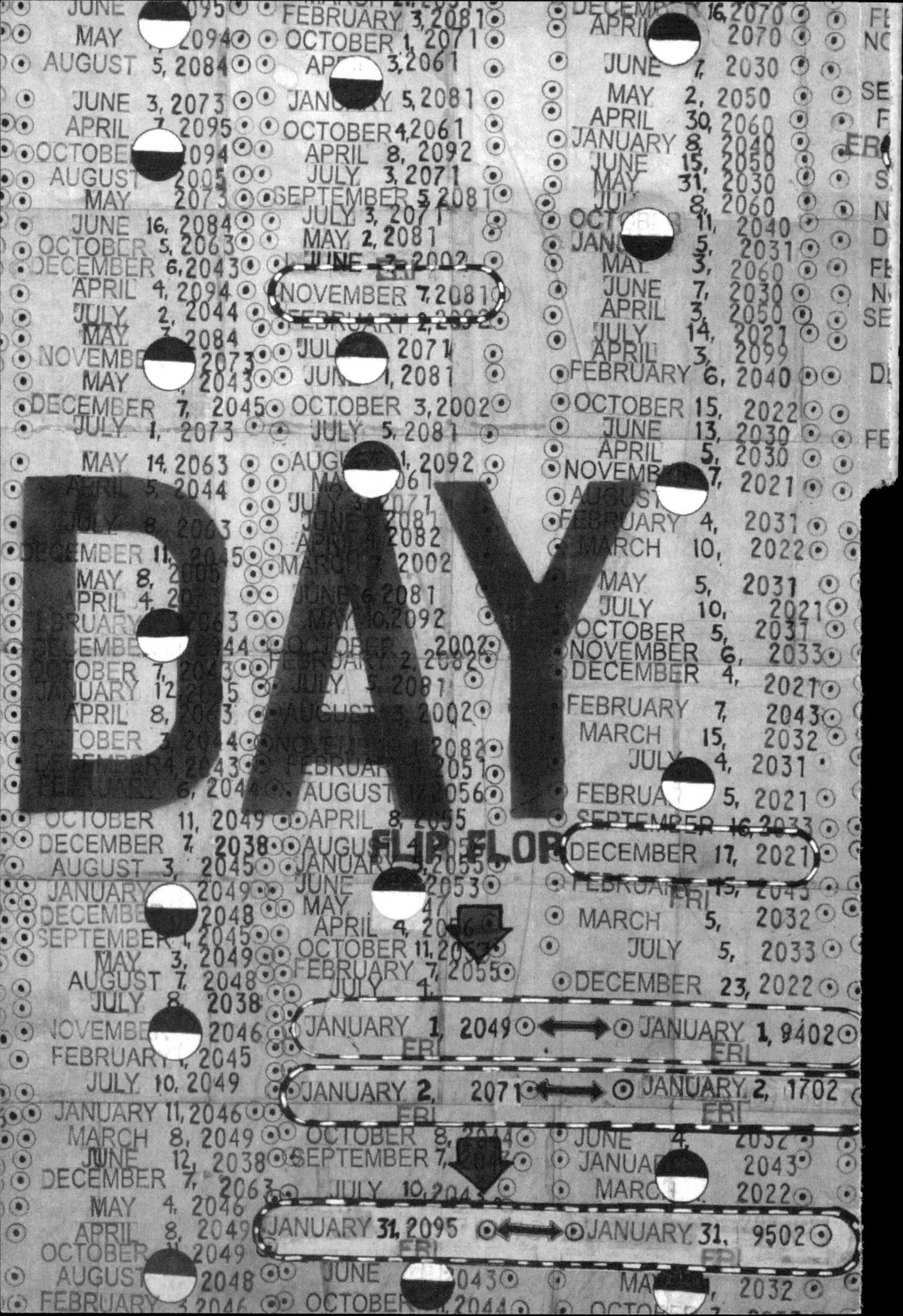

JUNE ..., 2095
MAY ..., 2094
AUGUST 5, 2084
JUNE 3, 2073
APRIL 7, 2095
OCTOBER ..., 2094
AUGUST ..., 2005
MAY ..., 2073
JUNE 16, 2084
OCTOBER 5, 2063
DECEMBER 6, 2043
APRIL 4, 2094
JULY 2, 2044
MAY ..., 2084
NOVEMBER ..., 2073
MAY ..., 2043
DECEMBER 7, 2045
JULY 1, 2073
MAY 14, 2063
APRIL 5, 2044
JULY 8, 2063
DECEMBER 11, 2045
MAY 8, 2005
APRIL 4, 20...
FEBRUARY ..., 2063
DECEMBER ..., 2044
OCTOBER 7, 204...
JANUARY 12, 20.5
APRIL 8, 2063
OCTOBER ..., 2044
DECEMBER 4, 2043
FEBRUARY 6, 2044
OCTOBER 11, 2049
DECEMBER 7, 2038
AUGUST 3, 2045
JANUARY ..., 2049
DECEMBER ..., 2048
SEPTEMBER ..., 2045
MAY 3, 2049
AUGUST 7, 2048
JULY 8, 2038
NOVEMBER ..., 2046
FEBRUARY ..., 2045
JULY 10, 2049
JANUARY 11, 2046
MARCH 8, 2049
JUNE 12, 2038
DECEMBER 7, 2063
MAY 4, 2046
APRIL 8, 2049
OCTOBER ..., 2049
AUGUST ..., 2048
FEBRUARY ...

FEBRUARY 3, 2081
OCTOBER 1, 2071
APRIL 3, 2061
JANUARY 5, 2081
OCTOBER 4, 2061
APRIL 8, 2092
JULY 3, 2071
SEPTEMBER 5, 2081
JULY 3, 2071
MAY 2, 2081
JUNE 7, 2002
NOVEMBER 7, 2081
FEBRUARY 2, 2002
JULY ..., 2071
JUNE 1, 2081
OCTOBER 3, 2002
JULY 5, 2081
AUGUST 1, 2092
MAY ..., 2061
JULY 3, 2071
JUNE ..., 2081
APRIL 4, 2082
MARCH 7, 2002
JUNE 6, 2081
MAY 10, 2092
OCTOBER 2, 2002
FEBRUARY 2, 2002
JULY 5, 2081
AUGUST 3, 2002
NOVEMBER ..., 2081
FEBRUARY 2, 2051
AUGUST ..., 2056
APRIL 8, 2055
AUGUST ..., 2055
JANUARY ..., 2055
JUNE ..., 2053
MAY ..., 47
APRIL 4, 2066
OCTOBER 11, 20...
FEBRUARY 7, 2055
JULY 4, ...

DECEMBER 16, 2070
APRIL ..., 2070
JUNE 7, 2030
MAY 2, 2050
APRIL 30, 2060
JANUARY 8, 2040
JUNE 15, 2050
MAY 31, 2030
JULY 8, 2060
OCTOBER 11, 2040
JANUARY 5, 2031
MAY 3, 2060
JUNE 7, 2030
APRIL 3, 2050
JULY 14, 2021
APRIL 3, 2099
FEBRUARY 6, 2040
OCTOBER 15, 2022
JUNE 13, 2030
APRIL 5, 2030
NOVEMBER 7, 2021
AUGUST ...,
FEBRUARY 4, 2031
MARCH 10, 2022
MAY 5, 2031
JULY 10, 2021
OCTOBER 5, 2031
NOVEMBER 6, 2033
DECEMBER 4, 2021
FEBRUARY 7, 2043
MARCH 15, 2032
JULY 4, 2031
FEBRUARY 5, 2021
SEPTEMBER 16, 2033
DECEMBER 17, 2021
FEBRUARY 15, 2045
MARCH 5, 2032
JULY 5, 2033
DECEMBER 23, 2022

JANUARY 1, 2049 ←→ JANUARY 1, 9402
FRI   FRI

JANUARY 2, 2071 ←→ JANUARY 2, 1702
FRI   FRI

OCTOBER 8, 2044
SEPTEMBER 7, ...
JULY 10, 204...
JUNE 4, 2032
JANUARY ..., 2043
MARCH ..., 2022

JANUARY 31, 2095 ←→ JANUARY 31, 9502
FRI   FRI

JUNE ..., 2043
OCTOBER ..., 2044
MARCH ..., 2032

DAY
FLIP FLOP